17 99

KEY QUOTATIONS IN SOCIOLOGY

'In this unique collection, Thompson gives us much more than a book of "quotable quotes". He has found extraordinarily articulate statements of sociology's key ideas, and he has arranged them in an historically and theoretically coherent way. In so doing, he has managed to tell the story of sociology in a compact, fresh and compelling manner, and also to describe society itself.'

Jeffrey C. Alexander, *University of California at Los Angeles*

Jean Baudrillard on consumption:

'It is not defined by the food we eat, the clothes we wear, the car we drive . . . but in the organization of all this as signifying substance . . . Consumption, in so far as it is meaningful, is a systematic act of the manipulation of signs.'

Auguste Comte on science and sociology:

'From science comes prevision; from prevision comes action [*Savoir pour prévoir et prévoir pour pouvoir*].'

Émile Durkheim on suicide:

'If religion protects a man from the desire to kill himself, it is not because it preaches respect for his person based on arguments *sui generis*, but because it is a society.'

Do you have any difficulty in finding a relevant quotation for an essay or exam paper in sociology? If so this useful little book, which contains a core of essential quotations for anyone interested in sociology, will provide you with all you need. Quotations are taken from the classic texts of the so-called 'Founding Fathers', the writings of more recent influential figures, and the most authoritative experts in special fields.

The book is divided into two fully cross-referenced parts: Key Concepts and Topics and Key Sociological Thinkers.

Kenneth Thompson is Professor in Sociology at the Open University.

KEY QUOTATIONS IN SOCIOLOGY

Kenneth Thompson

London and New York

First published 1996
by Routledge
11 New Fetter Lane, London EC4P 4EE

Simultaneously published in the USA and Canada
by Routledge
29 West 35th Street, New York, NY 10001

Typeset in Times by Keystroke, Jacaranda Lodge,
Wolverhampton

Printed and bound in Great Britain by
Biddles Ltd, Guildford and Kings Lynn

British Library Cataloguing in Publication Data
A catalogue record for this book is available from the British Library

Library of Congress Cataloging in Publication Data
A catalogue record for this book has been requested

ISBN 0–415–13517–6 (hbk)
ISBN 0–415–05761–2 (pbk)

This book is dedicated to the memory of my father,
the late Alfred Thompson, who died just as I
finished it, and to Margaret and Clare,
who make it all worthwhile.

CONTENTS

PREFACE

This book aims to provide the core of essential quotations for students and teachers of sociology. It does not pretend to be exhaustive, nor can it provide long passages of text such as those to be found in the various anthologies. The length of the quotations varies depending on the subject-matter and the style of writing. The choice of quotations has been made on the basis of several criteria: to represent the more 'classic' or influential writings and authors in sociology; to provide theoretical statements rather than empirical findings; to cover the key concepts and most central topics in sociology. The quotations are arranged in two sections: the first section deals with concepts and topics; the second covers some key sociological theorists who often feature in theory courses (although those same individuals may also be quoted in the first section, and are cross-referenced where appropriate).

Any choice of quotations is bound to have a subjective element, reflecting personal interests and experience, and also it is affected by a set of objective constraints, such as those of time and accessibility. I have been fortunate in being based at the Open University, which provides courses for many thousands of students throughout the world, and in having had experience of teaching or examining university students in several countries, and in different types of institutions, ranging from the University of California, Los Angeles, and Smith College, Massachusetts, to distance teaching institutions in Hong Kong. Despite the institutional and cultural differences, I hope and believe that it is possible to select a core of essential sociological quotations acceptable and useful to many students and teachers in those different institutions.

In initiating this project I am indebted to Chris Rojek, when he was at Routledge. At the Open University I have been assisted by my secretary, Molly Freeman. I would like to thank Stuart Hall, at the Open University, and Jeffrey Alexander, at UCLA, for intellectual stimulation during the course of compiling this collection.

Kenneth Thompson, 1995
The Open University, Milton Keynes

ACKNOWLEDGEMENTS

The author would like to thank the following:

The Institute of Psycho-Analysis and The Hogarth Press, for permission to quote from The Standard Edition of the Complete Psychological Works of Sigmund Freud, translated and edited by James Strachey.

W.W. Norton & Company, Inc., for permission to quote from *Civilization and its Discontents* by Sigmund Freud, translated from the German by James Strachey. Copyright © 1961 by James Strachey.

Blackwell Publishers and Stanford University Press for permission to quote from Pierre Bourdieu, *The Logic of Practice*, translated by Richard Nice, © 1990 Polity Press; and from Niklas Luhmann, *Love as Passion: The Codification of Intimacy*, translated by J. Gaines and D.L. Jones, 1986, Polity Press.

The Free Press, an imprint of Simon & Schuster, Inc., for permission to quote from Max Weber, *The Theory of Social and Economic Organization*, translated by A.M. Henderson and Talcott Parsons, edited by Talcott Parsons, Oxford University Press, 1947. Copyright © 1947, copyright renewed 1975 by Talcott Parsons.

The University of Chicago Press for permission to quote from G. Simmel, 'The Stranger', excerpt in *On Individuality and Social Forms: Selected Writings*, edited by D.K. Levine, University of Chicago Press, 1971.

While the publisher has made every effort to contact all copyright holders, if any have been inadvertently omitted the publisher will be pleased to make the necessary arrangements at the first opportunity.

Part 1

KEY CONCEPTS AND TOPICS

ACTION

See also WEBER, PARSONS

In 'action' is included all human behaviour when and in so far as the acting **1** individual attaches a subjective meaning to it. Action in this sense may be either overt or purely inward or subjective; it may consist of positive intervention in a situation, or of deliberately refraining from such intervention or passively acquiescing in the situation. Action is social in so far as, by virtue of the subjective meaning attached to it by the acting individual (or individuals) it takes account of the behaviour of others and is thereby oriented in its course.
Max Weber, *The Theory of Social and Economic Organization*, trans. A. M. Henderson and T. Parsons, New York, Oxford University Press, 1947; New York, Free Press (pbk), 1964, p. 88. First published in German in 1922.

Action consists of the structures and processes by which human beings form **2** meaningful intentions and, more or less successfully, implement them in concrete situations. The word 'meaningful' implies the symbolic or cultural level of representation and reference. Intentions and implementation taken together imply a disposition of the action system – individual or collective – to modify its relation to its situation or environment in an intended direction.

We prefer the term 'action' to 'behavior' because we are interested not in the physical events of behavior for their own sake but in their patterning, their patterned meaningful products (physical, cultural, and other), ranging from implements to works of art, and the mechanisms and processes that control such patterning.

Human action is 'cultural' in that meanings and intentions concerning acts are formed in terms of symbolic systems (including the codes through which they operate in patterns) that focus most generally about the universal of human societies, language.
Talcott Parsons, *Societies: Evolutionary and Comparative Perspectives*, Englewood Cliffs, New Jersey, Prentice-Hall, 1966, p. 5.

The most fundamental assumptions that inform any social scientific theory **3** concern the nature of action and order. Every theory of society assumes an image of man as an actor, assumes an answer to the question, 'What is action?' Every theory contains an implicit understanding of motivation. Is it efficient and rational, concerned primarily with objective calculation? Or is it nonrational and subjective, oriented towards moral concerns or altruism, strongly affected, perhaps, by internal emotional concerns? The problem of action is concerned, in other words, with epistemology, with the relative materialism and idealism of action. Action has vexed and divided classical thinkers from Plato and Aristotle to Augustine and Hobbes, and

it continues to do so today. Modern social science was born from the eighteenth- and nineteenth-century struggles between Enlightenment rationalists and traditionalists, and later between romantics and utilitarians. This struggle was, to an important degree, a fight about whether – and how – action was 'rational' . . .
Jeffrey C. Alexander, *Action and Its Environments*, New York, Columbia University Press, 1988, p. 13.

4 The presuppositions of any social theory are the positions a theory takes about the nature of human action and the manner in which plural actions are interrelated. The problem of action refers basically to epistemological questions: to problems of idealism and materialism, which are usually formulated sociologically in terms of the relative 'rationality' of the prototypical actor in any theoretical system. The problem of order, on the other hand, refers to the problem of how consistent patterns of such rational or nonrational actions are created: are patterns of action the result of continuous negotiation between relatively separated individuals or is this patterning – at least in part – the result of the imposition (either consensually or coercively) on individuals of a sui generis, prior structure or pattern?
Ibid., p. 223.

ADOLESCENCE

See also FAMILY

Much psychological research has suggested the very great importance to the individual of his affective ties, established in early childhood, to other members of his family of orientation. When strong affective ties have been formed, it seems reasonable to believe that situational pressures which force their drastic modification will impose important strains upon the individual.

Since all known kinship systems impose an incest tabu, the transition from asexual intrafamilial relationships to the sexual relation of marriage – generally to a previously relatively unknown person – is general. But with us this transition is accompanied by a process of 'emancipation' from the ties both to parents and to siblings, which is considerably more drastic than in most kinship systems, especially in that it applies to both sexes about equally, and includes emancipation from solidarity with *all* members of the family of orientation about equally, so that there is relatively little continuity with *any* kinship ties established by birth for anyone.

The effect of these factors is reinforced by two others. Since the effective kinship unit is normally the conjugal family, the child's emotional attachments to kin are confined to relatively few persons instead of being distributed more widely. Especially important, perhaps, is the fact that no other adult woman has a role remotely similar to that of the mother. Hence the average intensity of affective involvement in family relations is likely to be high. Secondly, the child's relations outside the family are only to a small extent ascribed. Both in the play group and in the school he must to a large extent 'find his own level' in competition with others. Hence the psychological significance of his security within the family is heightened.

We have then a situation where at the same time the inevitable importance of family ties is intensified and a necessity to become emancipated from them is imposed. This situation would seem to have a good deal to do with the fact that with us adolescence – and beyond – is, as has been frequently noted, a 'difficult' period in the life cycle. In particular, associated with this situation is the prominence in our society of what has been called a 'youth culture', a distinctive pattern of values and attitudes of the age groups between childhood and the assumption of full adult responsibilities. This youth culture, with its irresponsibility, its pleasure-seeking, its 'rating and dating', and its intensification of the romantic love pattern, is not a simple matter of 'apprenticeship' in adult values and responsibilities. It bears many of the marks of reaction to emotional tension and insecurity, and in all probability has among its functions that of easing the difficult process of adjustment from childhood emotional dependency to full 'maturity'. In it we find still a third element underlying the prominence of the romantic love complex in American society.

Talcott Parsons, 'The Kinship System of the Contemporary United States', *Essays in Sociological Theory*, New York, Free Press, 1954, pp. 189–90.

AGEING

At the point of retirement, we may make a generalized picture of the male. He has a well-ingrained self-image as competent, successful at some level of work, usefully productive, self-supporting, and able to provide for his family. This image has been built-up over years of time by the favorable reactions of his family, friends, co-workers, and those segments of society whose opinions he values. He has, moreover, found a kind of work – a social role – that permits him to express his self-image satisfactorily, and he is firmly incorporated into a physical environment and a group of co-workers which make it possible for him to carry out his role.

Using the concepts employed above, let us consider what happens at the point of compulsory retirement. First, the means of carrying out the social role disappears: the man is a lawyer without a case, a bookkeeper without books, a machinist without tools. Second, he is excluded from his group of former co-workers; as an isolated person he may be completely unable to function in his former role. Third, as a retired person, he begins to find a different evaluation of himself in the minds of others from the evaluation he had as an employed person. He no longer sees respect in the eyes of former

5

subordinates, praise in the faces of former superiors, and approval in the manner of former co-workers. The looking-glass composed of his former important groups throws back a changed image: he is done for, an old-timer, old fashioned, on the shelf. Fourth, he cannot accept this new evaluation for several reasons. He has had the old self-image for so many years that it has become part and parcel of him and is no longer dependent upon the current reflection of himself that he sees in the words and gestures of others. Long ago he internalized satisfying group reflections which now form a kind of independent self-conception. His self-image therefore is in conflict with the reflection he now finds in the attitudes and actions of others. Any movement toward solving the conflict is made difficult because the new self-image offered by those around him is of lower valuation than his internalized self-image.

Therefore at retirement we have a man still motivated by his old self-conception, but separated from his previous roles and many of his previous evaluative groups. He is a true social isolate. Moreover, the faint traces of a new self-image that he sees reflected in old and perhaps new groups is distasteful and unrewarding. His emotional reactions are likely to be distressing.

Ruth Shonle Cavan, 'Self and Role in Adjustment during Old Age', in A. M. Rose (ed.), *Human Behavior and Social Processes: An Interactionist Approach*, Boston, Houghton Mifflin, 1962, pp. 527–8.

ALIENATION

See also MARX

1   The alienation imputable to private ownership of the instruments of production manifests itself in the fact that work – the essentially human activity which defines man's humanity, as it were – has lost its human characteristics, because for the wage earner it has become merely a means of obtaining the wage necessary to maintain his existence. Instead of work being the expression of man himself, work has been degraded into an instrument, a means of livelihood. The entrepreneurs themselves are in a sense alienated, because the commodities they produce do not answer needs which are truly experienced by others but are put on the market in order to procure a profit for the entrepreneur. Thus the entrepreneur becomes a slave to an unpredictable market which is at the mercy of the hazards of competition. Exploiting the wage earner, he is not thereby humanized in his work, since he himself is alienated in the interests of the anonymous mechanism of the market.

Raymond Aron, *Main Currents in Sociological Thought* (2 vols), Harmondsworth, Penguin, 1970, vol. 1, p. 148.

In what does this alienation of labour consist? First, that the work is *external*   **2**
to the worker, that it is not part of his nature, that consequently he does not
fulfil himself in his work but denies himself, has a feeling of misery, not of
well-being, does not develop freely a physical and mental energy, but is
physically exhausted and mentally debased. The worker therefore feels
himself at home only during his leisure, whereas at work he feels homeless.
His work is not voluntary but imposed, *forced labour*. It is not the satisfaction of a need, but only a *means* for satisfying other needs. Its alien
character is clearly shown by the fact that as soon as there is no physical
or other compulsion it is avoided like the plague. Finally, the alienated
character of work for the worker appears in the fact that it is not his work
but work for someone else, that in work he does not belong to himself but
to another person.
Karl Marx, *Economic and Philosophical Manuscripts* [1844]; trans. T. Bottomore in
E. Fromm (ed.), *Marx's Concept of Man*, New York, Frederick Ungar, 1961, pp. 98–9.

The alienation of the worker in his product means not only that his labour   **3**
becomes an object, takes on its own existence, but that it exists outside him,
independently, and alien to him, and that it stands opposed to him as an
autonomous power.
Ibid., p. 96.

ANOMIE

See also DURKHEIM

Anomie is easy to define etymologically, but not semantically. The etymo-   **1**
logical definition of anomie is fixed and is obvious to anyone who knows its
Greek origin, *anomia* – absence of law. But such a definition is so broad as
to be almost useless. The semantic definition, instead, is obtained from the
contextual use of the word at different historical times – it is more specific,
but also varies greatly throughout the literature, reflecting specific concerns
of different epochs and cultures. Anomie means ruthlessness and *hybris*
in Euripides, anarchy and intemperance in Plato, sin and wickedness in
the Old Testament, unrighteousness or unwritten law in Paul's letters,
irregularity or formal transgression in Bishop Bramhall's treatises, a positive
characteristic of modern morality in Jean Marie Guyau's books, and a
human condition of insatiability in Durkheim.
Marco Orrù, *Anomie: History and Meanings*, Boston and London, Allen & Unwin,
1987, p. 2.

Society is the guardian of order and meaning not only objectively in its   **2**
institutional structures, but subjectively as well in its structuring of
individual consciousness.

It is for this reason that radical separation from the social world, or anomy, constitutes such a powerful threat to the individual.

Peter L. Berger, *The Sacred Canopy*, New York, Doubleday, 1967, pp. 21–2. Published in Britain as *The Social Reality of Religion*, London, Faber & Faber, 1969.

3   If the division of labour does not produce solidarity in all these cases, it is because the relations of the organs are not regulated, because they are in a state of anomy.

Émile Durkheim, *The Division of Labour*, trans. George Simpson, New York, Macmillan, 1933, p. 368. First published in French in 1893.

4   We repeatedly insist in the course of this book upon the state of juridical and moral anomy in which economic life actually is found.

Ibid., pp. 1–2.

5   With increased prosperity desires increase. At the very moment when traditional rules have lost their authority, the richer prize offered these appetites stimulates them and makes them more exigent and impatient of control. The state of de-regulation or anomy is thus further heightened by passions being less disciplined, precisely when they need more disciplining.

Émile Durkheim, *Suicide*, trans. J. A. Spaulding and G. Simpson, Glencoe, Illinois, Free Press, 1951, p. 253. First published in French 1897.

6   No society lacks norms governing conduct. But societies do differ in the degree to which folkways, mores and institutional controls are effectively integrated with the goals which stand high in the hierarchy of cultural values. The culture may be such as to lead individuals to center their emotional convictions upon the complex of culturally acclaimed ends, with far less emotional support for prescribed methods of reaching out for these ends. With such differential emphases upon goals and institutional procedures, the latter may be so vitiated by the stress on goals as to have the behavior of many individuals limited only by considerations of technical expediency. In this context, the sole significant question becomes: Which of the available procedures is most efficient in netting the culturally approved value? The technically most effective procedure, whether culturally legitimate or not, becomes typically preferred to institutionally prescribed conduct. As this process of attenuation continues, the society becomes unstable and there develops what Durkheim called 'anomie' (normlessness).

Robert K. Merton, *Social Theory and Social Structure* [1949], London and New York, Free Press, 1968, p. 189.

AUTHORITY

See also BUREAUCRACY, WEBER

Any social order is a tissue of authorities. In contemporary society these **1**
authorities range from the mild and provident authority of a mother over
her infant to the absolute, unconditional, and imprescriptible authority of
the national state. Some system or pattern of authority is involved in any
continuing social aggregate. The moment two or more persons find themselves in a relationship that involves, in whatever degree of informality or
formality, the distribution of responsibilities, duties, needs, privileges, and
rewards, a pattern of authority is present.
Robert A. Nisbet, *The Social Bond*, New York, Alfred A. Knopf, 1970, p. 113.

When there is no organization there is no authority. Authority appears **2**
only in organized groups – the associations – of society, never in unorganized
groups or in the unorganized community. An absence of organization
implies an absence of authority. There is authority only within an association, never in the interstices between associations. The exercise of
authority, furthermore, never extends beyond the limits of the association
in which it is institutionalized and which gives it support and sanction.
Robert Bierstedt, 'The Problem of Authority', in M. Berger, T. Abel and C. H.
Page (eds), *Freedom and Control in Modern Society*, New York, Van Nostrand,
1954, pp. 67–81. Quoted in R. A. Nisbet, *The Social Bond*, New York, Alfred A.
Knopf, 1970, p. 117.

BUREAUCRACY

See also WEBER

Legal authority: the pure type with employment of a bureaucratic adminis- **1**
trative staff . . .
   The following may thus be said to be the fundamental categories of
rational legal authority:

1   A continuous organization of official functions bound by rules.
2   A specified sphere of competence . . .
3   The organization of offices follows the principle of hierarchy . . .
4   The rules which regulate the conduct of an office may be technical rules
    or norms. In both cases, if their application is to be fully rational,
    specialized training is necessary . . .
5   In the rational type it is a matter of principle that the members of the
    administrative staff should be completely separated from ownership of
    the means of production or administration . . .

9

6 In the rational case, there is also a complete absence of appropriation of his official position by the incumbent ...

7 Administrative acts, decisions and rules are formulated and recorded in writing ...

8 Legal authority can be exercised in a variety of different forms ... The purest type of exercise of legal authority is that which employs a bureaucratic administrative staff ...

Max Weber, *The Theory of Social and Economic Organization*, trans. A. M. Henderson and T. Parsons, New York, Free Press, 1947, pp. 330–2. First published in German in 1922.

2 The purest type of exercise of legal authority is that which employs a bureaucratic staff ... who are appointed and function according to the following criteria:

1 They are personally free and subject to authority only with respect to their impersonal official obligations.

2 They are organized in a clearly defined hierarchy of offices.

3 Each office has a clearly defined sphere of competence in the legal sense.

4 The office is filled by a free contractual relationship ...

5 Candidates are selected on the basis of technical qualifications ...

6 They are remunerated by fixed salaries in money ...

7 The office is treated as the sole, or at least the primary, occupation of the incumbent.

8 It constitutes a career ...

9 The official works entirely separated from ownership of the means of administration ...

10 He is subject to strict and systematic discipline and control in the conduct of the office.

Ibid., pp. 333–4.

3 The development of the modern form of organization of corporate groups in all fields is nothing less than identical with the development and continued spread of bureaucratic administration.
Ibid., p. 337.

4 Bureaucracy is the sworn enemy of individual liberty, and of all bold initiative in matters of internal policy. The dependence upon superior authorities characteristic of the average employee suppresses individuality and gives to the society in which employees predominate a narrow petty-bourgeois and philistine stamp. The bureaucratic spirit corrupts character and engenders moral poverty. In every bureaucracy we may observe place-hunting, a mania for promotion, and obsequiousness towards those on whom promotion depends; there is an arrogance towards inferiors and servility towards superiors ... We may even say that the more conspicuously a bureaucracy is distinguished by its zeal, by its sense of duty, and by its devotion, the more also will it show itself to be petty, narrow, rigid, and illiberal.

Robert Michels, *Political Parties: A Sociological Study of Oligarchical Tendencies of Modern Democracy*, New York, Free Press, 1949, p. 189. First published in German in 1911.

Such inadequacies in orientation which involve trained incapacity clearly **5** derive from structural sources. The process may be briefly recapitulated. (1) An effective bureaucracy demands reliability of response and strict devotion to regulations. (2) Such devotion to the rules leads to their transformation into absolutes; they are no longer conceived as relative to a set of purposes. (3) This interferes with ready adaptation under special conditions not clearly envisaged by those who drew up the general rules. (4) Thus, the very elements which conduce toward efficiency in general produce inefficiency in specific instances.

Robert K. Merton, 'Bureaucratic Structure and Personality' [1949]; reprinted in R. K. Merton, *Social Theory and Social Structure*, New York, Free Press, 1968, p. 254.

CAPITALISM

Capitalist production requires exchange relations, commodities, and **1** money, but its *differentia specifica* is the purchase and sale of labour power. For this purpose, three basic conditions must become generalized throughout society. First, workers are separated from the means with which production is carried on, and can gain access to them only by selling their labour power to others. Second, workers are freed of legal constraints, such as serfdom or slavery, that prevent them from disposing of their own labour power. Third, the purpose of the employment of the worker becomes the expansion of a unit of capital belonging to the employer, who is thus functioning as a capitalist. The labour process therefore begins with a contract or agreement governing the conditions of the sale of labour power by the worker and its purchase by the employer. It is important to take note of the historical character of this phenomenon. While the purchase and sale of labour power has existed from antiquity, a substantial class of wage-workers did not begin to form in Europe until the fourteenth century, and did not become numerically significant until the rise of industrial capitalism (that is the *production* of commodities on a capitalist basis, as against mercantile capitalism, which merely exchanged the surplus products of prior forms of production) in the eighteenth century.

Harry Braverman, *Labor and Monopoly Capital*, New York, Monthly Review Press, 1974, pp. 52–3.

The capitalistic economy of the present day is an immense cosmos into **2** which the individual is born, and which presents itself to him, at least as an individual, as an unalterable order of things in which he must live. It forces the individual, in so far as he is involved in the system of market relationships, to conform to capitalistic rules of action. The manufacturer who, in the long run, acts counter to these norms, will just as inevitably be eliminated from the economic scene as the worker who cannot or will not adapt himself to them will be thrown into the streets without a job.

Max Weber, *The Protestant Ethic and the Spirit of Capitalism*, trans. T. Parsons, London, Allen & Unwin, 1930, pp. 54–5. First published in German in 1904–5.

CAREER

See also GOFFMAN

1 Traditionally the term *career* has been reserved for those who expect to enjoy the rises laid out within a respectable profession. The term is coming to be used, however, in a broadened sense to refer to any social strand of any person's course through life . . .

One value of the concept of career is its two-sidedness. One side is linked to internal matters held dearly and closely, such as image of self and felt identity; the other side concerns official position, jural relations, and style of life, and is part of a publicly accessible institutional complex. The concept of career, then, allows one to move back and forth between the personal and the public, between the self and its significant society, without having to rely overly for data upon what the person says he thinks he imagines himself to be.

Erving Goffman, *Asylums: Essays on the Social Situation of Mental Patients and Other Inmates*, New York, Doubleday, 1961, p. 127.

2 Subjectively career is the moving perspective in which a person sees his life as a whole, and interprets his attributes, actions and the things which happen to him . . . objectively it is a series of statuses and clearly defined offices . . . typical sequences of position, responsibility and even of adventure.

Everett Hughes, 'Institutional Office and the Person', *American Journal of Sociology*, vol. 43, 1937, pp. 409–10.

CHARISMA

'Charisma' shall be understood to refer to an extraordinary quality of a person, regardless of whether this quality is actual, alleged, or presumed. 'Charismatic authority', hence, shall refer to a rule over men, whether predominantly external or predominantly internal, to which the governed submit because of their belief in the extraordinary quality of the specific person.

Max Weber, 'The Social Psychology of the World Religions', in H. H. Gerth and C. Wright Mills (eds), *From Max Weber*, New York, Oxford University Press, 1946, p. 295.

CHURCH

See also SECT

The church is that type of organization which is overwhelmingly conservative, which to a certain extent accepts the secular order, and dominates the masses; in principle, therefore, it is universal, i.e. it desires to cover the whole life of humanity. The sects, on the other hand, are comparatively small groups; they aspire after personal inward perfection, and they aim at a direct personal fellowship between the members of each group.
Ernst Troeltsch, *The Social Teaching of the Christian Churches* (2 vols), London, Allen & Unwin, 1931, vol. 1, p. 331.

CITIZENSHIP

I shall be running true to type as a sociologist if I begin by saying that I **1** propose to divide citizenship into three parts. But the analysis is, in this case, dictated by history even more clearly than by logic. I shall call these three parts, or elements, civil, political and social. The civil element is composed of the rights necessary for individual freedom – liberty of the person, freedom of speech, thought and faith, the right to own property and to conclude valid contracts, and the right to justice. The last is of a different order from the others, because it is the right to defend and assert all one's rights on terms of equality with others and by due process of law. This shows us that the institutions most directly associated with civil rights are the courts of justice. By the political element I mean the right to participate in the exercise of political power, as a member of a body invested with political authority or as an elector of the members of such a body. The corresponding institutions are parliament and councils of local government. By the social element I mean the whole range from the right to a modicum of economic welfare and security to the right to share to the full in the social heritage and to live the life of a civilised being according to the standards prevailing in the society. The institutions most closely connected with it are the educational system and the social services.
T. H. Marshall, *Citizenship and Social Class and Other Essays*, Cambridge, Cambridge University Press, 1950. Extract in J. Allen, P. Braham and P. Lewis (eds), *Political and Economic Forms of Modernity*, Cambridge, Polity Press, 1992, pp. 218–19.

2 Is it still true that basic equality, when enriched in substance and embodied in the formal rights of citizenship, is consistent with the inequalities of social class? I shall suggest that our society today assumes the two are still compatible, so much so that citizenship has itself become, in certain respects, the architect of legitimate social inequality.

Ibid., p. 50.

3 The word 'citizen' derives from the Latin *civitas* (meaning 'citizenship', 'body of citizens' and, more rarely, 'city'). In its classical origins, the notion of citizenship was intimately connected with membership of a city. Roman citizens enjoyed certain rights (e.g. voting in assemblies) and acquired certain responsibilities (e.g. military service) as a consequence of belonging to Rome. Initially limited to those belonging to the city of Rome, the rights of citizenship were later extended throughout the Roman Empire. Citizenship was thus associated from an early stage with membership of a state and the word has retained this sense in modern times, so that current usage is synonymous with membership of a nation-state, with being an enfranchised inhabitant of a country.

Denise Riley, 'Citizenship and the Welfare State', in J. Allen, P. Braham and P. Lewis (eds), *Political and Economic Forms of Modernity*, Cambridge, Polity Press, 1992, p. 181.

4 The extremely difficult problem faced by women in their attempt to win full citizenship I shall call 'Wollstonecraft's dilemma'. The dilemma is that the two routes toward citizenship that women have pursued are mutually incompatible within the confines of the patriarchal welfare state, and, within that context, they are impossible to achieve. For three centuries, since universal citizenship first appeared as a political ideal, women have continued to challenge their alleged natural subordination within private life. From at least the 1790s they have also struggled with the task of trying to become citizens within an ideal and practice that have gained universal meaning through their exclusion. Women's response has been complex. On the one hand, they have demanded that the ideal of citizenship be extended to them, and the liberal-feminist agenda for a 'gender-neutral' social world is the logical conclusion of one form of this demand. On the other hand, women have also insisted, often simultaneously, as did Mary Wollstonecraft, that as women they have specific capacities, talents, needs and concerns, so that the expression of their full citizenship will be differentiated from that of men. Their unpaid work providing welfare could be seen, as Wollstonecraft saw women's tasks as mothers, as women's work as citizens, just as their husbands' paid work is central to men's citizenship.

Carole Pateman, *The Disorder of Women: Democracy, Feminism and Political Theory*, Cambridge, Polity Press, 1989, p. 197.

CIVILIZING PROCESS

An investigation lasting several years now published under the overall title *The Civilizing Process*, showed, to put it very briefly, that the social standard of conduct and sentiment, particularly in some upper-class circles, began to change fairly drastically from the sixteenth century onwards in a particular direction. The ruling of conduct and sentiment became stricter, more differentiated and all-embracing, but also more even, more temperate, banishing excesses of self-castigation as well as of self-indulgence. The change found its expression in a new term launched by Erasmus of Rotterdam and used in many other countries as a symbol of the new refinement of manners, the term 'civility', which later gave rise to the verb 'to civilize'. Further research made it probable that state-formation processes and particularly the subjection of warrior classes to stricter control, the 'courtization' of nobles in continental countries, had something to do with the change in the code of sentiment and conduct.

As it happened, research into the development of sport showed an overall development of the code of conduct and sentiment in the same direction. If one compares the folk-games played with a ball in the late Middle Ages or even in early modern times with soccer and rugby, the two branches of English football which emerged in the nineteenth century, one can notice an increasing sensitivity with regard to violence. The same direction of change can be seen, for instance, in the development of boxing . . .

If one tries to discover why the tempering of violence in pastimes, which is one of the distinguishing characteristics of sport, made its appearance first among the English upper classes during the eighteenth century, one cannot avoid looking rather closely at the development of tensions and violence involving these classes in society at large. Once a country has gone through cycles of violence, of which revolutions are examples, it usually takes a long time for the groups involved in such an experience to forget it. Many generations must pass before the antagonistic groups can trust each other sufficiently to live peacefully side by side and to allow, if they are members of one and the same state, a parliamentary regime to function properly . . .

In that respect, a parliamentary regime shows some affinity with sport-games. A specific type of leisure activities, among them hunting, boxing, racing and some ball games, assumed the characteristics of sport and, in fact, were first called sport, in England during the eighteenth century, that is, in the same period in which the ancient estate assemblies, the House of Lords and the House of Commons, representing small, privileged sections of society, formed the principal battle-ground where it was determined who should form the government. Among the chief requirements of a parliamentary regime as it emerged in England in the course of the eighteenth century was the readiness of a faction or party in government to hand over office to its opponents without the use of violence if the rules of the parliamentary game required it.

Norbert Elias, 'Introduction', in Norbert Elias and Eric Dunning, *Quest for Excitement: Sport and Leisure in the Civilizing Process* [1986], Oxford, Blackwell, 1993 (pbk edn), pp. 20–8.

CIVIL SOCIETY

1   'Civil society' refers to those agencies, institutions, movements, cultural forces and social relationships which are both privately or voluntarily organized and which are not directly controlled by the state. This includes households, religious groups, trade unions, private companies, political parties, humanitarian organizations, environmental groups, the women's movement, Parent–Teacher Associations and so on. In simple terms, 'civil society' refers to the realm of private power and private organizations whereas the state is the realm of public power and public organizations. Of course, this is by no means a fixed or finely calibrated distinction since the public and the private can never be so readily differentiated. Feminists, for instance, would argue that power relations in the household are significantly structured by the welfare and regulatory activities of the state and so are not constituted solely in the private sphere. Through its powers to make law as well as its spending, taxing, employment, education, health and social security policies, the state is deeply enmeshed in the institutions and processes of civil society. In effect, through its actions or inactions, the state effectively establishes the contours and constructs the framework of civil society. It is therefore possible to argue that the state constitutes civil society because of its power to define and redefine the legal and political boundaries between the public and private spheres.

Anthony McGrew, 'The State in Advanced Capitalist Societies', in J. Allen, P. Braham and P. Lewis (eds), *Political and Economic Forms of Modernity*, Cambridge, Polity Press, 1992, p. 69.

2   Assuming the need for these mechanisms of supervision of necessary political power, must we not from here on speak of the 'road to socialism' not as the abolition of the (contractarian) distinction between civil society and the state, as Marx would have it, but rather as the *deepening* of this distinction? In other words, should not democratic socialist movements be concerned to constitute or reinforce public spheres within regions of social power now presently in distress and seriously endangered by the activities of state and corporate bureaucracies? Is it not only through a plurality of public spheres within the domain of society that individuals and groups could autonomously defend themselves from arbitrary power? Can we therefore speak of the need for a postliberal reconstruction of civil society – of a 'socialist civil society' of nonpatriarchal public spheres that relate to state institutions only at the level of criticism, negotiation, and compromise?

Could the relations between autonomous public spheres within a socialist civil society come to resemble relations between federated and highly differentiated local communities, which temporarily surrender and entrust only such part of their powers as is necessary for the realization of their aims? So conceived, might not autonomous publics legitimately exercise their rights to secede from this federation? Might autonomous publics with good reason redefine areas of life as private, as beyond the scope of legitimate state activity?
John Keane, *Public Life and Late Capitalism*, Cambridge, Cambridge University Press, 1984, p. 257.

Civil society has the following components: **3**
(1) *Plurality*: families, informal groups, and voluntary associations whose plurality and autonomy allow for a variety of forms of life; (2) *Publicity*: institutions of culture and communication; (3) *Privacy*: a domain of individual self-development and moral choice; and (4) *Legality*: structures of general laws and basic rights needed to demarcate plurality, privacy, and publicity from at least the state and, tendentially, the economy.
Jean L. Cohen and Andrew Adato, *Civil Society and Political Theory*, Cambridge, Massachusetts, and London, MIT Press, 1992, p. 346.

CLASS

See also MARX, WEBER

It will be useful at this juncture to state what class is *not*. First, a class is **1** not a specific 'entity' – that is to say, a bounded social form in the way in which a business firm or a university is – and a class has no publicly sanctioned identity. It is extremely important to stress this, since established linguistic usage often encourages us to apply active verbs to the term 'class'; but the sense in which a class 'acts' in a certain way, or 'perceives' elements in its environment on a par with an individual actor, is highly elliptical, and this sort of verbal usage is to be avoided wherever possible. Similarly, it is perhaps misleading to speak of 'membership' of a class, since this might be held to imply participation in a definite 'group'. This form of expression, however, is difficult to avoid altogether, and I shall not attempt to do so in what follows. Secondly, class has to be distinguished from 'stratum', and class theory from the study of 'stratification' as such. The latter, comprising what Ossowski terms a gradation scheme, involves a criterion or set of criteria in terms of which individuals may be ranked descriptively along a scale. The distinction between class and stratum is again a matter of some significance, and bears directly upon the problem of class 'boundaries'. For the divisions between strata, for analytical purposes, may be drawn very precisely, since they may be set upon a measurement scale – as, for

example, with 'income strata'. The divisions between classes are *never* of this sort; nor, moreover, do they lend themselves to easy visualisation, in terms of any ordinal scale of 'higher' and 'lower', as strata do – although, once more, this sort of imagery cannot be escaped altogether. Finally, we must distinguish clearly between class and elite. Elite theory, as formulated by Pareto and Mosca, developed in part as a conscious and deliberate repudiation of class analysis. In place of the concept of class relationships, the elite theorists substituted the opposition of 'elite' and 'mass'; and in place of the Marxian juxtaposition of class society and classlessness they substituted the idea of the cyclical replacement of elites *in perpetuo*.
Anthony Giddens, *The Class Structure of the Advanced Societies*, London, Hutchinson, 2nd edn 1980, p. 106.

2   What are social classes in Marxist theory? They are groups of social agents, of men defined *principally* but not exclusively by their place in the *production process*, i.e. by their place in the economic sphere. The economic place of the social agents has a *principal* role in determining social classes. But from that we cannot conclude that this economic place is sufficient to determine social classes. Marxism states that the economic does indeed have the determinant role in a mode of production or a social formation; but the political and the ideological (the superstructure) also have an important role. For whenever Marx, Engels, Lenin and Mao analyse social classes, far from limiting themselves to the economic criteria alone, they make explicit reference to political and ideological criteria. We can thus say that a social class is defined by its *place* in the ensemble of social practices, i.e. by its place in the ensemble of the division of labour which includes political and ideological relations. This place corresponds to *the structural determination* of classes, i.e. the manner in which determination by the structure (relations of production, politico-ideological domination/subordination) operates on class practices – for classes have existence only in the class struggle.
Nicos Poulantzas, 'On Social Classes', *New Left Review*, vol. 78, 1973, p. 27.

3   Three clusters of positions within the social division of labour can be characterized as occupying contradictory locations within class relations ... 1. *managers and supervisors* occupy a contradictory location between the bourgeoisie and the proletariat; 2. certain categories of *semi-autonomous employees* who retain relatively high levels of control over their immediate labour process occupy a contradictory location between the working class and the petty bourgeoisie; 3. *small employers* occupy a contradictory location between the bourgeoisie and the petty bourgeoisie.
Erik Olin Wright, *Class, Crisis and the State*, London, New Left Books, 1978, p. 61.

4   Working from very similar premises, several quite independent investigations have suggested that there seem to be two very broad ways in which individuals conceptualise class structure: 'power' or 'conflict' or

'dichotomous' models on the one hand; and 'prestige' or 'status' or 'hierarchical' models on the other. Further it has been proposed that the social ideology of the working class tends to take the form of a power model whereas that of the middle class approximates the hierarchical model. Although some of these studies have noted variations in social imagery within the working class, they have concentrated chiefly on explaining the variations between the classes. Thus the power or dichotomous ideology of the working class and the hierarchical ideology of the middle class have been accounted for primarily in terms of differences in the industrial life chances and life experiences of manual and non-manual employees. While the similarity of these various investigations is very striking, it is also quite clear from other studies that the industrial and community milieux of manual workers exhibit a very considerable diversity and it would be strange if there were no correspondingly marked variations in the images of society held by different sections of the working class. Indeed, on the basis of existing research, it is possible to delineate at least three different types of workers and to infer that the work and community relationships by which they are differentiated from one another may also generate very different forms of social consciousness. The three types are as follows: first, the traditional worker of the 'proletarian' variety whose image of society will take the form of a power model; secondly, the other variety of traditional worker, the 'deferential', whose perception of social inequality will be one of status hierarchy; and, thirdly, the 'privatised' worker, whose social consciousness will most nearly approximate what may be called a 'pecuniary' model of society.

David Lockwood, 'Sources of Variation in Working-Class Images of Society', *Sociological Review*, vol. 14, 1966, p. 249.

Exclusion and usurpation may therefore be regarded as the two main 5 generic types of social closure, the latter always being a consequence of, and collective response to, the former.

Strategies of exclusion are the predominant mode of closure in all stratified systems. Where the excluded in their turn also succeed in closing off access to remaining rewards and opportunities, so multiplying the number of substrata, the stratification order approaches the furthest point of contrast to the Marxist model of class polarisation. The traditional caste system and the stratification of ethnic communities in the United States provide the clearest illustration of this closure pattern, though similar processes are easily detectable in societies in which class formation is paramount. Strategies of usurpation vary in scale from those designed to bring about marginal redistribution to those aimed at total expropriation. But whatever their intended scale they nearly always contain a potential challenge to the prevailing system of allocation and to the authorized version of distributive justice.

All this indicates the ease with which the language of closure can be translated into the language of power. Modes of closure can be thought of as different means of mobilizing power for the purpose of engaging in distributive struggle. To conceive of power as a built-in attribute of closure is at the very least to dispense with those fruitless searches for its 'location' inspired by Weber's more familiar but completely unhelpful definition in terms of the ubiquitous struggle between contending wills. Moreover, to speak of power in the light of closure principles is quite consistent with the analysis of class relations. Thus, to anticipate the discussion, the familiar distinction between bourgeoisie and proletariat, in its class as well as in its modern guise, may be conceived of as an expression of conflict between classes defined not specifically in relation to their place in the productive process but in relation to their prevalent modes of closure, exclusion and usurpation, respectively.

Frank Parkin, *The Marxist Theory of Class: A Bourgeois Critique*, London, Tavistock, 1979, pp. 45–6.

6   The capitalist class transformed into the managerial class.
Pitrim Sorokin, 'What Is a Social Class?', in R. Bendix and S. M. Lipset (eds), *Class, Status and Power*, Glencoe, Illinois, Free Press, 1953, p. 90.

7   The basic phenomenon seems to have been the shift in control of enterprise from the property interests of founding families to managerial and technical personnel who as such have not had a comparable vested interest in ownership.
Talcott Parsons, 'A Revised Analytical Approach to the Theory of Social Stratification', in R. Bendix and S. M. Lipset (eds), *Class, Status and Power*, Glencoe, Illinois, Free Press, 1953, pp. 122–3.

8   Our review of discrepant findings on the alleged separation of ownership and control in the large corporation in the United States, and of the problems entailed in obtaining reliable and valid evidence on the actual ownership interests involved in a given corporation, should make it clear that the absence of control by proprietary interests in the largest corporations is by no means an 'unquestionable', 'incontrovertible', 'singular', or 'critical' social 'fact'. Nor can one any longer have confidence in such assurances as the following by Robert A. Dahl (1970): 'Every literate person now rightly takes for granted what Berle and Means established four decades ago in their famous study, *The Modern Corporation and Private Property*' (p. 125). On the contrary, I believe that the 'separation of ownership and control' may well be one of those rather critical, widely accepted, pseudofacts with which all sciences occasionally have found themselves burdened and bedevilled.
Maurice Zeitlin, 'Corporate Ownership and Control: The Large Corporation and the Capitalist Class', *American Journal of Sociology*, vol. 79, no. 5, 1974, p. 1107.

Capitalist production, therefore, under its aspect of a continuous connected **9** process, of a process of reproduction, produces not only commodities, not only surplus-value, but it also produces and reproduces the capital relation; on the one side the capitalist, on the other the wage-labourer . . .

For the study of power in society the perspective of reproduction means that the commanding question of all the variants of the subjectivist approach – Who rules, a unified elite or competing leadership groups? Is the economic elite identical with or in control of the political elite? – is displaced by the question: What kind of society, what fundamental relations of production, are being reproduced? By what mechanisms? What role do the structure and actions and nonactions of the state (or of local government) play in this process of reproduction, furthering it, merely allowing it, or opposing it?

The analysis of reproduction makes possible an answer to the question of how the different moments of exercise of power in society are interrelated, even if there is no conscious, interpersonal interrelation. They are interrelated by their reproductive effects. A given kind of relations of production may be reproduced without the exploiting (dominant) class defined by them being in 'control' of the government in any usual and reasonable sense of the word, even though the interventions of the state further and/or allow these relations of production to be reproduced. And yet the fact that a specific form of exploitation and domination is being reproduced, is an example of class rule and is an important aspect of power in society.

Göran Therborn, 'What Does the Ruling Class Do When It Rules?', *Insurgent Sociologist*, vol. 6, no. 3, 1970, pp. 3–16. Extract in A. Giddens and D. Held (eds), *Classes, Power and Conflict*, London, Macmillan, 1982, pp. 232–3.

Class analysis, in our sense, has as its central concern the study of rela- **10** tionships among class structure, class mobility, class-based inequalities, and class-based action. More specifically, it explores the interconnections between positions defined by employment relations in labour markets and production units in different sectors of national economies; the processes through which individuals and families are distributed and redistributed among these positions over time; and the consequences thereof for their life-chances and for the social identities that they adopt and the social values and interests that they pursue. Understood in this way, class analysis does not entail a commitment to any particular theory of class but, rather, to a *research programme* – in, broadly, the sense of Lakatos (1970) – within which different, and indeed rival, theories may be formulated and then assessed in terms of their heuristic and explanatory performance . . . The programme is attractive in that it represents a specific way of investigating interconnections of the kind that have always engaged the sociological imagination: that is, between historically formed macrosocial structures,

on the one hand, and, on the other, the everyday experience of individuals within their particular social milieux, together with the patterns of action that follow from this experience. These are precisely the sort of inter-connections that, in C. Wright Mills' (1959) words, allow one to relate biography to history and 'personal troubles' to 'public issues'. From an analytical standpoint, the programme also promises economy of explana-tion: the ability to use a few well-defined concepts such as class position, class origins, class mobility or immobility, in order to explain a good deal both of what happens, or does not happen, to individuals across different aspects of their social lives and of how they subsequently respond.
J. H. Goldthorpe and G. Marshall, 'The Promising Future of Class Analysis: A Response to Recent Critiques', *Sociology*, vol. 26, no. 3, 1992, p. 382.

11 The key point in theoretical terms about the underclass seems to me to be that it is precisely not a class. Classes are essentially necessary social forces. It is no accident that Marx tried to link classes, not just to relations but to forces of production; he saw classes as being based on certain central social needs, one class which presides over the existing values and laws and rules and mode of production and the other class which represents some new opportunity for the future, some chances of development. The whole point about the underclass or the category of those who have dropped through the net is that they are not needed in this sense. Can I say in parenthesis that the real equivalent of the underclass on an international scale is the very poor countries. Their position in a world society and the extent to which they are needed or not needed presents analogous challenges, as does the extent to which there is an actual interest on the part of the richer countries in doing something for the poor or not. There may not be such an interest; there certainly is no massive and identifiable interest on the part of the official classes of the advanced societies to do something about the underclass. They could live quite happily with an underclass of 5, 10, 12, 15 per cent for a very long time and if they are rich enough and have arrangements like the Federal Republic of Germany, they can feed the underclass and not bother about the fact that they are not part of the labour market or indeed may not be part of political or social life in general. At the same time, it seems to me that tolerating a group of people for whom this is true, while professing values like those of work or the family, means that one tolerates a not insignificant group which has no stake in the accepted general values. If one tolerates a group which has no stake in the accepted general values, one cannot be surprised if people at the margin, and many others, increasingly cast doubt on these values and the values themselves begin to become much more tenuous and precarious than is sustainable for any length of time.
Ralf Dahrendorf, 'Footnotes to the Discussion', in David J. Smith (ed.), *Understanding the Underclass*, London, P.S.I., 1992, pp. 55–6.

COMMUNICATIONS

See also CULTURE, HABERMAS

Everyone, from politicians to academics, now agrees that public communi- **1**
cations systems are part of the 'cultural industries'. The popularity of this
tag points to a growing awareness that these organizations are both similar
to and different from other industries. On the one hand, they clearly have
a range of features in common with other areas of production and are
increasingly integrated into the general industrial structure. On the other
hand, it is equally clear that the goods they manufacture – the newspapers,
advertisements, television programmes, and feature films – play a pivotal
role in organizing the images and discourses through which people make
sense of the world. A number of writers acknowledge this duality rhetorically,
but go on to examine only one side, focusing either on the construction and
consumption of meanings (e.g. Fiske) or on the economic organization of
media industries (e.g. Collins, Garnham and Locksley). What distinguishes
the critical political economy perspective outlined here, is precisely its focus
on the interplay between the symbolic and economic dimensions of public
communications. It sets out to show how different ways of financing and
organizing cultural production have traceable consequences for the range of
discourses and representations in the public domain and for audiences'
access to them.
Peter Golding and Graham Murdock, 'Culture, Communications, and Political
Economy', in James Curran and Michael Gurevitch (eds), *Mass Media and Society*,
London and New York, Edward Arnold, 1991, p. 15.

Work on communications from within a cultural studies perspective 'is **2**
centrally concerned with the communication of meaning – how it is produced
in and through particular expressive forms and how it is continually negotiated and deconstructed through the practices of everyday life'.
Graham Murdock, 'Cultural Studies: Missing Links', *Critical Studies in Mass
Communication*, vol. 6, no. 4, December, 1989, p. 436. Quoted in J. Curran and M.
Gurevitch (eds), *Mass Media and Society*, London and New York, Edward Arnold,
1991, p. 16.

COMMUNITY

See also FOLK SOCIETY, *GEMEINSCHAFT* AND *GESELLSCHAFT*

Essentially the many and varied definitions of community are reducible to **1**
three.

1 Community as a fixed and bounded *locality* – that is, as a geographical

expression, denoting a human settlement located within a particular local territory. This is not really a sociological usage of community because, apart from the observation that they are all living together in a particular place, there is no consideration of the inhabitants at all, nor of how or, indeed, whether they interact with one another.

2 Community as a *local social system* – that is, as a set of social relationships which take place wholly, or mostly, within a locality. This is a more sociological usage of community since some indication is given of the social life of the area. Thus a community in this sense may be said to exist when a network of inter-relationships is established between those people living in the same locality (for example, where everyone knows everyone else). But note that nothing is being stated about the *content* of these relationships, merely the fact that individuals relate to one another. It may be, for example, that everyone knows everyone else in the locality, but that they all hate one another! Even if they were in constant conflict, however, they would still constitute a community in this second sense of the word.

3 Community as a *type of relationship*. More particularly, community is defined as a sense of identity between individuals (even though, in some cases, their mutual identification may never have resulted from any personal contact). This third definition corresponds most closely with the colloquial usage of community – the idea of a spirit of community, a sense of commonality among a group of people. In this meaning community may have no geographical (local) referent at all; a 'community spirit' may exist between individuals who are very widely scattered geographically. This notion of community, with its overtones of common identity, is perhaps best called *communion* since this word more clearly conveys what is involved. Most references to a loss of community in the modern world are in fact references to a loss of communion, a loss of meaningful identity with other people and the shared experiences which often accompany this identification.

Howard Newby, *Community*, Study Section 20 in the course *An Introduction to Sociology* (D207), Milton Keynes, The Open University Press, 1980, p. 13.

2 The local area is not a community in any sense, in the highly urban parts of the city; it is a community 'of limited liability' in the suburbs. Communication and participation are as apt to be segmented as in any formal organization that is extraterritorial. And many are utterly uninvolved, even in the strongest spatially defined communities.
Scott Greer, *The Emerging City*, New York, Collier Macmillan, 1962, p. 103.

3 Elsewhere I have argued that the identities of local neighbourhoods exist in tenuous opposition to one another and that relative rather than absolute differences give them their distinctive reputation. Obviously the main lines

of differentiation are the dimensions of stratification which are pervasive to the entire society: race, ethnicity, income, education, and the like. Indeed most communities in the United States can be and are described in these terms. Ethnically and racially homogeneous neighbourhoods are perhaps the most obvious examples, but far less distinctive neighbourhoods find a marginal difference to emphasize and to distinguish between 'us' and 'them' . . .

So far I have taken a narrow view of the local urban community by regarding it as the defended neighbourhood which segregates people to avoid danger, insult, and the impairment of status claims. This is, I think, a sufficient basis for explaining community differentiation, but it is not all that communities are or become . . .

The search for tree-lined streets, for a small community, and for a quiet place to live are in part a search for collectivities which at least have the earmarks of a place for the authentic expression of self. There is a certain irony in this symbolism because the original meaning which Tönnies gave community or Gemeinschaft emphasized its ascriptive character and independence of sentiments except as people adapted to necessity. This meaning lingers in sociology, and the freedom of people to move and be indifferent to their residential group seems almost antithetical to the traditional local community. Indeed, community seems to have undergone a transformation in the minds of Americans, and what people see in it is not Tönnies's community but Schmalenbach's communion. The community is a place to share feelings and expose one's tender inner core. The freedom of people (or at least some people) to choose where they live is an essential ingredient to this meaning of the local community. Communion rests on its voluntariness, and as Schmalenbach pointed out, it was antithetical to the traditional community which coerced membership and loyalty. With the loss of the ascribed local community, the entire concept is transformed into a sort of social movement for relations which are intimate enough to be self-revealing.
G. D. Suttles, *The Social Construction of Community*, Chicago, University of Chicago Press, 1972, pp. 247, 264–6.

The idea of a social movement as an interpretive community should not **4** lead to an undifferentiated monadical view of the group from which it wins active support. The strength of symbols is their multi-accentuality and malleability. Sharing a common body of symbols created around notions of 'race', ethnicity or locality, common history or identity does not dictate the sharing of the plural meanings which may become attached to those symbols and cluster around them. Community is as much about difference as it is about similarity and identity. It is a relational idea which suggests, for British blacks at least, the idea of antagonism – domination and subordination between one community and another. The word directs analysis to the boundary between these groups. It is a boundary which is presented primarily by symbolic means and therefore a broad range of meanings can co-exist around it, reconciling individuality and commonality and competing definitions of what the movement is about.

Paul Gilroy, *There Ain't No Black in the Union Jack*, London, Hutchinson, 1987, pp. 234–7.

CONFLICT THEORY

The most fruitful tradition of explanatory theory is the conflict tradition, running from Machiavelli and Hobbes to Marx and Weber. If we abstract out its main causal propositions from extraneous political and philosophical doctrines, it looks like the following.

Machiavelli and Hobbes initiated the basic stance of cynical realism about human society. Individuals' behaviour is explained in terms of their self-interests in a material world of threat and violence. Social order is seen as being founded on organized coercion. There is an ideological realm of belief (religion, law), and an underlying world of struggles over power; ideas and morals are not prior to interaction but are socially created, and serve the interests of parties to the conflict.

Marx added more specific determinants of the lines of division among conflicting interests and indicated the material conditions that mobilize particular interests into action and that make it possible for them to articulate their ideas . . .

For conflict theory, the basic insight is that human beings are sociable but conflict-prone animals. Why is there conflict? Above all else, there is conflict because violent coercion is always a potential resource, and it is a zero-sum sort. This does not imply anything about the inherence of drives to dominate; what we do know firmly is that being coerced is an intrinsically unpleasant experience, and hence that any use of coercion, even by a small minority, calls forth conflict in the form of antagonism to being dominated. Add to this the fact that coercive power, especially as represented in the state, can be used to bring one economic goods and emotional gratification – and to deny them to others – and we can see that the availability of co-ercion as a resource ramifies conflicts throughout the entire society. The simultaneous existence of emotional bases for solidarity – which may well be the basis of co-operation, as Durkheim emphasized – only adds group divisions and tactical resources to be used in these conflicts.

Randall Collins, *Conflict Theory: Toward an Explanatory Science*, New York, Academic Press, 1975, pp. 56–9.

CONSUMPTION

See also BAUDRILLARD

The essential activity of consumption is thus not the actual selection, **1**
purchase or use of products, but the imaginative pleasure-seeking to which
the product image lends itself, 'real' consumption being largely a resultant
of this 'mentalistic' hedonism ... The idea that contemporary consumers
have an insatiable desire to acquire objects represents a serious misunderstanding of the mechanism which impels people to want goods. Their basic
motivation is the desire to experience in reality the pleasurable dramas
which they have already enjoyed in imagination, and each 'new' product is
seen as offering a possibility of realizing this ambition.
Colin Campbell, *The Romantic Ethic and the Spirit of Modern Consumerism*,
Oxford, Blackwell, 1987, pp. 189–90.

We may distinguish both true and false needs. 'False' are those which are **2**
superimposed upon the individual by particular social interests in his
repression: the needs which perpetuate toil, aggressiveness, misery and
injustice ... Most of the prevailing needs to relax, to have fun, to behave
and consume in accordance with advertisements, to love and hate what
others love and hate, belong to this category of false needs.

   The people recognize themselves in their commodities; they find their
soul in their automobile, hi-fi set, split-level home, kitchen equipment. The
very mechanism which ties the individual to his society has changed; and
social control is anchored in the new needs which it has produced.
Herbert Marcuse, *One Dimensional Man*, London, Routledge & Kegan Paul, 1964,
pp. 5, 9.

During the earlier stages of economic development, consumption of goods **3**
without stint, especially consumption of the better grades of goods – ideally
all consumption in excess of the subsistence minimum – pertains normally
to the leisure class. This restriction tends to disappear, at least formally, after
the later peaceable stage has been reached with private ownership of goods
and an industrial system based on wage labour or on the petty household
economy ...

   High-bred manners and ways of living are items of conformity to the norm
of conspicuous leisure and conspicuous consumption ... Conspicuous
consumption of valuable goods is a means of reputability to the gentlemen
of leisure.
Thorstein Veblen, *The Theory of the Leisure Class* [1899], New York, Mentor,
1953, pp. 64, 75.

It is impossible to look at modern advertising without realizing that the **4**
material object being sold is never enough: this indeed is the crucial cultural

quality of its modern forms. If we were sensibly materialist, in that part of our living in which we use things, we should find most advertising to be of an insane irrelevance. Beer would be enough for use, without the additional promise that in drinking it we show ourselves to be manly, young in heart, or neighbourly. A washing-machine would be a useful machine to wash clothes, rather than an indication that we are forward-looking or an object of envy to our neighbours. But if these associations sell beer and washing-machines, as some of the evidence suggests, it is clear that we have a cultural pattern in which the objects are not enough but must be validated, if only in fantasy, by association with social and personal meanings which in a different cultural pattern might be more directly available. The short description of the pattern we have is *magic*: a highly organized and professional system of magical inducements and satisfactions, functionally very similar to magical systems in simpler societies, but rather strangely coexistent with a highly developed scientific technology.

Raymond Williams, *Problems in Materialism and Culture*, London, Verso, 1980. Extract in S. During (ed.), *The Cultural Studies Reader*, London, Routledge, 1993, p. 335.

CONVERSATIONAL ANALYSIS

See also GARFINKEL

Conversational analysis is, if we may put it this way, more concerned with utterances than with speakers and hearers. It is much less concerned with talk as a relation between persons than it is with conversation as a relation between utterances. It is in line with what we have just been saying about self-organizing settings, devoted to examining the ways in which utterances can relate to one another, with the ways in which utterances can make up interwoven patterns and with the ways in which utterances, in the inter-relation, build up those patterns. Hence, if one finds that conversations are units, that they have a beginning, middle and end, and that this is a standard, reproduced feature of conversation, just how do those things involve movement from the beginning to the middle of a conversation, and once a conversation is in full flow, what kinds of sayings will bring it to an orderly conclusion? Such answers require us to examine the various kinds of utterances that there are, and the organizational implications that their properties have. Thus, in Schegloff's account of the opening of telephone conversation . . . he was examining the openings of conversational sequences through the study of the answering of telephone calls. He came to analyse the answering of the telephone in terms of an utterance pair, summons and answers. Such utterances go together in the sense that summons requires an answer, a summons is done (so to speak) in search of an answer.

The neat thing about this pair, from the point of view of initiating an exchange of talk, is that if a summons is answered, then the summoner is required to speak again: thus, a summons–answer pair has the organizational potential to generate further talk. It is in this sense that conversational analysis is more concerned with utterances than speakers, being concerned with the ways in which utterances can combine themselves into unified, internally organized, developing exchanges.

Wes Sharrock and Bob Anderson, *The Ethnomethodologists*, London and New York, Tavistock, 1986, pp. 68–9.

CRIME

See also DEVIANCE, DURKHEIM

For orthodox criminology crime occurs because of a lack of conditioning   **1**
into values: the criminal, whether because of evil (in the conventional model) or lack of parental training (in the welfare model), lacks the virtues which keep us all honest and upright. In left idealism, crime occurs not because of lack of value but simply because of lack of material goods: economic deprivation drives people into crime. In the conventional viewpoint on crime, the criminal is flawed; he or she lacks human values and cognition. In the radical interpretation of this, the very opposite is true. The criminal, not the honest person, has the superior consciousness: he or she has seen through the foolishness of the straight world. To be well conditioned is to be well deceived. The criminal then enters into a new world of value – a sub-culture, relieved in part of the mystifications of the conventional world. We reject both these positions. The radical version smacks of theories of absolute deprivation; we would rather put at the centre of our theory notions of relative deprivation. And a major source of one's comparisons – or indeed the feeling that one should, in the first place, 'naturally' compete and compare oneself with others – is capitalism itself . . .

The values of an equal or meritocratic society which capitalism inculcates into people are constantly at loggerheads with the actual material inequalities in the world. And, contrary to the conservatives, it is the well-socialised person who is the most liable to crime. Crime is endemic to capitalism because it produces both egalitarian ideals and material shortages. It provides precisely the values which engender criticism of the material shortages which the radicals pinpoint. A high crime rate occurs in precise conditions: where a group has learnt through its past that it is being dealt with invidiously; where it is possible for it easily to pick up the contradictions just referred to and where there is no political channel for these feelings of discontent to be realised. There must be economic and political discontent and there must be an absence of economic and political opportunities ...

If we look at the official crime statistics in any Western capitalist country we see a remarkable similarity: the young are consistently seen to offend more than the old, the working class more than the middle class, black more than white, and men more than women.

J. Lea and J. Young, *What Is to Be Done about Law and Order?*, London, Penguin, 1984, pp. 95–104.

2 Detective fictions regularly distort or unmask the world so that asociality and crime become the everyday norm, but which at the same time charm away the seductive and ominous challenge through the inevitable triumph of order.

T. W. Adorno, *Prisms*, London, Neville Spearman, 1967, p. 32.

3 In other words, it is the values and sentiments intrinsic to social relations – and the passions aroused when these are violated – which form the broad context within which legal punishments operate. These sentiments and passions help shape penal institutions, giving them their form as well as their force.

D. Garland, 'Frameworks of Inquiry in the Sociology of Punishment', *British Journal of Sociology*, vol. 14, no. 1, 1990, p. 8.

CULTURE

See also IDEOLOGY

1 Culture is one of the two or three most complicated words in the English language ... This is so partly because of its intricate historical development, in several European languages, but mainly because it has now come to be used for important concepts in several distinct and incompatible systems of thought.

Raymond Williams, *Keywords*, London, Fontana, 1983, p. 87.

2 Culture consists of patterns, explicit and implicit, of and for behaviour, acquired and transmitted by symbols, constituting the distinctive achievement of human groups, including their embodiments in artifacts; the essential core of culture consists of traditional (i.e. historically derived and selected) ideas and especially their attached values; culture systems may, on the one hand, be considered as products of action, on the other as conditioning elements of further action.

A. L. Kroeber and C. Kluckhohn, *Culture: A Critical Review of Concepts and Definitions*, New York, Vintage Books, 1963, p. 181.

3 A culture is an historically created system of explicit and implicit designs

for living, which tends to be shared by all or specially designated members of a group at a specified point in time.
C. Kluckhohn and W. H. Kelley, 'The Concept of Culture', in Ralph Linton (ed.), *The Science of Man in the World Crisis*, New York, Columbia University Press, 1945, p. 98.

The 'culture' of a group or class, is the peculiar and distinctive 'way of **4** life' of the group or class, the meanings, values and ideas embodied in institutions, in social relations, in systems of beliefs, in *mores* and *customs*, in the uses of objects and material life. Culture is the distinctive shapes in which this material and social organization of life expresses itself. A culture includes the 'maps of meaning' which make things intelligible to its members. These 'maps of meaning' are not simply carried around in the head: they are objectivated in the patterns of social organization and relationship through which the individual becomes a 'social individual'. Culture is the way the social relations of a group are structured and shaped: but it is also the way those shapes are experienced, understood and interpreted.
J. Clark, S. Hall, T. Jefferson and B. Roberts, 'Subcultures, Cultures and Class', in S. Hall and T. Jefferson (eds), *Resistance through Rituals*, London, Hutchinson, 1976, p. 10.

The dominant culture of a complex society is never a homogeneous **5** structure. It is layered, reflecting different interests within the dominant class (e.g. an aristocratic versus a bourgeois outlook), containing different traces from the past (e.g. religious ideas within a largely secular culture), as well as emergent elements in the present. Subordinate cultures will not always be in open conflict with it. They may, for long periods, coexist with it, negotiate the spaces and gaps in it, make inroads into it, 'warrening it from within'. However, though the nature of this struggle over culture can never be reduced to a simple opposition, it is crucial to replace the notion of 'culture' with the more concrete, historical concept of 'cultures'; a redefinition which brings out more clearly the fact that cultures always stand in relations of domination – and subordination – to one another, are always, in some sense, in struggle with one another. The singular term, 'culture', can only indicate, in the most general and abstract way, the large cultural configurations at play in a society at any historical moment. We must move at once to the determining relationships of domination and subordination in which these configurations stand; to the processes of incorporation and resistance which define the cultural dialectic between them; and to the institutions which transmit and reproduce 'the culture' (i.e. the dominant culture) in its dominant or 'hegemonic' form.
Ibid., pp. 12–13.

The sociological theory that the loss of the support of objectively established **6** religion, the dissolution of the last remnants of precapitalism, together with technological and social differentiation or specialization, have led to cultural chaos is disproved every day; for culture now impresses the same stamp on everything . . .

The ruthless unity in the culture industry is evidence of what will happen in politics. Marked differentiations such as those of A and B films, or of stories in magazines in different price ranges, depend not so much on subject matter as on classifying, organizing, and labelling consumers. Something is provided for all so that none may escape; the distinctions are emphasized and extended. The public is catered for with a hierarchical range of mass-produced products of varying quality, thus advancing the rule of complete quantification. Everybody must behave (as if spontaneously) in accordance with his previously determined and indexed level, and choose the category of mass product turned out for his type . . .

Theodor Adorno and Max Horkheimer, *Dialectic of Enlightenment*, trans. J. Cumming, New York, The Seabury Press, 1972, pp. 120–3. First published in Germany in 1947.

7   The culture industry perpetually cheats its consumers of what it perpetually promises . . . The culture industry does not sublimate; it represses.
Ibid., p. 139.

8   What is decisive today is no longer Puritanism, although it still asserts itself in the form of women's organizations, but the necessity inherent in the system not to leave the customer alone, not for a moment to allow him any suspicion that resistance is possible. The principle dictates that he should be shown all his needs as capable of fulfilment, but that those needs should be so pre-determined that he feels himself to be the eternal consumer, the object of the culture industry. Not only does it make him believe that the deception it practises is satisfaction, but it goes further and implies that, whatever the state of affairs, he must put up with what is offered. The escape from every-day drudgery which the whole culture industry promises may be compared to the daughter's abduction in the cartoon: the father is holding the ladder in the dark. The paradise offered by the culture industry is the same old drudgery. Both escape and elopement are predesigned to lead back to the starting point. Pleasure promotes the resignation which it ought to help to forget.
Ibid., pp. 141–2.

9   While in no way wanting to limit research to 'following only those leads which emerge from content analysis', we must recognise that the discursive form of the message has a privileged position in the communicative exchange (from the viewpoint of circulation), and that the moments of 'encoding' and 'decoding', though only 'relatively autonomous' in relation to the communicative process as a whole, are *determinate* moments. A 'raw' historical event cannot, *in that form*, be transmitted by, say, a television newscast. Events can only be signified within the aural–visual forms of the

television discourse. In the moment when a historical event passes under the sign of discourse, it is subject to all the complex formal 'rules' by which language signifies. To put it paradoxically, the event must become a 'story' before it can become a *communicative event*. In that moment the formal sub-rules of discourse are 'in dominance', without, of course, subordinating out of existence the historical event so signified, the social relations in which the rules are set to work or the social and political consequences of the event having been signified in this way. The 'message form' is the necessary 'form of appearance' of the event in its passage from source to receiver. Thus the transposition into and out of the 'message form' (or the mode of symbolic exchange) is not a random 'moment', which we can take up or ignore at our convenience. The 'message form' is a determinate moment; though, at another level, it comprises the surface movements of the communications system only and requires, at another stage, to be integrated into the social relations of the communication process as a whole, of which it forms only a part.

Stuart Hall 'Encoding, Decoding', in S. Hall, D. Hobson, A. Love and P. Willis (eds), *Culture, Media, Language: Working Papers in Cultural Studies*, London, Hutchinson, 1980, p. 129.

Two theoretical poles have governed the consideration of action and order **10** since scientific consideration of societies began. The mechanistic conception of action has likened human behavior to a machine which responds automatically, 'objectively', and predictably to the stimuli of its environment. The order which is linked to this mechanical action is, correspondingly, seen as a coercive one, affecting action from without by virtue of its powerful force.

In opposition to this view there has arisen a subjective approach to action and order. According to this approach, action is motivated by something inside the person, by feeling, by perception, by sensibility. The order corresponding to such action is an ideational one. It is composed of nothing other than what exists in people's heads. There is subjective order rather than merely subjective action because subjectivity is here conceived as framework rather than intention, an idea held in common rather than an individual wish, a framework which can be seen as both the cause and the result of a plurality of interpretive interactions rather than a single interpretive act *per se*. Experience and the meaning of experience become central for this approach.

The concept of culture comes into play to the degree that meaning is conceived of as ordered in this way. Culture is the 'order' corresponding to meaningful action. Subjective, anti-mechanistic order is conceived of as followed for voluntary reasons rather than because of necessity in the mechanistic, objective sense . . .

Recent developments in cultural studies converge in their emphasis on the autonomy of culture from social structure. The meaning of ideology or belief system cannot be read off social behavior; it must be studied as a pattern in and of itself. Approaches to culture differ from one another in describing precisely what such autonomy implies. Some argue that knowledge of this independently organized cultural system is sufficient for understanding the motives and meaning of social behavior, others that this system must be understood as having been modeled upon processes that already exist in the social system itself. The concrete processes for relating culture, social structure, and action are also decidedly different, ranging from religious ritual, socialization, and education to dramaturgical innovation and the formation of class consciousness. Finally, there is extraordinary disagreement over what is actually inside of the cultural system itself. Is culture a set of logically interrelated symbols or is it values that assert desirable social qualities? Is it emotionally charged symbols about the sacred and profane or metaphysical ideas about other-worldly salvation? . . .

We cannot understand culture without reference to subjective meaning and we cannot understand it without reference to social structural constraints. We cannot interpret social behavior without acknowledging that it follows codes which it does not invent; at the same time, human invention creates a changing environment for every cultural code. Inherited metaphysical ideas form an inextricable web for modern social structures, yet powerful groups often succeed in transforming cultural structures into merely legitimating means.

Jeffrey C. Alexander, 'Analytic Debates', Introduction to Jeffrey Alexander and Steven Seidman (eds), *Culture and Society: Contemporary Debates*, Cambridge, Cambridge University Press, 1990, pp. 1–2, 25–6.

11   There are two notable differences between our contemporary European ideas of defilement and those, say, of primitive cultures. One is that dirt avoidance for us is a matter of hygiene or aesthetics and is not related to our religion ... The second difference is that our idea of dirt is dominated by the knowledge of pathogenic organisms. The bacterial transmission of disease was a great nineteenth-century discovery. It produced the most radical revolution in the history of medicine. So much has it transformed our lives that it is difficult to think of dirt except in the context of pathogenicity. Yet obviously our ideas of dirt are not so recent. We must be able to make the effort to think back beyond the last 100 years and to analyse the bases of dirt-avoidance, before it was transformed by bacteriology; for example, before spitting deftly into a spittoon was counted unhygienic.

If we can abstract pathogenicity and hygiene from our notion of dirt, we are left with the old definition of dirt as matter out of place. This is a very suggestive approach. It implies two conditions: a set of ordered relations and a contravention of that order. Dirt, then, is never a unique, isolated event. Where there is dirt there is system. Dirt is the by-product of a systematic ordering and classification of matter, in so far as ordering involves rejecting inappropriate elements. This idea of dirt takes us straight into the field of symbolism and promises a link-up with more obviously symbolic systems of purity.

We can recognize in our own notions of dirt that we are using a kind of omnibus compendium which includes all the rejected elements of ordered systems. It is a relative idea. Shoes are not dirty in themselves, but it is dirty to place them on the dining-table; food is not dirty in itself, but it is dirty to leave cooking utensils in the bedroom, or food bespattered on clothing; similarly, bathroom equipment in the drawing room; clothing lying on chairs; out-door things in-doors; upstairs things downstairs; under-clothing appearing where over-clothing should be, and so on. In short, our pollution behaviour is the reaction which condemns any object or idea likely to confuse or contradict cherished classifications . . .

Culture, in the sense of the public, standardised values of a community, mediates the experience of individuals. It provides in advance some basic categories, a positive pattern in which ideas and values are tidily ordered. And above all, it has authority, since each is induced to assent because of the assent of others.

Mary Douglas, *Purity and Danger*, London, Routledge, and New York, Praeger, 1966, pp. 35–9.

CULTURE OF POVERTY

As an anthropologist I have tried to understand poverty and its associated **1** traits as a culture or, more accurately, as a subculture with its own structure and rationale, as a way of life which is passed down from generation to generation along family lines. This view directs attention to the fact that the culture of poverty in modern nations is not only a matter of economic deprivation, of disorganization or of the absence of something. It is also something positive and provides some rewards without which the poor could hardly carry on.

The culture of poverty can come into being in a variety of historical contexts. However, it tends to grow and flourish in societies with the following set of conditions: (1) a cash economy, wage labor and production for profit; (2) a persistently high rate of unemployment and underemployment for unskilled labor; (3) low wages; (4) the failure to provide social, political and economic organization, either on a voluntary basis or by government imposition, for the low-income population; (5) the existence of a bilateral kinship system rather than a unilateral one; and finally, (6) the existence of a set of values in the dominant class which stresses the accumulation of wealth and property, the possibility of upward mobility and thrift, and explains low economic status as the result of personal inadequacy or inferiority.

The way of life which develops among some of the poor under these conditions is the culture of poverty ... The culture of poverty is both an adaptation and a reaction of the poor to their marginal position in a class-stratified, highly individuated, capitalistic society. It represents an effort to cope with feelings of powerlessness and despair which develop from the realization of the improbability of achieving success in terms of the values and goals of the larger society. Indeed, many of the traits of the culture of poverty can be viewed as attempts at local solutions for problems not met by existing institutions and agencies because the people are not eligible for them, cannot afford them, or are ignorant or suspicious of them ...

The culture of poverty, however, is not only an adaptation to a set of objective conditions of the larger society. Once it comes into existence it tends to perpetuate itself from generation to generation because of its effect on the children. By the time slum children are age six or seven they have usually absorbed the basic values and attitudes of their subculture and are not psychologically geared to take full advantage of changing conditions or increased opportunities which may occur in their lifetime.

Oscar Lewis, *La Vida: A Puerto Rican Family in the Culture of Poverty*, New York, Random House, 1965, pp. xl–xli.

2   A major difficulty with the use of the culture concept in conjunction with poverty (or with any question relating to complex societies) is that the concept of culture has varied and changed over time. Although accepted as basic, the concept has never been successfully defined in a universally accepted way by anthropologists.

In Lewis's use of the culture concept when dealing with poverty, he emphasized the self-perpetuation of the culture of poverty – the notion that children are doomed to the culture of poverty by age six. The use of early childhood socialization as the explanatory device for the transmission of culture has been characteristic of anthropology since its beginning ... More recent studies have focused upon this process as a central research problem in order to determine when early socialisation is important and when it is not. Lewis, on the other hand, simply accepts early childhood cultural transmission as the only significant enculturation process, without recognizing the issues involved.

In recent times, one sees two emergent views of culture. In one view, culture is a system of cognitive categories or cognitive maps, which individuals carry around in their heads and transmit through symbolic codes. The *sum* of the overlapping elements of individual cognitive maps is *culture*. The other point of view sees culture as a set of adaptive strategies for survival, usually linked to a particular setting of available resources and external constraints. This is an ecological approach to culture.

Lewis does not recognize these two trends and uses a traditional definition of culture as a 'way of life'. Thus, the ecological approach – the generation of culture and continued culture change resulting from inter-action with the ecosystem – is not found in Lewis's formulation. Lewis views the culture of poverty more as a set of cognitive maps. He presents a view of the carbon copy recapitulation of a way of life, generation after generation, without any notion of the interaction of this way of life with changing external systems . . .

It should be noted that at the time Lewis was writing about the concept, a major thrust of American domestic policy was the eradication of poverty. The various programs that were developed in the 1960s to deal with this problem were subsumed under the notion of the 'War on Poverty'. For those involved in determining what programs could be established to eliminate poverty conditions, there were two major alternatives: either attack the economic system, which created unemployment and underemployment, *or* attack the values and behavior of the poor, which were assumed to be inter-generationally transmitted and which *by themselves* perpetuated poverty by interfering with upward mobility. Although Lewis did accept the larger social system as generating poverty, his emphasis on the self-perpetuation of the culture of poverty was the point of departure for the elaboration by those developing anti-poverty programs. Thus, many programs of the War on Poverty were designed to change the behavior and values of the poor.

Edward Eames and Judith Granich Goode, *Anthropology of the City: An Introduction to Urban Anthropology*, Englewood Cliffs, New Jersey, Prentice-Hall, 1977, pp. 304–19.

DEVIANCE

Social groups create deviance by making rules whose infraction constitutes **1** deviance, and by applying those rules to particular people and labelling them as outsiders. From this point of view, deviance is not a quality of the act the person commits, but rather a consequence of the application by others of rules and sanctions to an 'offender'. The deviant is one to whom that label has successfully been applied; deviant behaviour is behaviour that people so label.

Howard Becker, *Outsiders: Studies in the Sociology of Deviance*, New York, Free Press, 1963, p. 9.

Deviance is not a property inherent in certain forms of behaviour; it is a **2** property conferred upon these forms by the audiences which directly or indirectly witness them. The critical variable in the study of deviance, then, is the social audience rather than the individual actor, since it is the audi-ence which eventually determines whether or not any episode or behaviour or any class of episodes is labelled deviant.

Kai T. Erikson, 'Notes on the Sociology of Deviance', in H. Becker (ed.), *The Other Side: Perspectives on Deviance*, New York, Free Press, 1964, p. 11.

3 We find five logically possible, alternative modes of adjustment or adaptation by individuals within the culture-bearing society or group. These are schematically presented in the following table, where (+) signifies 'acceptance', (−) signifies 'elimination', and (− +) signifies 'rejection and substitution of new goals and standards'.

		Culture goals	Institutionalized means
I.	Conformity	+	+
II.	Innovation	+	−
III.	Ritualism	−	+
IV.	Retreatism	−	−
V.	Rebellion	− +	− +

Robert K. Merton, 'Social Structure and Anomie', *American Sociological Review*, vol. 3, 1938, p. 676.

4 Through a complex process that is not yet fully understood by students of mass communication, the mere reporting of one event has, under certain circumstances, the effect of triggering off events of a similar order. This effect is much easier to understand and is better documented in regard to the spread of crazes, fashions, fads and other forms of collective behaviour, such as mass delusion or hysteria, than in cases of deviance. The main reason why this process has been misunderstood in regard to deviance – particularly collective and novel forms – is that too much attention has been placed on the supposed direct effects (imitation, attention, gratification, identification) on the deviants, rather than the effects of the control system and culture (via such processes as amplification) on the deviance.
Stanley Cohen, *Folk Devils and Moral Panics*, London, Martin Robertson, 1980, pp. 162–3.

5 One of the most fascinating problems about human behavior is why men violate the laws in which they believe. This is the problem that confronts us when we attempt to explain why delinquency occurs despite a greater or lesser commitment to the usages of conformity. A basic clue is offered by the fact that social rules or norms calling for valued behavior seldom if ever take the form of categorical imperatives. Rather, values or norms appear as *qualified* guides for action, limited in their applicability in terms of time, place, persons, and social circumstances . . .

The individual can avoid moral culpability for his criminal action – and thus avoid the negative sanctions of society – if he can prove that criminal intent was lacking. *It is our argument that much delinquency is based on what is essentially an unrecognized extension of defences to crimes in the form of justifications for deviance that are seen as valid by the delinquent but not by the legal system or society at large.*

These justifications are commonly described as rationalizations. They are viewed as following deviant behavior and as protecting the individual from self-blame and the blame of others after the act. But there is also reason to believe that they precede deviant behavior and make deviant behavior possible ... Disapproval flowing from internalized norms and conforming others in the social environment is neutralized, turned back, or deflected in advance. Social controls that serve to check or inhibit deviant motivational patterns are rendered inoperative, and the individual is freed to engage in delinquency without serious damage to his self-image. In this sense, the delinquent both has his cake and eats it too, for he remains committed to the dominant normative system and yet so qualifies its imperatives that violations are 'acceptable' if not 'right'. Thus the delinquent represents not a radical opposition to law-abiding society but something more like an apologetic failure, often more sinned against than sinning in his own eyes ... In analyzing these techniques, we have found it convenient to divide them into five major types:

Insofar as the delinquent can define himself as lacking responsibility for his deviant actions, the disapproval of self or others is sharply reduced in effectiveness as a restraining influence ...

A second major technique of neutralization centers on the injury or harm involved in the delinquent act ... For the delinquent, however, wrongfulness may turn on the question of whether or not anyone has clearly been hurt by his deviance, and this is open to a variety of interpretations ...

Even if the delinquent accepts the responsibility for his deviant actions and is willing to admit that his deviant actions involve an injury or hurt, the moral indignation of self and others may be neutralized by an insistence that the injury is not wrong in light of the circumstances. The injury, it may be claimed, is not really an injury; rather, it is a form of rightful retaliation or punishment ...

A fourth technique of neutralization would appear to involve a condemnation of the condemners or ... a rejection of the rejecters ...

Fifth, and last, internal and external social controls may be neutralized by sacrificing the demands of the larger society for the demands of the smaller social groups to which the delinquent belongs, such as the sibling pair, the gang, or the friendship clique.

Gresham M. Sykes and David Matza, 'Techniques of Neutralization: A Theory of Delinquency', *American Sociological Review*, vol. 22, 1957. Extract in D. H. Kelly (ed.), *Deviant Behavior*, New York, St Martin's Press, 1979, pp. 103–7.

DISCOURSE

See also FOUCAULT

A discourse is a group of statements which provide a language for talking about – i.e. a way of representing – a particular kind of knowledge about a topic. When statements about a topic are made within a particular discourse, the discourse makes it possible to construct the topic in a certain way. It also limits the other ways in which the topic can be constructed.

A discourse does not consist of one statement, but of several statements working together to form what the French social theorist, Michel Foucault, calls a 'discursive formation'. The statements fit together because any one statement implies a relation to all the others.
Stuart Hall, 'The West and the Rest: Discourse and Power', in S. Hall and B. Gieben (eds), *Formations of Modernity*, Cambridge, Polity, 1992, p. 291.

DIVISION OF LABOUR

1 The division of labour is a central concept in social and economic thought. It provides the means by which the connections between economic processes and social relationships can be identified. It forms a basis of hierarchies of power and advantage . . . I use division of labour to refer to the differentiation of work tasks, imposed and remunerated in some specific manner and organized in structured patterns of activity. (Though unpaid labour in the household and community are important aspects of the division of labour, for the present, I will be concerned with paid employment.) When contemporary social scientists have investigated the division of labour, their studies have tended to come under one or other of the following headings: (1) sectoral patterns of employment in agriculture, manufacture, etc.; (2) the occupational or skill structure of the labour force; (3) the organization of tasks in the workplace.
Elizabeth Garnsey, 'The Rediscovery of the Division of Labour', in *Theory and Society*, vol. 10, 1981, p. 337.

2 The owner of stock which employs a great number of labourers necessarily endeavours, for his own advantage, to make such a proper division and distribution of employment that they may be enabled to produce the greater quantity of work possible.
Adam Smith, *The Wealth of Nations* [1776, Book I, ch. VIII]; Oxford University Press, 1976, p. 104.

3 Every undertaker in manufacture finds that the more he can subdivide the tasks of his workmen and the more hands he can employ on separate articles, the more are his expenses diminished and his profits increased.
Adam Ferguson, *An Essay on the History of Civil Society*, [1767]; ed. Duncan Forbes, Edinburgh University Press, 1966, p. 181.

EDUCATION

The educational system helps integrate youth into the economic system, we **1** believe, through a structural correspondence between its social relations and those of production. The structure of social relations in education not only inures the student to the discipline of the workplace, but develops the types of personal demeanour, modes of self-presentation, self-image, and social-class identification which are the crucial ingredients of job adequacy. Specifically, the social relationships of education – the relationships between administrators and teachers, teachers and students, students and students, and students and their work – replicate the hierarchical division of labour.
S. Bowles and H. Gintis, *Schooling in Capitalist America*, London, Routledge & Kegan Paul, 1976, p. 131.

The difficult thing to explain about how middle class kids get middle class **2** jobs is why others let them. The difficult thing to explain about how working class kids get working class jobs is why they let themselves.
Paul Willis, *Learning to Labour*, London, Saxon House, 1977, p. 1.

Teachers themselves are very often unaware of the way they allocate their **3** time and it is not uncommon to ask teachers whether they give more attention to one sex than the other, and to have them vehemently protest that they do not and that they treat both sexes equally. But when their next lesson is taped it is often found that over two-thirds of their time was spent with the boys who comprised less than half of the class. Most teachers do not consciously want to discriminate against girls, they say they do want to treat the sexes fairly, but our society and education is so structured that 'equality' and 'fairness' mean that males get more attention.
Dale Spender, *Invisible Women: The Schooling Scandal*, Writers and Readers Co-operative, 1982, p. 54.

Two general types of code can be distinguished: *elaborated* and *restricted*. **4** They can be defined on a linguistic level, in terms of the probability of predicting for any one speaker which syntactic elements will be used to organize meaning across a representative range of speech. In the case of an elaborated code, the speaker will select from a relatively extensive range of alternatives, and the probability of predicting the organizing elements is considerably reduced. In the case of a restricted code the number of alternatives is often severely limited and the probability of predicting the elements is greatly increased ...

Children socialized within the middle class and associated strata can be expected to possess both an elaborated *and* a restricted code, whilst children socialized within some sections of the working-class strata, particularly the lower working class, can be expected to be *limited* to a restricted code. If a child is to succeed as he progresses through school it

41

becomes critical for him to possess, or at least to be oriented towards, an elaborated code. The relative backwardness of lower-working-class children may well be a form of culturally induced backwardness transmitted to the child through the implications of the linguistic process. The code the child brings to the school symbolizes his social identity. It relates him to his kin and to his local social relations. The code orients the child progressively toward a pattern of relationships which constitutes for the child his psychological reality and this reality is reinforced every time he speaks.

Basil Bernstein, 'A Socio-Linguistic Approach to Social Learning', in J. Gould (ed.), *Penguin Survey of the Social Sciences 1965*, Harmondsworth, Penguin, 1965, pp. 145, 166.

5 How a society selects, classifies, distributes, transmits and evaluates the educational knowledge it considers to be public, reflects both the distribution of power and the principles of social control. From this point of view, differences within and change in the organization, transmission and evaluation of educational knowledge should be a major area of sociological interest.

Basil Bernstein, *Class, Codes and Control*, vol. 3, London, Routledge & Kegan Paul, 1977, p. 83.

6 [E]ach family transmits to its children, indirectly rather than directly, a certain *cultural capital* and a certain *ethos*. The latter is a system of implicit and deeply interiorized values which, among other things, helps to define attitudes towards the cultural capital and educational institutions. The cultural heritage, which differs from both points of view according to social class, is the cause of the initial inequality of children when faced with examinations and tests, and hence of unequal achievement . . .

In fact, to penalize the underprivileged and favour the most privileged, the school has only to neglect, in its teaching methods and techniques and its criteria when making academic judgements, to take account of the cultural inequalities between children of different social classes. In other words, by treating all pupils, however unequal they may be in reality, as equal in rights and duties, the educational system is led to give its *de facto* sanction to initial cultural inequalities. The formal equality which governs pedagogical practice is in fact a cloak for and justification of indifference to the real inequalities with regard to the body of knowledge taught or rather demanded. Thus, for example, the 'pedagogy' used in secondary or higher education is, objectively, an 'arousing pedagogy', in Weber's words, aimed at stimulating the 'gifts' hidden in certain exceptional individuals by means of certain incantatory techniques, such as the verbal skills and powers of the teacher. As opposed to a rational and really universal pedagogy, which would take nothing for granted initially, would not count as acquired what some, and only some, of the pupils in question had inherited, would do all things for all and would be organized with the explicit aim of providing all with the means of acquiring that which, although apparently a natural gift, is only given to the children of the educated classes, our own pedagogical tradition is in fact, despite external appearances of irreproachable equality and universality, only there for the benefit of pupils who are in the particular position of possessing a cultural heritage conforming to that demanded by the school . . .

Pierre Bourdieu, 'The School as a Conservative Force', in J. Eggleston (trans. and ed.), *Contemporary Research in the Sociology of Education*, London, Methuen, 1974, pp. 32–8.

What schools do ideologically, culturally, and economically is very com-　**7** plicated and cannot be fully understood by the application of any simple formula. There *are* very strong connections between the formal and informal knowledge within the school and the larger society with all its inequalities. But since the pressures and demands of dominant groups are highly mediated by the internal histories of educational institutions and by the needs and ideologies of people who actually work in them, the aims and results will often be contradictory as well.

M. W. Apple, *Ideology and Curriculum*, London, Routledge, 1990, pp. x–xi.

The major impetus for the creation of national education systems lay in　**8** the need to provide the state with trained administrators, engineers and military personnel; to spread dominant national cultures and inculcate popular ideologies of nationhood; and so to forge the political and cultural unity of burgeoning nation states and cement the ideological hegemony of their dominant classes.

Andy Green, *Education and State Formation*, London, Macmillan, 1990, p. 309.

The most common modern interpretation of the role of education is that　**9** it meets the demand for technical skills. Most contemporary evidence, however, contradicts this interpretation. The content of most modern education is not very practical; educational attainment and grades are not much related to work performance, and most technical skills are learned on the job. Although work skills are more complex in some modern jobs than in most pre-industrial jobs, in many modern jobs they are not . . .

In historical perspective education has been used more often for organizing status groups than for other purposes. Since the defining locus of status-group activity is leisure and consumption, status-group education has been sharply distinguished from practical education by the exclusion of materially productive skills. Because status groups have used a common culture as a mark of group membership, status-group education has taken the form of a club and has included much ceremony to demonstrate group solidarity and to publicly distinguish members from non-members . . .

Historical evidence indicates that mass, compulsory education was first created not for industrial, but for military and political discipline.

Randall Collins, 'Some Comparative Principles of Educational Stratification', *Harvard Educational Review*, vol. 47, no. 1, 1977, pp. 5–9.

ETHNICITY

See also RACE

1 We shall call 'ethnic groups' those human groups that entertain a subjective belief in their common descent because of similarities of physical type or of customs or both, or because of memories of colonization and migration; this belief must be important for the propagation of group formation; conversely it does not matter whether or not an objective blood relationship exists.
Max Weber, *Economy and Society* (3 vols), ed. and trans. G. Roth and C. Wittich, New York, Bedminster Press, 1968, vol. 1, p. 389. First published in German in 1925.

2 An ethnic group consists of those who conceive of themselves as being alike by virtue of their common ancestry, real or fictitious, and who are so regarded by others.
Tamotsu Shibutani and Kian Kwan, *Ethnic Stratification: A Comparative Approach*, London, Macmillan, 1965, p. 47.

3 Ethnic identity consists of feelings of (1) community – through neighborhood, peer-group, and leisure-time pursuits; (2) association – participation in work, educational and charitable organizations dominated by people of a common ancestry; (3) tribalism – a sense of peoplehood and common origin, a feeling of primordial ties; and (4) common religion.
John Wilson, *Religion in American Society*, Englewood Cliffs, New Jersey, Prentice-Hall, 1978, p. 309.

4 An ethnic group, as I will use the term, is a segment of a larger society whose members are thought, by themselves and/or others, to have a common origin and to share important segments of a common culture and who, in addition, participate in shared activities in which the common origin and culture are significant ingredients . . .

The definition of an ethnic group that I have suggested has three ingredients: (1) The group is perceived by others in the society to be different in some combinations of the following traits: language, religion, race, and ancestral homeland with its related culture; (2) the members also perceive themselves as different; and (3) they participate in shared activities built around their (real or mythical) common origin and culture. Each of these is a variable, of course; hence we need to work toward a scale of ethnicity. One can be fully ethnic or barely ethnic . . .

If we concentrate on the relationship of ethnic groups to the societies of which they are part, a different way of looking at ethnic variation appears from the one that we see when attention is given to the three variables in the definition. At least four major types can be found among multi-ethnic societies in the contemporary world:

44

A   A society can be built out of formally equal ethnic groups.
B   A society can be characterised by a major national cultural group, separated from one or more ethnic groups by a highly permeable boundary.
C   One or more ethnic groups can be strongly oriented toward an outside mother society.
D   One or more ethnic groups can be 'imprisoned' as disprivileged minorities within the larger society.

J. Milton Yinger, 'Ethnicity in Complex Societies: Structural, Cultural, and Characterological Factors', in Lewis A. Coser and Otto N. Larsen (eds), *The Uses of Controversy in Sociology*, New York, Free Press, 1976, pp. 200–2.

ETHOS

In recent anthropological discussion, the moral (and aesthetic) aspects of a given culture, the evaluative elements, have commonly been summoned up in the term 'ethos', while the cognitive, existential aspects have been designated by the term 'world view'. A people's ethos is the tone, character, and quality of their life, its moral and aesthetic style and mood; it is the underlying attitude toward themselves and their world that life reflects.
Clifford Geertz, 'Ethos, World View, and the Analysis of Sacred Symbols', *The Antioch Review*, vol. 17, no. 4, 1957. Reprinted in C. Geertz, *The Interpretation of Cultures*, London, Hutchinson, and New York, Basic Books, 1973, pp. 126–7.

EXCHANGE

In the systems of the past we do not find simple exchange of goods, wealth   **1**
and produce through markets established among individuals. For it is groups, and not individuals, which carry on exchange, make contracts, and are bound by obligations; the persons represented in the contracts are moral persons – clans, tribes, and families; the groups, or the chiefs as intermediaries for the groups, confront and oppose each other. Further, what they exchange is not exclusively goods and wealth, real and personal property, and things of economic value. They exchange rather courtesies, entertainments, ritual, military assistance, women, children, dances and feasts; and fairs in which the market is but one element and the circulation of wealth but one part of a wide and enduring contract. Finally, although the prestations and counter-prestations take place under a voluntary guise they are in essence strictly obligatory, and their sanction is private or open warfare. We propose to call this the system of *total prestations*.
Marcel Mauss, *The Gift*, trans. Ian Cunnison, Glencoe, Illinois, Free Press, 1954, p. 8.

2   The institutionalized form the exchange of gifts frequently assumes in simpler societies highlights the two general functions of social, as distinct from strictly economic, exchange, namely, to establish bonds of friendship and to establish superordination over others ...

The basic principles underlying the conception of exchange may be briefly summarized. An individual who supplies rewarding services to another obligates him. To discharge this obligation, the second must furnish benefits to the first in turn. Concern here is with extrinsic benefits, not primarily with the rewards intrinsic to the association itself, although the significance of the social 'commodities' exchanged is never perfectly independent of the interpersonal relation between the exchange partners. If both individuals value what they receive from the other, both are prone to supply more of their own services to provide incentives for the other to increase his supply and to avoid becoming indebted to him. As both receive increasing amounts of the assistance they originally needed rather badly, however, their need for still further assistance typically declines ...

'Social exchange', as the term is used here, refers to voluntary actions of individuals that are motivated by the returns they are expected to bring and typically do in fact bring from others. Action compelled by physical coercion is not voluntary, although compliance with other forms of power can be considered a voluntary service rendered in exchange for the benefits such compliance produces, as already indicated. Whereas conformity with internalized standards does not fall under the definition of exchange presented, conformity to social pressures tends to entail indirect exchanges. Men make charitable donations, not to earn the gratitude of the recipients, whom they never see, but to earn the approval of their peers who participate in the philanthropic campaign. Donations are exchanged for social approval, though the recipients of the donations and the suppliers of the approval are not identical, and the clarification of the connection between the two requires an analysis of the complex structures of indirect exchange.

Social exchange differs in important ways from strictly economic exchange. The basic and most crucial distinction is that social exchange entails *unspecified* obligations ...

It seems to be typical of social associations that the individuals who establish them have some common and some conflicting interests. A stable social relationship requires that individuals make some investments to bring it into being and maintain it in existence, and it is to the advantage of each party to have the other or others assume a disproportionate share of the commitments that secure their continuing association. Hence the common interest of individuals in sustaining a relation between them tends to be accompanied by conflicting interests as to whose investment should contribute most to its sustenance.

Peter M. Blau, *Exchange and Power in Social Life*, New York, Wiley, 1964, pp. 88–114.

FAMILY

See also GENDER, MARRIAGE

The pairing family, itself too weak and unstable to make an independent **1** household necessary, or even desirable, did not by any means dissolve the communistic household transmitted from earlier times. But the communistic household implies the supremacy of women in the house, just as the exclusive recognition of a natural mother, because of the impossibility of determining the natural father with certainty, signifies high esteem for the women, that is, for the mothers. That woman was the slave of man at the commencement of society is one of the most absurd notions that have come down to us from the period of the Enlightenment of the eighteenth century. Woman occupied not only a free but also a highly respected position among all savages and all barbarians of the lower and middle stages and partly even of the upper stage . . .

As wealth increased, it, on the one hand, gave the man a more important status in the family than the woman, and, on the other hand, created a stimulus to utilise this strengthened position in order to overthrow the traditional order of inheritance in favour of his children. But this was impossible as long as descent according to mother right prevailed. This had, therefore, to be overthrown, and it was overthrown; and it was not so difficult to do this as it appears to us now. For this revolution – one of the most decisive ever experienced by mankind – need not have disturbed one single living member of a gens. All the members could remain what they were previously. The simple decision sufficed that in future the descendants of the male members should remain in the gens, but those of the females were to be excluded from the gens and transferred to that of their father. The reckoning of descent through the female line and the right of inheritance through the mother were hereby overthrown and male lineage and right of inheritance from the father instituted. We know nothing as to how and when this revolution was effected among the civilised peoples. It falls entirely within prehistoric times. That it was actually effected is more than proved by the abundant traces of mother right which have been collected, especially by Bechofen . . .

The overthrow of mother right was the world-historic defeat of the female sex. The man seized the reins in the house also, the woman was degraded, enthralled, the slave of the man's lust, a mere instrument for breeding children. This lowered position of women, especially manifest among the Greeks of the Heroic and still more of the Classical Age, has become gradually embellished and dissembled and, in part, clothed in milder form, but by no means abolished . . .

Friedrich Engels, 'The Origins of Family, Private Property, and State' [1884];

excerpt in Robert C. Tucker (ed.), *The Marx–Engels Reader*, 2nd edn, New York, W. W. Norton, 1978, pp. 735–6.

2   The form of the family corresponding to civilisation and under it becoming the definitely prevailing form is monogamy, the supremacy of the man over the woman, and the individual family as the economic unit of society.
Ibid., p. 757.

3   The emphasis which has here been placed on the multilineal symmetry of our kinship structure might be taken to imply that our society was characterized by a correspondingly striking assimilation of the roles of the sexes to each other. It is true that American society manifests a high level of the 'emancipation' of women, which in important respects involves relative assimilation to masculine roles, in accessibility to occupational opportunity, in legal rights relative to property holding, and in various other respects undoubtedly the kinship system constitutes one of the important sets of factors underlying this emancipation since it does not, as do so many kinship systems, place a structural premium on the role of either sex in the maintenance of the continuity of kinship relations.

But the elements of sex-role assimilation in our society are conspicuously combined with elements of segregation which in many respects are even more striking than in other societies, as for instance in the matter of the much greater attention given by women to style and refinement of taste in dress and personal appearance. This and other aspects of segregation are connected with the structure of kinship, but not so much by itself as in its interrelations with the occupational system.

The members of the conjugal family in our urban society normally share a common basis of economic support in the form of money income, but this income is not derived from the co-operative efforts of the family as a unit – its principal source lies in the remuneration of occupational role performed by individual members of the family. Status in an occupational role is generally, however, specifically segregated from kinship status – a person holds a 'job' as an individual, not by virtue of his status in a family.

Among the occupational statuses of members of a family, if there is more than one, much the most important is that of the husband and father, not only because it is usually the primary source of family income, but also because it is the most important single basis of the status of the family in the community at large. To be the main 'breadwinner' of his family is a primary role of the normal adult man in our society. The corollary of this role is his far smaller participation than that of his wife in the internal affairs of the household. Consequently, 'housekeeping' and the care of children is still the primary functional content of the adult feminine role in the middle-classes, in the great majority of cases not one which in status or remuneration competes closely with those held by men of her own class.

Hence there is a typically asymmetrical relation of the marriage pair to the occupational structure.

This asymmetrical relation apparently both has exceedingly important positive functional significance and is at the same time an important source of strain in relation to the patterning of sex roles.

Talcott Parsons, 'The Kinship System of the Contemporary United States', *Essays in Sociological Theory*, New York, Free Press, 1954, pp. 190–1.

We are living, I believe, through a transitional and contested period of **4** family history, a period *after* the modern family order, but before what we cannot foretell. Precisely because it is not possible to characterize with a single term the competing sets of family cultures that co-exist at present, I identify this family regime as post-modern. The post-modern family is not a new model of family life, not the next stage in an orderly progression of family history, but the stage when the belief in a logical progression of stages breaks down. Rupturing evolutionary models of family history and incorporating both experimental and nostalgic elements, 'the' post-modern family lurches forward and backward into an uncertain future.

Judith Stacey, *Brave New Families*, New York, Basic Books, 1990, p. 18.

FOLK SOCIETY

Such a society is small, isolated, non-literate and homogeneous, with a strong sense of group solidarity. The ways of living are conventionalized into the coherent system which we call 'a culture'. Behavior is traditional, spontaneous, uncritical and personal: there is no legislation or habit of experiment and reflection for intellectual ends. Kinship, its relations and institutions, are the type categories of experience and the familial group is the unit of action. The sacred prevails over the secular; the economy is one of status rather than the market.

Robert Redfield, 'The Folk Society', *American Journal of Sociology*, vol. 52, no. 3, 1946, p. 293.

FORDISM

Fordism is an industrial era whose secret is to be found in the mass production systems pioneered by Henry Ford. These systems were based on four principles from which all else followed:

(a) products were standardised; this meant that each part and each task could also be standardised. Unlike craft production – where each part had to be specially designed, made and fitted – for a run of mass-produced cars, the same headlight could be fitted to the same model in the same way.

(b) if tasks are the same, then some can be mechanised; thus mass production plants developed special-purpose machinery for each model, much of which could not be switched from product to product.

(c) those tasks which remained were subject to scientific management or Taylorism, whereby any task was broken down into its component parts, redesigned by work-study specialists on time-and-motion principles, who then instructed manual workers on how the job should be done.

(d) flowline replaced nodal assembly, so that instead of workers moving to and from the product (the node), the product flowed past the workers.

... a culture of post-Fordist capitalism is emerging. Consumption has a new place. As for production the keyword is flexibility – of plant and machinery, as of products and labour. Emphasis shifts from scale to scope, and from cost to quality. Organizations are geared to respond to rather than regulate markets. They are seen as frameworks for learning as much as instruments of control. Their hierarchies are flatter and their structures more open. The guerrilla force takes over from the standing army. All this has liberated the centre from the tyranny of the immediate. Its tasks shift from planning to strategy, and to the promotion of the instruments of post-Fordist control – systems, software, corporate culture and cash.

Robin Murray, 'Fordism and Post-Fordism', in S. Hall and M. Jacques (eds), *New Times*, London, Lawrence & Wishart, 1989, pp. 38–47.

FUNCTION AND FUNCTIONALISM

See also PARSONS

1   The *function* of any recurrent activity, such as the punishment of a crime, or a funeral ceremony, is the part it plays in the social life as a whole and therefore the contribution it makes to the maintenance of the structural continuity.

The concept of function as here defined thus involves the notion of a *structure* consisting of a *set of relations* amongst *unit entities*, the *continuity* of the structure being maintained by a *life-process* made up of the *activities* of the constituent units.

A. R. Radcliffe Brown, 'On the Concept of Function in Social Science', *American Anthropologist*, vol. 37, 1935, p. 396.

2   A theory which does not present and include at every step the definitions of individual contributions and of their integration into collective action stands condemned. The fact that functionalism implies this problem constantly and consistently may be taken as a proof that, so far as it does, it does not neglect one of the most essential problems of social science.

Indeed, functionalism is, in its essence, the theory of transformation of organic – that is, individual – needs into derived cultural necessities and imperatives. Society by the collective wielding of the conditioning apparatus molds the individual into a cultural personality. The individual, with his physiological needs and psychological processes, is the ultimate source and aim of all tradition, activities, and organized behavior.

The word 'society' is used here in the sense of a co-ordinated set of differentiated groups. The juxtaposition and opposition of 'the individual' and 'the society', as an undifferentiated mass, is always fictitious and therefore fallacious . . .

From the structural approach we have found that social organization must always be analyzed into institutions – that is, definite groups of men united by a charter, following rules of conduct, operating together a shaped portion of the environment, and working for the satisfaction of definite needs. This latter defines the function of an institution.

Here, once again, we see that every institution contributes, on the one hand, toward the integral working of the community as a whole, but it also satisfies the derived and basic needs of the individual.

Bronislaw Malinowski, 'The Group and the Individual in Functional Analysis', *American Journal of Sociology*, vol. 44, 1939, p. 962.

GEMEINSCHAFT/GESELLSCHAFT

See also COMMUNITY

All intimate, private and exclusive living together is understood as life in *Gemeinschaft* (community). *Gesellschaft* (society) is public life – it is the world itself. In *Gemeinschaft* (community) with one's family, one lives from birth on bound to it in weal and woe. One goes into *Gesellschaft* (society) as one goes into a strange country. A young man is warned against bad *Gesellschaft* (society), but the expression bad *Gemeinschaft* (community) violates the meaning of the word. Lawyers may speak of domestic *Gesellschaft* (society) thinking only of the legalistic concept of a social association, but the domestic *Gemeinschaft* (community) or home life with its immeasurable influence upon the human soul has been felt by everyone who ever shared it. Likewise, each member of a bridal couple knows that he or she goes into marriage as a complete *Gemeinschaft* (community) of life. A *Gesellschaft* (society) of life would be a contradiction in and of itself. One keeps or enjoys another's *Gesellschaft* (society or company) but not his *Gemeinschaft* (community) in this sense. One becomes a part of a religious *Gemeinschaft* (community); religious *Gesellschaften* (associations, or societies), like any other groups formed for given purposes, exist only in so far as they, viewed from without, take their places among the institutions

of a political body or as they represent conceptual elements of a theory; they do not touch upon the religious *Gemeinschaft* as such. There exists a *Gemeinschaft* (community) of language, of folkways or mores, or of beliefs, but, by way of contrast, *Gesellschaft* (society or company) exists in the realm of business, travel or sciences. So of special importance are the commercial *Gesellschaften* (societies or companies), whereas, even though a certain familiarity and *Gemeinschaft* (community) may exist among business partners, one could indeed hardly speak of commercial Gemeinschaft (community). To make the word combination 'joint-stock *Gemeinschaft*' would be abominable. On the other hand, there exists a *Gemeinschaft* (community) of ownership in fields, forest and pasture. The *Gemeinschaft* (community) of property between man and wife cannot be called *Gesellschaft* (society) of property. Thus many differences become apparent ... *Gemeinschaft* (community) is old; *Gesellschaft* (society) is new as a name as well as a phenomenon ... All praise of rural life has pointed out that the *Gemeinschaft* (community) among people is stronger there and more alive; it is the lasting and genuine form of living together. In contrast to *Gemeinschaft, Gesellschaft* (society) is transitory and superficial. Accordingly, *Gemeinschaft* (community) should be understood as a living organism, *Gesellschaft* (society) as a mechanical aggregate and artifact.
Ferdinand Tönnies, *Community and Association*, London, Routledge & Kegan Paul, 1955, pp. 37–9. First published in German in 1887.

GENDER

See also FAMILY

1 Male orientation may so colour the organization of sociology as a discipline that the invisibility of women is a structured male view, rather than a superficial flaw. The male focus, incorporated into the definitions of subject areas, reduces women to a side issue from the start.
Anne Oakley, *The Sociology of Housework*, London, Martin Robertson, 1974, p. 4.

2 It is the specific properties (e.g. female-sexed body), qualities (a disposition to nurturance, a certain relation to the body, etc.), or necessary attributes (e.g. the experience of femaleness, of living in the world as female) that women have developed or have been bound to historically in their differently patriarchal sociocultural contexts which make them women not men.
T. De Lauretis, 'The Essence of the Triangle or, Taking the Risk of Essentialism Seriously: Feminist Theory in Italy, the US and Britain', *Differences*, 1989, vol. 1, no. 2, pp. 5–6.

3 Sir, a woman's preaching is like a dog's walking on his hinder legs. It is not done well; but you are surprised to find it done at all.
Samuel Johnson, 31 July 1763.

Every woman knows the torment of getting up to speak. Her heart racing, **4**
at times entirely lost for words, ground and language slipping away – that's
how daring a feat, how great a transgression it is for a woman to speak –
even just open her mouth – in public. A double distress, for even if she
transgresses, her words fall almost always upon deaf male ear, which hears
in language only that which speaks in the masculine.
Hélène Cixous, 'The Laugh of the Medusa', in E. Marks and I. de Courtivron (eds),
New French Feminisms, Brighton, Harvester, 1984, p. 251. First published in *Signs*,
summer, 1976.

I suggest female – or perhaps I should call it feminine – desire is to some **5**
extent the *lynch pin* of a consumerist society. Everywhere women are
offered pleasure – pleasure for losing weight, pleasure for preparing
beautiful meals, pleasure if we acquire something new – a new body, a new
house, a new outfit, a new relationship, a new baby. Pleasure is western
society's special offer for women. But some drive is required to take
up that offer. And it is female desire which makes us respond and take up
that offer. To be a woman is to be constantly addressed, to be constantly
scrutinized, to have our desire constantly courted – in the kitchen, on the
streets, in the world of fashion, in films and in fiction. Issuing forth from
books and magazines, from films and television, from the radio, there are
endless questions about what women desire, endless theories and opinions
offered. Desire is stimulated and endlessly defined. Everywhere it seems
female desire is sought, bought, packaged and consumed. Female desire is
courted with the promise of future perfection, by the lure of achieving
ideals – ideal legs, ideal hair, ideal homes, ideal cream cakes, ideal relationships. Such ideas don't exist in reality, except as the end product of some
elaborate photographic techniques or the work of complicated fantasies.
But these ideals are held out to women everywhere, all the time. Things
may be bad, life may be difficult, relationships may be unsatisfying, you
may be feeling undervalued or unfulfilled at work, but there's always the
promise of improvements, everything could be transformed, you'll almost
certainly feel better. It's not the social structure or men that are seen as
the problem, but your own failure to come up to scratch. Female dissatisfaction is constantly recast in the discourses surrounding and dominating
us, as desire. Constantly we are made to feel desire for something
more, for a perfect reworking of what has gone before – dissatisfaction is
displaced into desire for an ideal . . .
Rosalind Coward, 'Female Desire and Sexual Identity', in M. Diaz-Diocaretz and
I. Zavala (eds), *Women, Feminist Identity and Society in the 1980s*, Amsterdam and
Philadelphia, J. Benjamins 1991, pp. 25–9.

The problem lay buried, unspoken, for many years in the minds of American **6**
women. It was a strange stirring, a sense of dissatisfaction, a yearning that
women suffered in the middle of the twentieth century in the United States.

Each suburban wife struggled with it alone. As she made the beds, shopped for groceries, matched slipcover material, ate peanut butter sandwiches with her children, chauffeured Cub Scouts and Brownies, lay beside her husband at night – she was afraid to ask even of herself the silent question – 'Is this all?' For over fifteen years there was no word of this yearning in the millions of words written about women, for women, in all the columns, books and articles by experts telling women their role was to seek fulfilment as wives and mothers. Over and over women heard in voices of tradition and of Freudian sophistication that they could desire no greater destiny than to glory in their own femininity . . .

In the fifteen years after World War II, this mystique of feminine fulfil-ment became the cherished and self-perpetuating core of contemporary American culture.

Betty Friedan, *The Feminine Mystique*, New York, Dell, 1963, pp. 11–14.

7   I am distinguishing between two forms of patriarchy: private and public. They differ on a variety of levels: firstly, in terms of the relations between the structures and, secondly, in the institutional form of each structure. Further, they are differentiated by the main form of patriarchal strategy: exclusion-ary in private patriarchy and segregationist in public patriarchy. Private patriarchy is based upon household production, with a patriarch controlling women individually and directly in the relatively private sphere of the home. Public patriarchy is based on structures other than the household, although this may still be a significant patriarchal site. Rather, institutions conven-tionally regarded as part of the public domain are central in the maintenance of patriarchy. In private patriarchy it is a man in his position as husband or father who is the direct oppressor and beneficiary, individually and directly, of the subordination of women. This does not mean that household produc-tion is the sole patriarchal structure. Indeed it is importantly maintained by the active exclusion of women from public arenas by other structures. The exclusion of women from these spheres could not be perpetuated without patriarchal activity at these levels. Public patriarchy is a form in which women have access to both public and private arenas. They are not barred from the public arenas, but are nonetheless subordinated within them. The expropriation of women is performed more collectively than by individual patriarchs. The household may remain a site of patriarchal oppression, but it is no longer the main place where women are present.

Sylvia Walby, *Theorizing Patriarchy*, Oxford, Blackwell, 1990, pp. 178–9.

8   There is a paradox in women's labour force participation. On the one hand women are concentrated in the lowest grade, least skilled and lowest paid jobs with the poorest employment benefits and prospects. On the other hand women report high levels of satisfaction with their jobs, often greater satisfaction than that reported by men with their higher status and better paid jobs . . .

The paradox of women's high satisfaction with comparatively poor jobs can be explained by their having different life goals from men. Most women's preference has been for the home-maker role, with paid employment regarded as a secondary activity, to be fitted in as and when home-maker activities allow it ... Social scientists have been using a value-laden and biased definition of job quality, one that is based on the priorities and preferences of male breadwinners. Women who have chosen a homemaker career often have some paid work as well, but their job preferences emphasise convenience factors over the high pay and security of employment conventionally valued by men ...

More generally, future research on workforce participation, and its consequences, must recognize that working women are a heterogeneous group, comprising at least two qualitatively different groups. One group has work commitment similar to that of men, leading to long-term workplans and almost continuous full-time work, often in jobs with higher status and earnings than are typical for women. The second group has little or no commitment to paid work and a clear preference for the home-maker role; paid employment is a secondary activity, usually undertaken to earn a supplementary wage rather than as primary breadwinner, and is in low-skilled, low-paid, part-time, casual and temporary jobs more often than in skilled, permanent, full-time jobs. The distinctive character of the second group is sometimes recognized in theories of a reserve army of labour, although this is often seen as applying to part-time workers only. Sociologists need to recognize and refine the substantial qualitative differences between these two groups, rather than treating female labour supply as a single continuum measured by hours worked, as in economic theory.

Catherine Hakim, 'Grateful Slaves and Self-made Women: Fact and Fantasy in Women's Work Orientations', *The European Sociological Review*, vol. 7, no. 2, 1991, pp. 101–16.

How does birth look through the eyes of women? If birth is currently **9** thought of and described by medical texts as if it were work done by the uterus, and if women's bodies are consequently subjected to the same kinds of controls as workers in the workplace, do women, as workers often have, resist their conditions? ...

Do women's efforts to resist procedures that they experience as intrusions on their anatomy resemble the efforts of workers? Childbirth activist literature can be seen (and sometimes describes itself) as guides to 'self-defence in the hospital' and the methods women have developed are strikingly similar to those that workers have tried in the workplace ...

If doctors are like managers controlling the work that women's bodies do in birthing a baby, then will they stop short of actually removing the work force, the women themselves? This question leads us to an examination of the rapidly developing reproductive technologies. Many have suggested that these technologies contribute to birth being seen as commodity production: eggs, sperms, wombs, embryos, and even babies are increasingly being bought and sold. My analogy of birth and production shows that this analogy is a slight extension of existing tendencies: ever since labor in childbirth was defined as mechanical work done by the uterus, birth has been seen as the (re)production of goods. What is changing is our ability to harvest components of the goods (embryo, eggs) earlier and to know in greater detail what the quality of the goods is . . . On the one hand, technology allows the development of new standards for fetal growth. On the other hand, doctors, husbands and state governments are successfully using legal sanctions to force women to involuntarily alter their diets (stop taking drugs), alter their daily activity (be confined to a hospital for the last weeks of pregnancy), or undergo caesarean section to protect the rights of the fetus. Although one could argue that at least some of these restrictions might benefit the fetus, they certainly give the woman no choice about sacrificing her rights to those of the fetus. The possibility exists that the woman, the 'laborer', will increasingly drop out of sight as doctor-managers focus on 'producing' perfect 'products'.

Emily Martin, *The Women in the Body: A Cultural Analysis of Reproduction*, Milton Keynes, Open University Press, 1989, pp. 139–45.

10 The early relation to a primary caretaker provides in children of both genders both the basic capacity to participate in a relationship with the features of the early parent–child one, and the desire to create this intimacy. However, because women mother, the early experience and preoedipal relationship differ for boys and girls. Girls retain more concern with early childhood issues in relation to their mother, and a sense of self involved with these issues. Their attachments therefore retain more preoedipal aspects. The greater length and different nature of their pre-oedipal experience, and their continuing preoccupation with the issues of this period, mean that women's sense of self is continuous with others and that they retain capacities for primary identification, both of which enable them to experience the empathy and lack of reality sense needed by a cared-for infant. In men, these qualities have been curtailed, both because they are early treated as an opposite by their mother and because their later attachment to her must be repressed. The relational basis for mothering is thus extended in women, and inhibited in men, who experience themselves as more separate and distinct from others . . .

Social reproduction is thus asymmetrical. Women in their domestic role reproduce men and children physically, psychologically, and emotionally. Women in their domestic role as housekeepers reconstitute themselves physically on a daily basis and reproduce themselves as mothers, emotionally and psychologically, in the next generation. They thus contribute to the perpetuation of their own social roles and position in the hierarchy of gender.

Institutionalized features of family structure and the social relations of reproduction reproduce themselves. A psychoanalytic investigation shows that women's mothering capacities and commitments, and the general psychological capacities and wants which are the basis of women's emotional work, are built developmentally into feminine personality. Because women are themselves mothered by women, and grow up with the relational capacities and needs, and psychological definition of self-in-relationship, which commits them to mothering. Men, because they are mothered by women, do not. Women mother daughters who, when they become women, mother.
Nancy Chodorow, *Reproduction of Mothering: Psychoanalysis and the Sociology of Gender*, Berkeley, University of California Press, 1978, pp. 205–9.

The fact that masculinity may appear in different guises at different times **11** does not entitle us to draw the conclusion that we are dealing with an ephemeral quality which is sometimes present and sometimes not. In the final analysis, how men behave will depend upon the existing social relations of gender. By this I mean the way in which men and women confront each other ideologically and politically. Gender is never simply an arrangement in which the roles of men and women are decided in a contingent and haphazard way. At any given moment, gender will reflect the material interests of those who have power and those who do not. Masculinity, therefore, does not exist in isolation from femininity – it will always be an expression of the current image that men have of themselves in relation to women. And these images are often contradictory and ambivalent. Masculinity, from this point of view, is always local and subject to change. Obviously, some masculinities are long-lived whilst others are as ephemeral as fads in pop music. However, what does not easily change is the justification and naturalization of male power; that is, what remains relatively constant in the masculine ideology, masculinism or heterosexualism. What I am proposing here is that we must distinguish between three concepts which often tend to be confused in literature as well as in political and everyday discourse, namely masculinity, masculinism and patriarchy. Masculinity refers to those aspects of men's behaviour that fluctuate over time . . .

The implication here is that male identity is a fragile and tentative thing with no secure anchorage in the contemporary world. Such fragility makes it almost impossible to talk about masculinity as though it had some recognizable substantive basis. And yet, in everyday and academic discourse, we find that men are commonly described as aggressive, assertive, independent, competitive, insensitive, and so on. These attributes are based on the idea that there is something about men which transcends their local situation. Men are seen as having natures which determine their behaviour in all situations. Indeed, the habit of attributing some kind of exalted power to masculinity is so ingrained in our culture that it makes it very difficult to give credence to those explanations which stress its contextuality. This is precisely the point. Those people who speak of masculinity as an essence, as an inborn characteristic, are confusing masculinity with masculinism, masculine ideology. Masculinism is the ideology that justifies and naturalizes male domination. As such, it is the ideology of patriarchy. Masculinism takes it for granted that there is a fundamental difference between men and women, it assumes that heterosexuality is normal, it accepts without question the sexual division of labour, and it sanctions the political and dominant role of men in the public and private spheres.

Arthur Brittan, *Masculinity and Power*, Oxford, Blackwell, 1989, pp. 1–6.

GENERALIZED OTHER

See MEAD

GLOBALIZATION

1   The concept of globalization is best understood as expressing fundamental aspects of time–space distanciation. Globalization concerns the intersection of presence and absence, the interlacing of social events and social relations 'at a distance' with local contextualities.

Anthony Giddens, *Modernity and Self-Identity*, Cambridge, Polity Press, 1991, p. 21.

2   Globalization can thus be defined as the intensification of worldwide social relations which link distant localities in such a way that local happenings are shaped by events occurring many miles away and vice versa.

Anthony Giddens, *The Consequences of Modernity*, Cambridge, Polity Press, 1991 (pbk edn), p. 64.

HEALTH (AND MEDICINE)

See also PARSONS

1   In human society pain, like so many other physiological phenomena, acquires specific social and cultural significance, and accordingly, certain reactions to pain can be understood in the light of this significance ...

With these aims in mind the project was set up at the Kingsbridge Veterans Hospital, Bronx, New York, where four ethno-cultural groups were selected for an intensive study. These groups included patients of Jewish, Italian, Irish and 'Old American' stock. These groups – Jews,

Italian, and Irish – were selected because they were described by medical people as manifesting striking differences in their reaction to pain. Italians and Jews were described as tending to 'exaggerate' their pain, while the Irish were often depicted as stoical individuals who were able to take a great deal of pain. The fourth group, the 'Old Americans', were chosen because the values and attitudes of this group dominate in this country and are held by many members of the medical profession and by many descendants of the immigrants who, in the process of Americanization, tend to adopt American patterns of behavior . . .

Attitudes of Italian and Jewish patients toward pain-relieving drugs can serve as an indication of their attitude toward pain. When in pain the Italian calls for pain relief and is mainly concerned with the analgesic effects of the drugs which are administered to him. Once the pain is relieved the Italian patient easily forgets his sufferings and manifests a happy and joyful disposition. The Jewish patient, however, often is reluctant to accept the drug, and he explains this reluctance in terms of concern about the effects of the drug upon his health in general. He is apprehensive about the habit-forming aspects of the analgesic. Moreover, he feels that the drug relieves his pain only temporarily and does not cure him of the disease which may cause the pain . . .

It has been stated that the Italians and Jews tend to manifest similar behavior in terms of their reactions to pain. As both cultures allow for free expressions of feelings and emotions by words, sounds and gestures, both the Italians and Jews feel free to talk about their pain, complain about it and manifest their sufferings by groaning, moaning, crying, etc. They are not ashamed of this expression. They admit willingly that when they are in pain they do complain a great deal, call for help and expect sympathy and assistance from other members of their immediate social environment, especially from members of their family. When they are in pain they are reluctant to be alone and prefer the presence and attention of other people. This behavior, which is expected, accepted and approved by the Italian and Jewish cultures, often conflicts with the patterns of behavior expected from a patient by American or Americanized medical people. Thus they tend to describe the behavior of the Italian and Jewish patient regardless of whether they have the objective criteria for evaluating the actual amount of pain which the patient experiences. It seems that the uninhibited display of reaction to pain as manifested by the Jewish and Italian patient provokes distrust in American culture instead of provoking sympathy.

Mark Zborowski, 'Cultural Components in Responses to Pain', *Journal of Social Issues*, vol. 8, no. 4, 1952, pp. 16–30.

The takeover of birth by male doctors in America was an unusual **2** phenomenon in comparison to France and England, where traditional midwifery continued as a much more significant part of birth. Practice developed differently in America because the society itself expanded more rapidly and the medical profession grew more quickly to doctor in ever new communities. American mobility left fewer stable communities than in France or England, and thus networks of women to support midwives were more often broken. The standards of the American medical profession were not so high or so strictly enforced as standards in other countries, and thus there were both more 'educated' doctors and more self-proclaimed doctors in America to compete with midwives. So American midwives disappeared from view because they had less support from stable communities of women and more competition from male doctors.

Richard W. Wertz and Dorothy C. Wertz, *Lying In: The History of Childbirth in America*, New York, Macmillan, 1977. Extract in P. Conrad and R. Kern (eds), *The Sociology of Health and Illness*, New York, St Martin's Press, 1981, p. 181.

3   Some aspects of patriarchal strategies of demarcation are demonstrated most vividly by examining the relationship between female midwifery practices and male medical practice. First, there were attempts by members of the medical profession to renegotiate boundaries between midwifery and medical practice by fragmenting midwifery and incorporating certain aspects of midwifery into 'obstetrics' and by ensuring that midwives were restricted to the sphere of *normal* labour, seeking medical assistance for abnormal labour. These may be described as patriarchal strategies of *pre-emptive de-skilling*: the midwife's sphere of competence was narrowed and strictly bounded as aspects of midwifery practice were expropriated and placed within the exclusive sphere of competence of medical doctors. Second, a patriarchal strategy of *pre-emptive incorporation* was pursued in relation to the use of surgical instruments in childbirth, particularly the use of short forceps, and midwives were never able to incorporate these tasks within their own sphere of competence. Finally, strategies of *pre-emptive closure* ensured that midwives were unsuccessful in their attempts to organise on the same terms as physicians, surgeons and apothecaries, despite attempts to do so in the seventeenth century.

Anne Witz, 'Patriarchy and the Labour Market: Occupational Control Strategies and the Medical Divisions of Labour', in D. Knights and H. Willmott (eds), *Gender and the Labour Process*, Aldershot, Gower, 1986, p. 27.

4   Within the last decade medical professional practice has become a major threat to health. Depression, infection, disability, dysfunction, and other specific iatrogenic diseases now cause more suffering than all accidents from traffic or industry. Beyond this, medical practice sponsors sickness by the reinforcement of a morbid society which not only industrially preserves its defectives but breeds the therapist's client in a cybernetic way. Finally, the so-called health-professions have an indirect sickening power – a structurally health-denying effect. I want to focus on this last syndrome,

which I designate as medical Nemesis. By transforming pain, illness, and death from a personal challenge into a technical problem, medical practice expropriates the potential of people to deal with their human condition in an autonomous way and becomes the source of a new kind of un-health.
Ivan Illich, 'Medical Nemesis', *The Lancet*, 28 May 1974, p. 918.

Along with progressive medicalization, a process of demedicalization   5
seems also to be taking place in the society. To some extent the signs of demedicalization are reactions to what is felt by various individuals and groups to be a state of '*over*-medicalization'.

One of the most significant manifestations of this counter-trend is the mounting concern over implications that have arisen from the continuously expanding conception of 'sickness' in the society ... many observers from diverse professional backgrounds have published works in which they express concern about the 'coercive' aspects of the 'label' illness and the treatment of illness by medical professionals and in medical institutions ... This emerging view emphasizes the degree to which what is defined as health and illness, normality and abnormality, sanity and insanity varies from one society, culture, and historical period to another. Thus, it is contended, medical diagnostic categories such as 'sick', 'abnormal', and 'insane' are not universal, objective, or necessarily reliable. Rather they are culture-, class-, and time-bound, often ethnocentric, and as much artifacts of the preconceptions of socially biased observers as they are valid summaries of the characteristics of the observed. In this view, illness (especially mental illness) is largely a mythical construct, created and enforced by the society. The hospitals to which seriously ill persons are confined are portrayed as 'total institutions': segregated, encompassing, depersonalizing organizations, 'dominated' by physicians who are disinclined to convey information to patients about their conditions, or to encourage paramedical personnel to do so. These 'oppressive' and 'counter-therapeutic' attributes of the hospital environment are seen as emanating from the professional ideology of physicians and the kind of hierarchical relationships that they establish with patients and other medical professionals partly as a consequence of this ideology, as well as from the bureaucratic and technological features of the hospital itself. Whatever their source, the argument continues, the characteristics of the hospital and of the doctor–patient relationship increase the 'powerlessness' of the sick person, 'maintain his uncertainty', and systematically 'mortify' and 'curtail' the 'self' with which he enters the sick role and arrives at the hospital door.

This critical perspective links the labelling of illness, the 'imperialist' outlook and capitalist behavior of physicians, the 'stigmatizing' and 'dehumanizing' experiences of patients, and the problems of the health-care system more generally to imperfections and injustices in the society as a whole.

Renee C. Fox, 'The Medicalization and Demedicalization of American Society', *Daedalus*, Journal of the American Academy of Arts and Sciences, Boston, Massachusetts, winter, 1977. Extract in P. Conrad and K. Rochelle (eds), *The Sociology of Health and Illness*, New York, St Martin's Press, 1981, pp. 527–8.

6 Professional schools often receive a major share of the blame for producing this kind of cynicism – and none more than the medical school. The idealistic young freshman changes into a tough, hardened, unfeeling doctor; or so the popular view has it. Teachers of medicine sometimes rephrase the distinction between the clinical and pre-clinical years into one between the 'cynical' and 'pre-cynical' years. Psychological research supports this view, presenting attitude surveys which show medical students year by year scoring lower on 'idealism' and higher on 'cynicism'. Typically, this cynicism is seen as developing in response to the shattering of ideals consequent on coming face-to-face with the realities of professional practice . . .

Some of the students' determined idealism at the outset is reaction against the lay notion, of which they are uncomfortably aware, that doctors are money-hungry cynics; they counter this with an idealism of similar lay origin stressing the doctor's devotion to service. But this idealism soon meets a setback, as students find that it will not be relevant for a while, since medical school has, it seems, little relation to the practice of medicine, as they see it. As it has not been refuted, but only shown to be temporarily beside the point, the students 'agree' to set this idealism aside in favour of a realistic approach to the problem of getting through school. This approach, which we have labelled as the cynicism specific to the school experience, serves as protection for the earlier grandiose feelings about medicine by postponing their exposure to reality to a distant future. As that future approaches near the end of the four years and its possible mistreatment of their ideals moves closer, the students again worry about maintaining their integrity, this time in actual medical practice. They use some of the knowledge they have gained to plan careers which, it is hoped, can best bring their ideals to realization.

We can put this in propositional form by saying that when a man's ideals are challenged by outsiders and then further strained by reality, he may salvage them by postponing their application to a future time when conditions are expected to be more propitious.
Howard S. Becker and Blanche Geer, 'The Fate of Idealism in Medical School', *American Sociological Review*, vol. 23, 1958, pp. 50–6.

7 Our model bears upon that most central of sociological problems, namely, how a measure of order is maintained in the face of inevitable changes (derivable from sources both external and internal to the organization). Students of formal organization tend to underplay the processes of internal change as well as overestimate the more stable features of organizations – including its rules and its hierarchical statuses. We ourselves take our cue

from Mead (1936), who some years ago, when arguing for orderly and directed social change, remarked that the task turns about relationships between change and order:

> 'How can you bring those changes about in an orderly fashion and yet preserve order? To bring about change is seemingly to destroy the given order, and yet society does and must change. That is the problem, to incorporate the method of change into the order of society itself.'

Without Mead's melioristic concerns, one can yet assume that order is something at which members of any society, any organization must work. For the shared agreements, the binding contracts – which constitute the grounds for an expectable, non-surprising, taken-for-granted, even ruled orderliness – are not binding and shared for all time. Contracts, understandings, agreements, rules – all have appended to them a temporal clause . . . Such considerations have led us to emphasise the importance of negotiation – the processes of give-and-take, of diplomacy, of bargaining – which characterizes organizational life . . .

The model presented has pictured the hospital as a locale where personnel, mostly but not exclusively professionals, are enmeshed in a complex negotiative process in order to accomplish their individual purposes and to work – in an established division of labour – toward clearly as well as vaguely phrased institutional objectives. We have sought to show how differential professional training, ideology, career, and hierarchical position all affect the negotiation; but we have also attempted to show how nonprofessionals may affect the total process. We have outlined important relationships between daily working arrangement and the more permanent structure.

A. Strauss *et al.* 'The Hospital and Its Negotiated Order', in E. Friedson (ed.), *The Hospital in Modern Society*, New York, Macmillan, 1963, pp. 147–69. Extract in G. Salaman and K. Thompson (eds), *People and Organisations*, London, Longman, 1973, p. 318.

HEGEMONY

The methodological contention on which our own study must be based is **1** the following: that the supremacy of a social group manifests itself in two ways, as 'domination' and as 'intellectual and moral leadership'. A social group dominates antagonistic groups, which it tends to 'liquidate', or to subjugate perhaps even by armed force; it leads kindred and allied groups. A social group can, and indeed must, already exercise 'leadership' before winning governmental power (this indeed is one of the principal conditions for the winning of such power); it subsequently becomes dominant when it exercises power, but even if it holds it firmly in its grasp, it must continue to 'lead' as well.

Antonio Gramsci, *Selections from the Prison Notebooks*, London, Lawrence & Wishart, 1971, pp. 57–8.

2 In other words, the preponderance of civil society over the state in the West can be equated with the predominance of 'hegemony' over 'coercion' as the fundamental mode of bourgeois power in advanced capitalism. Since hegemony pertains to civil society, and civil society prevails over the State, it is the cultural ascendancy of the ruling class that essentially ensures the stability of the capitalist order. For in Gramsci's usage here, hegemony means the ideological subordination of the working class by the bourgeoisie, which enables it to rule by consent.
Perry Anderson, 'The Antinomies of Antonio Gramsci', *New Left Review*, no. 100, 1976/7, p. 26.

IDEAL TYPE

See also WEBER

An ideal type is formed by the one-sided accentuation of one or more points of view and by the synthesis of a great many diffuse, discrete, more or less present and occasionally absent concrete individual phenomena, which are arranged according to those one-sidedly emphasized viewpoints into a unified analytical construct. In its conceptual purity, this mental construct cannot be found empirically anywhere in reality. It is a utopia.
Max Weber, *The Methodology of the Social Sciences*, ed. Edward A. Shils and Henry A. Finch, New York, Free Press, 1949, p. 89. First published as 'Objectivity' in *Social Science and Social Policy*, in 1904.

IDENTITY

See also MEAD, COOLEY

For the purposes of exposition, I shall distinguish three very different conceptions of identity: those of the (a) Enlightenment subject, (b) sociological subject, and (c) post-modern subject. The Enlightenment subject was based on a conception of the human person as a fully centred, unified individual, endowed with the capacities of reason, consciousness and action, whose 'centre' consisted of an inner core which first emerged when the subject was born, and unfolded with it, while remaining essentially the same – continuous or 'identical' with itself – throughout the individual's existence. The essential centre of the self was a person's identity. I shall say more about this in a moment, but you can see that this was a very 'individualist' conception of the subject and 'his' (for Enlightenment subjects were usually described as male) identity.

The notion of the sociological subject reflected the growing complexity of the modern world and the awareness that this inner core of the subject was not autonomous and self-sufficient, but was formed in relation to 'significant others', who mediated to the subject the values, meanings and symbols – the culture – of the worlds he/she inhabited. G. H. Mead, C. H. Cooley, and the symbolic interactionists are the key figures in sociology who elaborated this 'interactive' conception of identity and the self. According to this view, which has become the classic sociological conception of the issue, identity is formed in the 'interaction' between self and society. The subject still has an inner core or essence that is 'the real me', but this is formed and modified in a continuous dialogue with the cultural worlds 'outside' and the identities which they offer.

Identity in this sociological conception, bridges the gap between the 'inside' and the 'outside' – between the personal and the public worlds. The fact that we project 'ourselves' into these cultural identities, at the same time internalizing their meanings and values, making them 'part of us', helps to align our subjective feelings with the objective places we occupy in the social and cultural world. Identity thus stitches (or, to use a current metaphor, 'sutures') the subject into the structure. It stabilizes both subjects and the cultural worlds they inhabit, making both reciprocally more unified and predictable.

Yet these are exactly what are now said to be 'shifting'. The subject, previously experienced as having a unified and stable identity, is becoming fragmented; composed not of a single, but of several, sometimes contradictory or unresolved identities . . . This produces the post-modern subject, conceptualized as having no fixed, essential or permanent identity. Identity becomes a 'moveable feast': formed and transformed continuously in relation to the ways we are represented or addressed in the cultural systems which surround us.

Stuart Hall, 'The Question of Cultural Identity', in S. Hall, D. Held and T. McGrew (eds), *Modernity and Its Futures*, Cambridge, Polity Press, 1992, pp. 275–6.

IDEOLOGY

See also MARX

The ideas of the ruling class are in every epoch the ruling ideas: i.e. the **1** class, which is the ruling material force of society, is at the same time its ruling intellectual force. The class which has the means of material production at its disposal, has control at the same time over the means of mental production, so that thereby, generally speaking, the ideas of those who lack the means of mental production are subject to it. The ruling ideas are nothing more than the ideal expression of the dominant material relationships, the dominant material relationships grasped as ideas; hence of the relationships which make the one class the ruling one, therefore the ideas of its dominance. The individuals composing the ruling class possess among other things consciousness, and therefore think. In so far, therefore, as they rule as a class and determine the extent and compass of an epoch, it is self-evident that they do this in their whole range, hence among other things rule also as thinkers, as producers of ideas, and regulate the production and distribution of the ideas of their age: thus their ideas are the ruling ideas of the epoch.

Karl Marx and Friedrich Engels, *The German Ideology* [1845–6], New York, International Publishers, 1963 (pbk edn), p. 39.

2 One must therefore distinguish between historically organic ideologies, those, that is, which are necessary to a given structure, and ideologies that are arbitrary, rationalistic, or 'willed'. To the extent that ideologies are historically necessary they have a validity which is 'psychological'; they 'organise' human masses, and create the terrain on which men move, acquire consciousness of their position, struggle, etc. To the extent that they are arbitrary they only create individual 'movements', polemics and so on (though even these are not completely useless, since they function like an error which by contrasting with truth, demonstrates it.).

Antonio Gramsci, *Selections from the Prison Notebooks*, ed. and trans. Q. Hoare and G. Nowell Smith, London, Lawrence & Wishart, 1971, pp. 376–7.

3 The claim, presented as an essential postulate of historical materialism, that every fluctuation of politics and ideology can be presented and expounded as an immediate expression of the structure, must be contested in theory as primitive infantilism, and combated in practice with the authentic testimony of Marx, the author of concrete political and historical works.

Ibid., p. 407.

4 Ideology represents the imaginary relationship of individuals to their real conditions of existence.

Louis Althusser, 'Ideology and Ideological State Apparatuses (Notes towards an Investigation)', trans. B. Brewster, in *Lenin, Philosophy and Other Essays*, London, New Left Books, 1971, p. 162. First published in French in 1970.

5 Thus, in order to represent why the category of the 'subject' is constitutive of ideology, which only exists by constituting concrete subjects as subjects, I shall employ a special mode of exposition: 'concrete' enough to be recognized, but abstract enough to be thinkable and thought, giving rise to a knowledge.

As a first formulation I shall say: *all ideology hails or interpellates concrete individuals as concrete subjects*, by the functioning of the category of the subject.

This is a proposition which entails that we distinguish for the moment between concrete individuals on the one hand and concrete subjects on the other, although at this level concrete subjects only exist insofar as they are supported by a concrete individual.

I shall then suggest that ideology 'acts' or 'functions' in such a way that it 'recruits' subjects among the individuals (it recruits them all), or 'transforms' the individuals into subjects (it transforms them all) by that very precise operation which I have called *interpellation* or hailing, and which can be imagined along the lines of the most commonplace everyday police (or other) hailing: 'Hey, you there!'

Assuming that the theoretical scene I have imagined takes place in the street, the hailed individual will turn round. By this mere one-hundred-and-eighty-degree physical conversion, he becomes a *subject*. Why? Because he has recognized that the hail was 'really' addressed to him, and that 'it was *really him* who was hailed' (and not someone else).
Ibid., pp. 173–4.

Whatever its origins among the French *philosophes*, ideology as a way of **6** translating ideas into action was given its sharpest phrasing by the left Hegelians, by Feuerbach and by Marx. For them, the function of philosophy was to be critical, to rid the present of the past. ('The tradition of all the dead generations weighs like a nightmare on the brain of the living', wrote Marx.) Feuerbach, the most radical of all the left Hegelians, called himself Luther II. Man would be free, he said, if we could demythologize religion. The history of all thought was a history of progressive disenchantment, and if finally, in Christianity, God had been transformed from a parochial deity to a universal abstraction, the function of criticism – using the radical tool of alienation, or self-estrangement – was to replace theology by anthropology, to substitute Man for God. Philosophy was to be directed at life, man was to be liberated from the 'spectre of abstractions' and extricated from the bind of the supernatural. Religion was capable only of creating 'false consciousness'. Philosophy would reveal 'true consciousness'. And by placing Man, rather than God, at the center of consciousness, Feuerbach sought to bring the 'infinite into the finite'.

If Feuerbach 'descended into the world', Marx sought to transform it. And where Feuerbach proclaimed anthropology, Marx, reclaiming a root insight of Hegel, emphasized History and historical context. The world was not generic Man, but men; and of men, classes of men. Men differed because of their class position. And truths were class truths. All truths, thus, were masks, or partial truths, but the real truth was the revolutionary truth. And this real truth was rational . . .
Daniel Bell, *The End of Ideology*, Glencoe, Illinois, Free Press, 1965 (pbk edn), pp. 393–4.

7   Ideology is the conversion of ideas into social levers . . .

What gives ideology its force is its passion. Abstract philosophical inquiry has always sought to eliminate passion, and the person, to rationalize all ideas. For the ideologue, truth arises in action, and meaning is given by experience by the 'transforming moment' . . .

The ideologies, therefore, which emerged from the nineteenth century had the force of the intellectual behind them. They embarked upon what William James called 'the faith ladder', which in its vision of the future cannot distinguish possibilities from probabilities, and converts the latter into certainties.

Today, these ideologies are exhausted . . .

And yet, the extraordinary fact is that while the old nineteenth-century ideologies and intellectual debates have become exhausted, the rising states of Asia and Africa are fashioning new ideologies with a different appeal for their peoples. These are the ideologies of industrialization, modernization, Pan-Arabism, color, and nationalism.
Ibid., pp. 400–3.

8   The particular conception of ideology is implied when the term denotes that we are sceptical of the ideas and representations advanced by our opponent. They are regarded as more or less conscious disguises of the real nature of a situation, the true recognition of which would not be in accord with his interests. These distortions range all the way from conscious lies to half-conscious and unwitting disguises; from calculated attempts to dupe others to self deception. This conception of ideology, which has only gradually become differentiated from the common-sense notion of the lie, is particular in several senses. Its particularity becomes evident when it is contrasted with the more inclusive total conception of ideology. Here we refer to the ideology of an age or of a concrete historico-social group, e.g. of a class, when we are concerned with the characteristics and composition of the total structure of the mind of this epoch or of this group . . .

Both of these conceptions of ideology, accordingly, make these so-called 'ideas' a function of him who holds them, and of his position in his social milieu. Although they have something in common, there are also significant differences between them. Of the latter we mention merely the most important:

(a) Whereas the particular conception of ideology designates only a part of the opponent's assertions as ideologies – and this only with reference to their content, the total conception calls into question the opponent's total *Weltanschauung* (including his conceptual apparatus), and attempts to understand these concepts as an outgrowth of the collective life of which he partakes.

(b) The particular conception of 'ideology' makes its analysis of ideas on a purely psychological level. If it is claimed for instance that an adversary is lying, or that he is concealing or distorting a given factual situation, it is still nevertheless assumed that both parties share common criteria of validity – it is still assumed that it is possible to refute lies and eradicate sources of error by referring to accepted criteria of objective validity common to both parties. The suspicion that one's opponent is the victim of an ideology does not go so far as to exclude him from discussion on the basis of a common theoretical frame of reference. The case is different with the total conception of ideology. When we attribute to one historical epoch one intellectual world and to ourselves another one, or if a certain historically determined social stratum thinks in categories other than our own, we refer not to the isolated cases of thought-content, but to fundamentally divergent thought-systems and to widely differing modes of experience and interpretation. We touch upon the theoretical or noological level whenever we consider not merely the content but also the form, and even the conceptual framework of a mode of thought as a function of the life-situation of the thinker . . .

(c) Corresponding to this difference, the particular conception of ideology operates primarily with a psychology of interests, while the total conception uses a more formal functional analysis, without any reference to motivations, confining itself to an objective description of the structural differences in minds operating in different social settings. The former assumes that this or that interest is the cause of a given lie or deception. The latter presupposes simply that there is a correspondence between a given social situation and a given perspective, point of view, or apperception mass. In this case, while an analysis of constellations of interests may often be necessary it is not to establish causal connections but to characterize the total situation. Thus interest psychology tends to be displaced by an analysis of the correspondence between the situation to be known and the forms of knowledge.

Karl Mannheim, *Ideology and Utopia: An Introduction to the Sociology of Knowledge* [1929]; ed. and trans. L. Wirth and E. Shils, New York, Harcourt Brace Jovanovich, 1936, pp. 1–3, 55–9.

There are currently two main approaches to the study of the social deter- **9**
minants of ideology: the interest theory and the strain theory. For the first, ideology is a mask and a weapon; for the second, a symptom and a remedy. In the interest theory, ideological pronouncements are seen against the background of a universal struggle for advantage, in the strain theory, against the background of a chronic effort to correct sociopsychological disequilibrium. In the one, men pursue power; in the other, they flee anxiety. As they may, of course, do both at the same time – and even one by means of the other – the two theories are not necessarily contradictory; but the strain theory (which arose in response to the empirical difficulties

encountered by the interest theory), being less simplistic, is more pene-
trating, less concrete, more comprehensive . . .

Where science is the diagnostic, the critical, dimension of culture, ideology is the justificatory, the apologetic, one – it refers to that part of culture
which is actively concerned with the establishment and defence of patterns
of belief and value.

Clifford Geertz, 'Ideology as a Cultural System', in D. Apter (ed.), *Ideology and
Discontent*, New York, Collier-Macmillan, 1964; reprinted in R. Bocock and K.
Thompson (eds), *Religion and Ideology*, Manchester, Manchester University Press,
1985, pp. 76, 83.

INSTITUTION

See also DURKHEIM, PARSONS

[T]he essential aspect of social structure lies in a system of patterned
expectations defining the *proper* behavior of persons playing certain roles,
enforced both by the incumbents' own positive motives for conformity
and by the sanctions of others. Such systems of patterned expectations,
seen in the perspective of their place in a total social system and sufficiently
thoroughly established in action to be taken for granted as legitimate, are
conveniently called 'institutions'. The fundamental, structurally stable element of social systems then, which, according to the present argument,
must play a crucial role in their theoretical analysis, is their structure of
institutional patterns defining the roles of their constituent actors.

Talcott Parsons, 'The Present Position and Prospects of Systematic Theory in
Sociology', in T. Parsons, *Essays in Sociological Theory* [1954], New York, Free
Press, 1964 (pbk edn), p. 231.

LABOUR PROCESS

The distinctive capacity of human labor power is therefore not its ability to
produce a surplus, but rather its intelligent and purposive character, which
gives it infinite adaptability and which produces the social and cultural conditions for enlarging its own productivity, so that its surplus product may
be continuously enlarged. From the point of view of the capitalist, this
many-sided potentiality of humans in society is the basis upon which is
built the enlargement of his capital. He therefore takes up every means of
increasing the output of the labor power he has purchased when he sets it
to work as labor. The means he employs may vary from the enforcement
upon the worker of the longest possible working day in the early period of
capitalism to the use of the most productive instruments of labor and the
greatest intensity of labor, but they are always aimed at realizing from the

potential inherent in labor power the greatest useful effect of labor, for it is this that will yield for him the greatest surplus and thus the greatest profit. But if the capitalist builds upon this distinctive quality and potential of human labor power, it is also this quality, by its very indeterminacy, which places upon him his greatest challenge and problem. The coin of labor has its obverse side: in purchasing labor power that can do much, he is at the same time purchasing an undefined quality and quantity. What he buys is infinite in potential, but in its realization it is limited by the subjective state of the workers, by their previous history, by the general social conditions under which they work as well as the particular conditions of the enterprise, and by the technical setting of their labor. The work actually performed will be affected by these and many other factors, including the organization of the process and the forms of supervision over it, if any ... Having been forced to sell their labor power to another, the workers also surrender their interest in the labor process, which has now been 'alienated'. *The labor process has become the responsibility of the capitalist.* In this setting of antagonistic relations of production, the problem of realizing the 'full usefulness' of the labor power he has bought becomes exacerbated by the opposing interests of those for whose purposes the labor process is carried on, and those who, on the other side, carry it on ... It thus becomes essential for the capitalist that control over the labor process pass from the hands of the worker into his own. This transition presents itself in history as the *progressive alienation of the process of production* from the worker; to the capitalist, it presents itself as the problem of *management.*

Harry Braverman, *Labor and Monopoly Capital*, New York, Monthly Review Press, 1974, pp. 56–8.

MARRIAGE

See also FAMILY

Ever since Durkheim it has been a commonplace of family sociology that marriage serves as a protection against anomie for the individual. Interesting and pragmatically useful though this insight is, it is but the negative side of a phenomenon of much broader significance. If one speaks of *anomic* states, then one ought properly to investigate also the *nomic* processes that, by their absence, lead to the aforementioned states. If, consequently, one finds a negative correlation between marriage and anomie, then one should be led to inquire into the character of marriage as a *nomos*-building instrumentality, that is, of marriage as a social arrangement that creates for the individual the sort of order in which he can experience his life as making sense ...

Every individual requires the ongoing validation of his world, including crucially the validation of his identity and place in this world, by those few who are his truly significant others. Just as the individual's deprivation of relationship with his significant others will plunge him into anomie, so their continual presence will sustain for him that *nomos* by which he can feel at home in the world at least most of the time. Again in a broad sense, all the actions of the significant others and even their simple presence serve this sustaining function. In everyday life, however, the principal method employed is speech. In this sense, it is proper to view the individual's relationships with his significant others as an ongoing conversation ...

If one concedes these points, one can now state a general sociological proposition: the plausibility and stability of the world, as socially defined, is dependent upon the strength and continuity of significant relationships in which conversation about this world can be continually carried on. Or, to put it a little differently: the reality of the world is sustained through conversation with significant others ...

With these preliminary assumptions stated we can now arrive at our main thesis here. Namely, we would contend that marriage occupies a privileged status among the significant validating relationships for adults in our society. Put slightly differently: marriage is a crucial nomic instrumentality in our society.

Peter L. Berger and Hansfried Kellner, 'Marriage and the Construction of Reality', *Diogenes*, no. 46 (Summer), 1964, pp. 1–23. Extract in Rose L. Coser (ed.), *The Family, Its Structures and Functions*, New York, St Martin's Press, 1974, pp. 157–60.

MEDIA CULTURE

See also CULTURE, SEMIOLOGY

Culture in the broadest sense is a form of highly participatory activity, in which people create their societies and identities. Culture shapes individuals, drawing out and cultivating their potentialities and capacities for speech, action, and creativity. Media culture is also involved in these processes, yet it is something new in the human adventure. Individuals spend tremendous amounts of time listening to the radio, watching television, going to see films, experiencing music, going shopping, reading magazines and newspapers, and participating in these and other forms of media culture. Thus, media culture has come to dominate everyday life, serving as the ubiquitous background and often the highly seductive foreground of our attention and activity, which many argue is undermining human potentiality and creativity ...

In general, it is not a system of rigid ideological indoctrination that induces consent to existing capitalist societies, but the pleasures of the media and consumer culture. Media entertainment is often highly pleasurable and uses sight, sound, and spectacle to seduce audiences into identifying with certain views, attitudes, feelings, and positions. Consumer culture offers a dazzling array of goods and services that induce individuals to participate in a system of commercial gratification. Media and consumer culture work hand in hand to generate thought and behavior that conform to existing values, institutions, beliefs, and practices.

Yet audiences may resist the dominant meanings and messages, create their own readings and appropriations of mass-produced culture, and use their culture as resources to empower themselves and to invent their own meanings, identities, and forms of life. Moreover, media culture itself provides resources which individuals can appropriate, or reject, in form-ing their own identities against dominant models. Media culture thus induces individuals to conform to the established organization of society, but it also provides resources that can empower individuals against that society.

Douglas Kellner, *Media Culture*, London and New York, Routledge, 1995, p. 3.

MODERNITY

See also POSTMODERN

Two images of what it feels like to live in the world of modernity have **1** dominated the sociological literature, yet both of them seem less than adequate. One is that of Weber, according to which the bonds of rationality are drawn tighter and tighter, imprisoning us in a featureless cage of bureau-cratic routine. Among the three major founders of sociology, Weber saw most clearly the significance of expertise in modern social development and used it to outline a phenomenology of modernity. Everyday experience, according to Weber, retains its colour and spontaneity, but only on the perimeter of the 'steel-hard' cage of bureaucratic rationality. The image has a great deal of power and has, of course, featured strongly in fictional literature in the twentieth century as well as in more directly sociological discussions. There are many contexts of modern institutions which are marked by bureaucratic fixity. But they are far from all-pervasive, and even in the core settings of its application, namely, large-scale organizations, Weber's characterization of bureaucracy is inadequate. Rather than tend-ing inevitably to rigidity, organizations produce areas of autonomy and spontaneity – which are actually often less easy to achieve in smaller groups. We owe this counter insight to Durkheim, as well as to subsequent empirical study of organizations. The closed climate of opinion within some small groups and the modes of direct sanction available to its members fix the horizons of action much more narrowly and firmly than in larger organizational settings.

The second is the image of Marx – and of many others, whether they regard themselves as Marxist or not. According to this portrayal, modernity is seen as a monster. More limpidly perhaps than any of his contemporaries, Marx perceived how shattering the impact of modernity would be, and how irreversible. At the same time, modernity was for Marx what Habermas has aptly called an 'unfinished project'. The monster can be tamed, since what human beings have created they can always subject to their own control. Capitalism, simply, is an irrational way to run the modern world, because it substitutes the whims of the market for the controlled fulfilment of human need.

For these images I suggest we should substitute that of the juggernaut – a runaway engine of enormous power which, collectively as human beings, we can drive to some extent but which also threatens to rush out of our control and which could rend itself asunder.

Anthony Giddens, *The Consequences of Modernity*, Stanford, California, Stanford University Press, 1990, pp. 137–8.

2   The project of modernity, formulated in the 18th century by the philosophers of the Enlightenment, consisted in their efforts to develop objective science, universal morality and law, and autonomous art according to their inner logic. At the same time, this project intended to release the cognitive potential of each of these domains from their esoteric forms. The Enlightenment philosophers wanted to utilize this accumulation of specialized culture for the enrichment of everyday life – that is to say, for the rational organization of everyday social life.

Jürgen Habermas, 'Modernity versus Postmodernity', *New German Critique*, no. 22, 1981, p. 9.

MORAL PANIC

Societies appear to be subject every now and then to periods of moral panic. A condition, episode, person or group of persons emerges to become defined as a threat to societal values and interests; its nature is presented in a stylized and stereotypical fashion by the mass media; the moral barricades are manned by editors, bishops, politicians and other right-thinking people; socially accredited experts pronounce their diagnoses and solutions; ways of coping are evolved or ... resorted to; the condition then disappears, submerges or deteriorates and becomes more visible. Sometimes the subject of the panic is quite novel and at other times it is something which has been in existence long enough, but suddenly appears in the limelight. Sometimes the panic passes over and is forgotten, except in folklore and collective memory; at other times it has more serious and long-lasting repercussions

and might produce such changes as those in legal and social policy or even in the way society conceives itself.
Stanley Cohen, *Folk Devils and Moral Panics*, Harmondsworth, Penguin, 1972, p. 9.

NATION

If the concept of 'nation' can in any way be defined unambiguously, it **1** certainly cannot be stated in terms of empirical qualities common to those who count as members of the nation. In the sense of those using the term at a given time, the concept undoubtedly means, above all, that it is proper to expect from certain groups a specific sentiment of solidarity in the face of other groups. Thus the concept belongs to the sphere of values. Yet, there is no agreement on how these groups should be delimited or about what concerted action should result from such solidarity. In ordinary language, 'nation' is, first of all, not identical with the 'people of a state', that is with the membership of a given polity. Numerous polities comprise groups who emphatically assert the independence of their 'nation' in the face of other groups; or they comprise merely parts of a group whose members declare themselves to be one homogeneous 'nation' . . .
Max Weber, *Economy and Society* (3 vols), ed. and trans. G. Roth and C. Wittich, New York, Bedminster Press, 1968, vol. 2, p. 922. First published in German in 1925.

Nationalism is not the awakening of nations to self-consciousness; it **2** invents nations where they did not exist.
Ernest Gellner, *Thought and Change*, London, Weidenfeld & Nicolson, 1964, p. 169.

In an anthropological spirit, then, I propose the following definition of the **3** nation: it is an imagined political community – and imagined as both inher-ently limited and sovereign. It is *imagined* because the members of even the smallest nation will never know most of their fellow-members, meet them, or even hear of them, yet in the mind of each lives the image of their communion . . . The nation is imagined as *limited* because even the largest of them, encompassing perhaps a billion living human beings, has finite, if elastic boundaries . . . It is imagined as *sovereign* because the concept was born in an age in which enlightenment and Revolution were destroying the legitimacy of the divinely-ordained, hierarchical dynastic realm . . . Finally, it is imagined as a *community*, because, regardless of the actual inequality and exploitation that may prevail in each, the nation is always conceived as a deep, horizontal comradeship.
Benedict Anderson, *Imagined Communities*, London, Verso, 1983, pp. 15–16.

ORIENTALISM

1 My contention is that, without examining Orientalism as a discourse, one cannot possibly understand the enormously systematic discipline by which European culture was able to manage – and even produce – the Orient politically, sociologically, militarily, ideologically, scientifically and imaginatively during the post-Enlightenment period. Moreover, so authoritative a position did Orientalism have that I believe no one writing, thinking, or acting on the Orient could do so without taking account of the limitations on thought and action imposed by Orientalism. In brief, because of Orientalism, the Orient was not (and is not) a free subject of thought and action. This is not to say that Orientalism unilaterally determines what can be said about the Orient, but that it is the whole network of interests inevitably brought to bear on (and therefore always involved in) any occasion when that peculiar entity 'the Orient' is in question.

Edward Said, *Orientalism: Western Concepts of the Orient*, Harmondsworth, Penguin, 1985, p. 3.

2 Within the perspective of Foucault's analysis of knowledge, we can now treat Orientalism as a discourse that creates typologies within which characters can be distributed: the energetic Occidental man versus the lascivious Oriental, the rational westerner versus the unpredictable Oriental, the gentle white versus the cruel yellow man. The notion of Orientalism as a discourse of power emerging in the context of a geo-political struggle between Europe and the Middle East provides the basis of one of the most influential studies of recent times, namely Edward Said's *Orientalism* (1978).

Orientalism as a discourse divides the globe unambiguously into Occident and Orient; the latter is essentially strange, exotic and mysterious, but also sensual, irrational and potentially dangerous. This Oriental strangeness can only be grasped by the gifted specialist in Oriental cultures and, in particular, by those with skills in philology, language and literature. The task of Orientalism was to reduce the bewildering complexity of Oriental societies and Oriental culture to some manageable, comprehensible level. The expert, through the discourse on the Orient, represented the mysterious East in terms of basic frameworks and typologies. The chrestomathy summarised the exotic Orient in a table of comprehensible items.

The point of Orientalism, according to Said, was to Orientalise the Orient and it did so in the context of fundamental colonial inequalities. Orientalism was based on the fact that we know or talk about the Orientals, whereas they neither know themselves adequately nor talk about us.

Bryan S. Turner, *Religion and Social Theory*, London, Heinemann Educational Books, 1983, p. 31.

PHENOMENOLOGY

Phenomenology, as generally defined in sociology, refers to the study of how the social world is constructed. We might think of how an architect blueprints a project and then oversees its realization. Phenomenology suggests that we are all, in a sense, collective architects of our identities, actions, communities, and social realities. Patterns of social life appear to exist independently of ourselves, but phenomenology seeks to reveal how people produce an apparently independent world in the course of their daily lives.

Myron Orleans, 'Phenomenological Sociology', in H. Etzkowitz and R. M. Glassman (eds), *The Renascence of Sociological Theory*, Itasca, Illinois, F. E. Peacock Publishers, 1991, p. 169.

POSTMODERN

I define postmodern as incredulity toward metanarratives.   1

Jean-François Lyotard, *The Postmodern Condition: A Report on Knowledge*, trans. G. Bennington and B. Massumi, Manchester, Manchester University Press, and Minnesota, University of Minnesota Press, 1984, p. xxiiif.

I would argue that the contemporary arts – in the widest possible sense,   2
whether they call themselves postmodernist or reject that label – can no longer be regarded as just another phase in the sequence of modernist and avantgardist movements which began in Paris in the 1850s and 1860s and which maintained an ethos of cultural progress and vanguardism through the 1960s. On this level, postmodernism cannot be regarded simply as a sequel to modernism, as the latest step in the never-ending revolt of modernism against itself. The postmodern sensibility of our time is different from both modernism and avantgardism precisely in that it raises the question of cultural tradition and conservation in the most fundamental way as an aesthetic and a political issue. It doesn't always do it successfully, and it often does it exploitatively. And yet, my main point about contemporary postmodernism is that it operates in a field of tension between tradition and innovation, conservation and renewal, mass culture and high art, in which the second terms are no longer automatically privileged over the first; a field of tension which can no longer be grasped in categories such as progress vs. reaction, Left vs. Right, present vs. past, modernism vs. realism, abstraction vs. representation, avant-garde vs. Kitsch. The fact that such dichotomies, which after all are central to the classical accounts of modernism, have broken down is part of the shift in the following terms: Modernism and the avant-garde were always closely related to social and industrial modernization. They were related to it as an adversary culture, yes, but they drew their energies, not unlike Poe's *Man of the Crowd*, from their proximity to the crises brought about by modernization and progress. Modernization

– such was the widely held belief, even when the word was not around – had to be traversed. There was a vision of emerging on the other side. The modern was a world-scale drama played out on the European and American stage, with mythic modern man as its hero and with modern art as a driving force, just as Saint-Simon had envisioned it already in 1825. Such heroic visions of modernity and of art as a force of social change (or, for that matter, resistance to undesired change) are a thing of the past, admirable for sure, but no longer in tune with current sensibilities, except perhaps with an emerging apocalyptic sensibility as the flip side of modernist heroism.

Andreas Huyssen, 'Mapping the Postmodern', in L. Nicholson (ed.), *Feminism/ Postmodernism*, New York, Routledge, 1990, pp. 269–71.

3 What does post-modernity ordinarily refer to? Apart from the general sense of living through a period of marked disparity from the past, the term usually means one or more of the following: that we have discovered that nothing can be known with any certainty, since all pre-existing 'foundations' of epistemology have been shown to be unreliable; that 'history' is devoid of teleology and consequently no version of 'progress' can plausibly be defended; and that a new social and political agenda has come into being with the increasing prominence of ecological concerns and perhaps new social movements generally. Scarcely anyone today seems to identify post-modernity with what it was once widely accepted to mean – the replacement of capitalism by socialism.

Anthony Giddens, *The Consequences of Modernity*, Cambridge, Polity Press, 1990, p. 46.

4 We are at the end of what is called The Modern Age. Just as Antiquity was followed by several centuries of Oriental ascendancy which Westerners provincially call The Dark Ages, so now The Modern Age is being succeeded by a post-modern period. Perhaps we may call it: The Fourth Epoch.

The ending of one epoch and the beginning of another is, to be sure, a matter of definition. But definitions, like everything social, are historically specific. And now our basic definitions of society and of self are being overtaken by new realities. I do not mean merely that we *feel* we are in an epochal kind of transition, I mean that too many of our explanations are derived from the great historical transition from the Medieval to the Modern Age; and that when they are generalized for use today, they become unwieldy, irrelevant, not convincing. And I mean also that our major orientations – liberalism and socialism – have virtually collapsed as adequate explanations of the world and of ourselves.

C. Wright Mills, 'Culture and Politics: The Fourth Epoch', in *The Listener* (published by the British Broadcasting Corporation), 12 March 1959. Reprinted in C. Wright Mills, *Power, Politics and People*, New York, Ballantine Books, 1963, p. 236.

The last few years have been marked by an inverted millenarianism, in **5**
which premonitions of the future, catastrophic or redemptive, have been
replaced by senses of the end of this or that (the end of ideology, art, or
social class; the 'crisis' of Leninism, social democracy, or the welfare state,
etc., etc.): taken together, all of these perhaps constitute what is increasingly called postmodernism. The case for its existence depends on the
hypothesis of some radical break or *coupure* traced back to the end of the
1950s or the early 1960s. As the word itself suggests, this break is most
often related to notions of the waning or extinction of the hundred-year-
old modern movement (or to its ideological or aesthetic repudiation).
Thus, abstract expressionisn in painting, existentialism in philosophy, the
final forms of representation in the novel, the films of the great auteurs, or
the modernist school of poetry (as institutionalized and canonized in the
works of Wallace Stevens): all these are now seen as the final extraordinary
flowering of a high modernist impulse which is spent and exhausted with
them. The enumeration of what follows then at once becomes empirical,
chaotic and heterogeneous . . .

The postmodernisms have in fact been fascinated precisely by this whole
'degraded' landscape of schlock and kitsch, of TV series and Readers' Digest
culture, of advertising and motels, of the late show and the grade B
Hollywood film, of so-called paraliterature with its airport paperback categories of the gothic and the romance, the popular biography, the murder
mystery and science-fiction or fantasy novel; materials they no longer simply
'quote', as a Joyce or Mahler might have done, but incorporate into their
very substance.

Nor should the break in question be thought of as a purely cultural affair;
indeed, theories of the postmodern – whether celebratory or couched in the
language of moral revulsion and denunciation – bear a strong family resemblance to all those more ambitious sociological generalizations which, at
much the same time, bring us the news of the arrival and inauguration of a
whole new type of society, most famously baptised 'post-industrial society'
(Daniel Bell), but often also designated consumer society, media society,
information society, electronic society or 'high tech', and the like. Such
theories have the obvious ideological mission of demonstrating, to their own
relief, that the new social formation in question no longer obeys the laws
of classical capitalism, namely the primacy of industrial production and the
omnipresence of class struggle. The Marxist tradition has therefore resisted
them with vehemence, with the signal exception of the economist Ernest
Mandel, whose book *Late Capitalism* sets out not merely to anatomize the
historic originality of this new society (which he sees as a third stage or
moment in the evolution of capital), but also to demonstrate that it is, if anything, a purer stage of capitalism than any of the moments that preceded it.
Fredric Jameson, 'Postmodernism, or The Cultural Logic of Late Capitalism', *New
Left Review*, no. 146, 1984, pp. 53–5.

POST-STRUCTURALISM

If structuralism divided the sign from the referent ... 'post-structuralism' goes a step further: it divides the signifier from the signified.

Another way of putting what we have just said is that meaning is not immediately present in a sign. Since the meaning of a sign is a matter of what the sign is not, its meaning is always in some sense absent from it too. Meaning, if you like, is scattered or dispersed along the whole chain of signifiers; it cannot be easily nailed down, it is never fully present in any sign alone, but is rather a kind of constant flickering presence and absence together. Reading a text is more like tracing this process of constant flickering than it is like counting the beads on a necklace.

Terry Eagleton, *Literary Theory: An Introduction*, Oxford, Blackwell, 1983, p. 128.

POWER

See also FOUCAULT, PARSONS, WEBER

1   *Power we define as the determination of others' behavior in accordance with one's own ends.* Any social structure can be viewed as a power system, and in speaking of stratification we often have in mind the general outline of this power system. Power, however, attaches not simply to the structure and positional personality, but also to the non-structural interaction and hence to role personalities. For example, power attaches to the patriarch as against the wife, but the wife's superior intelligence and energy may negate it. Structural power is necessarily most noticeable when behavior is chiefly determined by position, e.g. in formal legal relations, as contrasted to primary group relations. Social distance bolsters structural power at the expense of personal power.
Kingsley Davis, 'A Conceptual Analysis of Stratification', *American Sociological Review*, vol. 7, no. 3, 1942, pp. 315–16.

2   *The Iron Law of Oligarchy* ... Organization implies the tendency to oligarchy ... It may be enunciated as a general rule that the increase in the power of the leaders is directly proportional with the extension of the organization.
Robert Michels, *Political Parties: A Sociological Study of Oligarchical Tendencies of Modern Democracy*, New York, Free Press, 1949, p. 32.

3   It seems that conceptions of power may be divided into two very broad categories. On the one hand, there are those which are asymmetrical and tend to involve (actual or potential) conflict and resistance. Such conceptions appear to presuppose a view of social or political relations as competitive and inherently conflictual; as Hobbes remarked, 'because the power of a man resisteth and hindereth the effects of the power of another,

power simply is no more, but the excess of the power of one above that of another'. On the other hand, there are those conceptions which do not imply that some gain at others' expense but rather that all may gain: power is a collective capacity or achievement. Such conceptions appear to rest on a view of social or political relations as at least potentially harmonious and communal.

Steven Lukes, 'Power and Authority', in Tom Bottomore and Robert Nisbet (eds), *A History of Sociological Analysis*, New York, Basic Books, 1978, p. 636.

By the powerful we mean, of course, those who are able to realize their **4** will, even if others resist it.

C. Wright Mills, *The Power Elite*, New York and London, Oxford University Press, 1956, p. 9.

Power has to do with whatever decisions men make about the arrangements **5** under which they live, and about the events which make up the history of their times. Events that are beyond human decision do happen; social arrangements do change without benefit of explicit decision. But in so far as such decisions are made, the problem of who is involved in making them is the basic problem of power. In so far as they could be made but are not, the problem becomes who fails to make them?

We cannot today merely assume that in the last resort men must always be governed by their own consent. For among the means of power which now prevail is the power to manage and to manipulate the consent of men. That we do not know the limits of such power, and that we hope it does have limits, does not remove the fact that much power today is successfully employed without the sanction of the reason or the conscience of the obedient.

Surely nowadays we need not argue that, in the last resort, coercion is the 'final' form of power. But then, we are by no means constantly at the last resort. Authority (power that is justified by the beliefs of the voluntarily obedient) and manipulation (power that is wielded unbeknown to the powerless) must also be considered, along with coercion. In fact, the three types must be sorted out whenever we think about power.

C. Wright Mills, 'The Structure of Power in American Society', *British Journal of Sociology*, vol. IX, no. 1, March 1958, pp. 29–41. Reprinted in C. Wright Mills, *Power, Politics and People*, New York, Ballantine Books, 1963, p. 236.

Within limits, every student of social affairs is free to define important **6** concepts the way he prefers; there is no canonically 'correct' definition. But choosing one alternative will have consequences which differ from those implied in another, and this is the case with Mills' conception of power. The essential point at present is that, to Mills, power is not a facility for the performance of a function in, and on behalf of, the society as a system, but is interpreted exclusively as a facility for getting what one group, the holders of power, wants by preventing another group, the 'outs', from getting what it wants.

What this conception does is to elevate a secondary and derived aspect of a total phenomenon into the central place. A comparison may help to make this clear. There is obviously a distributive aspect of wealth and it is in a sense true that the wealth of one person or group by definition cannot also be possessed by another group. Thus the *distribution* of wealth is, in the nature of the case, a focus of conflicts of interest in a society. But what of the positive functions of wealth and of the conditions of its production? It has become fully established that the wealth available for distribution can only come about through the processes of production, and that those processes require the 'co-operation' or integration of a variety of different agencies – what economists call the 'factors of production'. Wealth, in turn, is a generalized class of facilities available to units of the society – individuals and various types and levels of collectivities – for whatever uses may be important to them. But even apart from the question of what share each gets, the fact that there should be wealth to divide, and how much, cannot be taken for granted as given except within a very limited context.

Very similar things can be said about power in a political sense. Power is a generalized facility or resource in the society. It has to be divided or allocated, but it also has to be produced and it has collective as well as distributive functions. It is the capacity to mobilize the resources of the society for the attainment of goals for which a general 'public' commitment has been made, or may be made. It is mobilization, above all, of the action of persons and groups, which is binding on them by virtue of their position in the society. Thus within a much larger complex, Mills concentrates almost exclusively on the distributive aspect of power. He is interested only in *who* has power and what *sectoral* interests he is serving with his power, not in how power comes to be generated or in what communal rather than sectoral interests are served.

Talcott Parsons, *Structure and Process in Modern Societies*, Glencoe, Illinois, Free Press, 1960, pp. 220–1.

PROFESSION

See also BUREAUCRACY

A sociological definition of the professions should limit itself, so far as possible, to the *differentia specifica* of professional behavior. For example, concepts like style of life, corporate solidarity and socialization structures and processes, which apply to all other groups as well as to professional ones, are not the *differentia specifica*.

There is no absolute difference between professional and other kinds of occupational behavior, but only relative differences with respect to certain attributes common to all occupational behavior. Some occupational behavior, seen in the light of these attributes, which we discuss below, is fully professional; other behavior is partly professional; and some can be thought of as barely or not at all professional. On this view, for example, there may be some professional elements in some kinds of business behavior. Similarly, on the same view, the medical profession is more professional than the nursing profession, and the medical doctor who does university research is more professional than the medical doctor who provides minor medical services in a steel plant. Professionalism is a matter of degree.

Professional behavior may be defined in terms of four essential attributes: a high degree of generalized and systematic knowledge; primary orientation to the community interest rather than to individual self-interest; a high degree of self-control of behavior through codes of ethics internalized in the process of work socialization and through voluntary associations organized and operated by the work specialists themselves; and a system of rewards (monetary and honorary) that is primarily a set of symbols of work achievement and thus ends in themselves, not means to some end of individual self-interest.

Bernard Barber, 'Some Problems in the Sociology of the Professions', *Daedalus*, vol. 92, no. 2, pp. 671–2.

RACE

Between me and the other world there is ever an unasked question: **1** unasked by some through feelings of delicacy; by others through the difficulty of rightly framing it. All, nevertheless, flutter around it. They approach me in a half-hesitant sort of way, eye me curiously or compassionately, and then, instead of saying directly, How does it feel to be a problem? they say, I know an excellent colored man in my town; or, I fought at Mechanicsville; or, Do not those Southern outrages make your blood boil? At these I smile, or am interested, or reduce the boiling to a simmer, as the occasion may require. To the real question, How does it feel to be a problem? I answer seldom a word . . .

After the Egyptian and Indian, the Greek and Roman, the Teuton and Mongolian, the Negro is a sort of seventh son, born with a veil, and gifted with second-sight in this American world – a world which yields him no true self-consciousness, but only lets him see himself through the revelation of the other world. It is a peculiar sensation, this double-consciousness, this sense of always looking at one's self through the eyes of others, of measuring one's soul by the tape of a world that looks on in amused contempt and pity. One ever feels his twoness – an American, a Negro; two souls, two thoughts, two unreconciled strivings; two warring ideals in one dark body, whose dogged strength alone keeps it from being torn asunder.

The history of the American Negro is the history of this strife – this longing to attain self-conscious manhood, to merge his double self into a

better and truer self. In this merging he wishes neither of his older selves to be lost. He would not Africanize America, for America has too much to teach this world and Africa. He would not bleach his Negro soul in a flood of white Americanism, for he knows that Negro blood has a message for the world. He simply wishes to make it possible for a man to be both a Negro and an American, without being cursed and spit upon by his fellows, without having the doors of Opportunity closed roughly in his face.
W. E. B. Du Bois, *The Soul of Black Folk* [1903]; New York, Bantam, 1989, pp. 1–9.

2 The American negro problem is a problem in the heart of the American. It is there that the interracial tension has its focus. It is there that the decisive struggle goes on. This is the central viewpoint of this treatise. Though our study includes economic, social, and political race relations, at bottom our problem is the moral dilemma of the American – the conflict between his moral valuations on various levels of consciousness and generality: The 'American Dilemma', referred to in the title of this book, is the ever-raging conflict between, on the one hand, the valuations preserved on the general plane which we shall call the 'American Creed', where the American thinks, talks, and acts under the influence of high national and Christian precepts, and, on the other hand, the valuations on specific planes of individual and group living, where personal and local interests, economic, social, and sexual jealousies; considerations of community prestige and conformity; group prejudice against particular persons or types of people; and all sorts of miscellaneous wants, impulses, and habits dominate his outlook.
Gunnar Myrdal, *An American Dilemma: The Negro Problem and Modern Democracy*, New York, Harper, 1944, pp. xlv–xlvii.

3 My basic thesis is that American society has experienced three major stages of black–white contact, and that each stage embodies a different form of racial stratification structured by the particular arrangement of both the economy and the polity. Stage one coincides with antebellum slavery and the early post-bellum era and may be designated the period of *plantation economy and racial-caste oppression*. Stage two begins in the last quarter of the nineteenth century and ends at roughly the New Deal era, and may be identified as the period of *industrial expansion, class conflict, and racial oppression*. Finally, stage three is associated with the modern, industrial, post-World War II era, which really began to crystallize during the 1960s and 1970s, and may be characterized as the period of *progressive transition from race inequalities to class inequalities*. The different periods can be identified as the preindustrial, industrial and modern industrial stages of American class relations, respectively . . .

Access to the means of production is increasingly based on educational criteria (a situation which distinguishes the modern industrial from the earlier industrial system of production) and thus threatens to solidify the position of the black underclass. In other words, a consequence of the rapid growth of the corporate and government sectors has been the gradual creation of a segmented labor market that currently provides vastly different mobility opportunities for different segments of the black population. On the one hand, poorly trained and educationally limited blacks of the inner city, including that growing number of black teenagers and young adults, see their job prospects increasingly restricted to the low-wage sector, their unemployment rates soaring to record levels (which remain high despite swings in the business cycle), their labor force participation rates declining, their movement out of poverty slowing, and their welfare roles increasing. On the other hand, talented and educated blacks are experiencing unprecedented job opportunities that are at least comparable to those of whites with equivalent qualifications. The improved job situation for the more privileged blacks in the corporate and government sectors is related both to the expansion of salaried white-collar positions and to the pressures of state affirmative action programs. In view of these developments, it would be difficult to argue that the plight of the black underclass is solely a consequence of racial oppression, that is, the explicit and overt efforts of whites to keep blacks subjugated, in the same way that it would be difficult to explain the rapid economic improvement of the more privileged blacks by arguing that the traditional forms of racial segregation and discrimination still characterize the labor market in American industries.

William Julius Wilson, *The Declining Significance of Race*, Chicago, University of Chicago Press, 1978, pp. 2–3, 151–2.

Race, as a meaningful criterion within the biological sciences, has long been **4** recognized to be a fiction. When we speak of 'the white race' or 'the black race', 'the Jewish race' or 'the Aryan race', we speak in biological misnomers and, more generally, in metaphors. Nevertheless, our conversations are replete with usages of race which have their sources in dubious pseudo-science of the eighteenth and nineteenth centuries ...

The sense of difference defined in popular usages of the term 'race' has both described and *inscribed* differences of language, belief system, artistic tradition, and gene pool, as well as all sorts of supposedly natural attributes such as rhythm, athletic ability, cerebration, usury, fidelity, and so forth. The relation between 'racial character' and these sorts of characteristics has been inscribed through tropes of race, lending the sanction of God, biology, or the natural order to even presumably unbiased descriptions of cultural tendencies and differences.

Henry Louis Gates, Jr, ' "Race" as the Trope of the World', in H. L. Gates (ed.), *'Race', Writing and Difference*, Chicago, University of Chicago Press, 1986, pp. 4–13.

We increasingly face a racism which avoids being recognized as such because **5** it is able to line up 'race' with nationhood, patriotism and nationalism.

A racism which has taken a necessary distance from crude ideas of biological inferiority and superiority now seeks to present an imaginary definition of the nation as a unified cultural community. It constructs and defends an image of national culture – homogeneous in its whiteness yet precarious and perpetually vulnerable to attack from enemies within and without.
Paul Gilroy, *There Ain't No Black in the Union Jack*, London, Hutchinson, 1987, p. 87.

RATIONAL CHOICE THEORY

Rational choice theory contains one element that differentiates it from nearly all other theoretical approaches in sociology. This element can be summed up in a single word: *optimization*. The theory signifies that in acting rationally, an actor is engaging in some kind of optimization. This is sometimes expressed as maximizing utility, sometimes as minimizing cost, sometimes in other ways. But however expressed, it is this that gives rational choice theory its power.
James Coleman and Thomas J. Feraro, *Rational Choice Theory*, London, Sage, 1992, p. xi.

REFERENCE GROUP

1   The related notions of 'relative deprivation' and 'reference group' both derive from a familiar truism: that people's attitudes, aspirations and grievances largely depend on the frame of reference within which they are conceived ...

A 'comparative' reference group is the group whose situation or attributes a person contrasts with his own. A 'normative' reference group is the group from which a person takes his standards ... The third sense of 'reference group' is the particular role a person has in mind in the context of the inequality which he feels – proletarian, a corporal, a Negro, a student and so on. This group may or may not be the source of his norms; but whether or not it fulfils the additional function of the normative reference group, it is the basis of the comparison which he makes. Everyone is, of course, in some sense a member of an almost infinite multiplicity of groups, for every attribute which a person shares with others makes him by definition the joint member, with them, of at least this one group. But most of these are irrelevant to any feelings of inequality. The 'membership reference group' is, as it were, the starting-line for the inequality with the comparative reference group by which a feeling of relative deprivation is engendered.
W. G. Runciman, *Relative Deprivation and Social Justice*, London, Routledge & Kegan Paul, 1966, pp. 9–12.

2   For any individual there are as many reference groups as there are communication networks in which he becomes regularly involved.

86

Tamotsu Shibutani, 'Reference Groups and Social Control', in A. Rose (ed.), *Human Behavior and Social Processes*, London, Routledge & Kegan Paul, 1962, p. 138.

RELIGION

See also SECULARIZATION, MARX, DURKHEIM

Religion is the human enterprise by which a sacred cosmos is established. **1** Put differently, religion is cosmization in a sacred mode. By sacred is meant here a quality of mysterious and awesome power, other than man and yet related to him, which is believed to reside in certain objects of experience.
Peter L. Berger, *The Social Reality of Religion*, London, Faber & Faber, 1969, p. 26. Published in America as *The Sacred Canopy*, New York, Doubleday, 1967.

Religious culture is that set of beliefs and symbols (and values deriving **2** directly therefrom) pertaining to a distinction between an empirical and a superempirical, transcendent reality; the affairs of the empirical being subordinated to the non-empirical.
Roland Robertson, *The Sociological Interpretation of Religion*, Oxford, Blackwell, 1970, p. 47.

A religion is: (1) a system of symbols which acts to (2) establish powerful, **3** pervasive and long-lasting moods and motivations in men by (3) formulating conceptions of a general order of existence and (4) clothing these conceptions with such an aura of factuality that (5) the moods and motivations seem uniquely realistic.
Clifford Geertz, 'Religion as a Cultural System', in M. Banton (ed.), *Anthropological Approaches to Religion*, London, Tavistock, 1966, pp. 1–46. Extract in R. Bocock and K. Thompson, *Religion and Ideology*, Manchester, Manchester University Press, 1985, p. 67.

The term 'religion' is derived from *religio*, the bond of social relations **4** between individuals; the term 'sociology' is derived from *socius*, the bond of companionship that constitutes societies. Following Durkheim (1961), we may define religion as a set of beliefs and practices, relating to the sacred, which create social bonds between individuals. We may define sociology, naively, as the 'science of community'. Sociology in general and the sociology of religion in particular, are thus concerned with the processes which unite and disunite, bind and unbind social relationships in space and time.
Bryan S. Turner, *Religion and Social Theory*, London, Sage, 1983, p. 8.

The religious world is but the reflex of the real world. And for a society based **5** upon the production of commodities, in which the producers in general enter into social relations with one another by treating their products as commodities and values, whereby they reduce their individual private labour to the standard of homogeneous human labour – for such a society, Christianity with its cultus of abstract man, more especially in its bourgeois developments, Protestantism, Deism, etc., is the most fitting form of religion ... The religious reflex of the real world can, in any case, only then finally vanish, when the practical relations of everyday life offer to man none but perfectly intelligible and reasonable relations with regard to his fellowmen and to nature.

Karl Marx, *Capital* [1867]; extract in K. Marx and F. Engels, *On Religion*, Moscow, Foreign Languages Publishing House, 1955, pp. 135–6.

REVOLUTION

1 Social revolutions are set apart from other sorts of conflicts and transformative processes above all by the combination of two coincidences: the coincidence of societal structural change with class upheaval; and the coincidence of political with social transformation ... What is unique to social revolution is that basic changes in social structure and in political structure occur together in a mutually reinforcing fashion ... This conception of social revolution differs from many other definitions of revolution ... [by identifying] a complex object of explanation of which there are relatively few historical instances.

Theda Skocpol, *States and Social Revolutions*, Cambridge, Cambridge University Press, 1979, pp. 4–5.

2 The state, in short, is fundamentally Janus-faced, with an intrinsically dual anchorage in class-divided socioeconomic structures and an international system of states. If our aim is to understand the breakdown and building-up of state organizations in revolutions, we must look not only at the activities of social groups. We must also focus upon the points of intersection between international conditions and pressures, on the one hand, and class-structured economics and politically organized interests, on the other hand. State executives and their followers will be found manoeuvring to extract resources and build administrative and coercive organizations precisely at this intersection. Here, consequently, is the place to look for the political contradictions that help launch social revolutions. Here, also, will be found the forces that shape the rebuilding of state organizations within social-revolutionary crises.

Ibid., p. 32.

RISK SOCIETY

1 This book is, then, about 'reflexive modernization' of industrial society. This guiding idea is developed from two angles. First, the intermingling

of continuity and discontinuity is discussed with the examples of *wealth production* and *risk production*. The argument is that, while in classical industrial society the 'logic' of wealth production dominates the 'logic' of risk production, in the risk society this relationship is reversed. The productive forces have lost their innocence in the reflexivity of modernization processes. The gain in power from techno-economic 'progress' is being increasingly overshadowed by the production of risks. In an early stage, these can be legitimated as 'latent side effects'. As they become globalized, and subject to public criticism and scientific investigation, they come, so to speak, out of the closet and achieve a central importance in social and political debates. This 'logic' of risk production and distribution is developed in comparison to the 'logic' of distribution of wealth (which has so far determined social-theoretical thinking). At the center lie the risks and consequences of modernization, which are revealed as irreversible threats to the life of plants, animals, and human beings. Unlike the factory-related or occupational hazards of the nineteenth and the first half of the twentieth centuries, these can no longer be limited to certain localities or groups, but rather exhibit a tendency to globalization which spans production and reproduction as much as national borders, and in this sense brings into being supra-national and non-class-specific global hazards with a new type of social and political dynamism.

Ulrich Beck, *Risk Society*, trans. M. Ritter, London, Sage, 1992, pp. 12–13. Originally published in German in 1986.

The concepts of 'industrial' or 'class society', in the broadest sense of Marx or **2** Weber, revolved around the issue of how socially produced wealth could be distributed in a socially unequal and *also* 'legitimate' way. This overlaps with the new *paradigm of risk society* which is based on the solution of a similar and yet quite different problem. How can the risks and hazards systematically produced as part of modernization be prevented, minimized, dramatized, or channeled? Where do they finally see the light of day in the shape of 'latent side effects', how can they be limited and distributed away so that they neither hamper the modernization process nor exceed the limits of that which is 'tolerable' – ecologically, medically, psychologically and socially?

We are therefore concerned no longer exclusively with making nature useful, or with releasing mankind from traditional constraints, but also and essentially with problems resulting from techno-economic development itself. Modernization is becoming reflexive; it is becoming its own theme. Questions of the development and employment of technologies (in the realms of nature, society and the personality) are being eclipsed by questions of the political and economic 'management' of the risks of actually or potentially utilized technologies – discovering, administering, acknowledging, avoiding or concealing such hazards with respect to specially defined horizons of relevance ...

The concept of risk is directly bound to the concept of reflexive modernization. *Risk* may be defined as a *systematic way of dealing with hazards and insecurities induced and introduced by modernization itself.* Risks, as opposed to older dangers, are consequences which relate to the threatening force of modernization and to its globalization of doubt. They are politically reflexive.
Ibid., pp. 19–21.

ROLE

See also STATUS, MEAD

1   A *role* represents the dynamic aspect of a status. The individual is socially aligned to a status and occupies it with relation to other statuses. When he puts the rights and duties which constitute the status into effect, he is performing a role ... There are no roles without statuses and no statuses without roles. Just as in the case of *status*, the term *role* is used with a double significance. Every individual has a series of roles deriving from the various patterns in which he participates, and at the same time a *role*, general, which represents the sum total of these roles and determines what he does for his society and what he can expect from it.

Although all statuses and roles derive from social patterns and are integral parts of patterns, they have an independent function with relation to the individuals who occupy particular statuses and exercise their roles. To such individuals the combined status and role represent the minimum attitudes and behavior which he must assume if he is to participate in the overt expression of the pattern. Status and role serve to reduce the ideal patterns for social life to individual terms. They become models for organizing the attitudes and behavior of the individuals so that these will be congruous to those of other individuals participating in the expression of the pattern.
Ralph Linton, *The Study of Man*, New York, Appleton-Century, 1936, pp. 113–14.

2   A particular social status involves, not a single associated role, but an array of associated roles. This is a basic characteristic of social structure. This fact can be registered by a distinctive term *role-set*, by which I mean that *complement of role relationships which persons have by virtue of occupying a particular social status.* As an example: the single status of medical student entails not only the role of student in relation to his teacher, but also an array of other roles relating the occupant of that status to other students, nurses, physicians, social workers, medical technicians, etc.
Robert K. Merton, *Social Theory and Social Structure*, Glencoe, Illinois, Free Press, 1968, p. 423.

Behavior is said to make sense when a series of actions is interpretable as **3** indicating that the actor has in mind some role which guides his behavior ... The isolated action becomes a datum for role analysis only when it is interpreted as the manifestation of a configuration. The individual acts as if he were expressing some role through his behavior and may assign a higher degree of reality to the assumed role than to his specific actions. The role becomes the point of reference for placing interpretations on specific actions, for anticipating that one line of action will follow upon another, and for making evaluations of individual actions. For example, the lie which is an expression of the role of a friend is an altogether different thing from the same lie taken as a manifestation of the role of confidence man.
R. H. Turner, 'Role-taking process versus conformity', in A. M. Rose (ed.), *Human Behavior and Social Processes*, New York, Houghton Mifflin, 1962, p. 24.

The idea of role-taking shifts emphasis away from the simple process of **4** enacting a prescribed role to devising a performance on the basis of an imputed other-role. The actor is not the occupant of a position for which there is a neat set of rules – a culture or set of norms – but a person who must act in the perspective supplied in part by his relationship to others whose actions reflect roles that he must identify.
Ibid., p. 23.

The unity of a role cannot consist simply in the bracketing of a set of **5** specific behaviors, since the same behavior can be indicative of different roles under different circumstances. The unifying element is to be found in some assignment of purpose or sentiment to the actor. Various actions by an individual are classified as intentional and unintentional (relevant or irrelevant) on the basis of a role designation ... Role-taking involves selective perception of the actions of another and a great deal of selective emphasis, organized about some purpose or sentiment attributed to the other.
Ibid., p. 28.

SECT

See also CHURCH

I should now like to propose a seven-fold classification of sects ... I define each type in terms of its response to the world, of the kind of reaction which dominates the customary practices and its members' beliefs ...

The *conversionist* sect is the typical sect of evangelistic, fundamentalist Christianity. Its reaction towards the outside world is to suggest that the latter is corrupted because man is corrupted. If men can be changed then the world will be changed ...

One recognizes the *revolutionary* type in the eschatological movements of the Christian tradition. Its attitude towards the outside world is summed up in a desire to be rid of the present social order when the time is ripe – if necessary by force and violence . . .

The pietist sects represent the *introversionist* type whose response to the world is neither to convert the population nor to expect the world's over-turn, but simply in retiring from it to enjoy the security gained by personal holiness . . .

Manipulationist sects, which I previously called gnostic, are those which insist especially on a particular and distinctive knowledge. They define themselves *vis-à-vis* the outside world essentially by accepting its goals. They frequently proclaim a more spiritualized and ethereal version of the cultural ends of global society but do not reject them.

Thaumaturgical sects are movements which insist that it is possible for men to experience the extraordinary effect of the supernatural on their lives. Within Christianity, their principal representatives are spiritualist groups whose main activity lies in seeking personal messages from the spirits, obtaining cures, effecting transformations and performing miracles. These sects define themselves in relation to the wider society by affirming that normal reality and causation can be suspended for the benefit of special and personal dispensations . . .

The *reformist* sects seem to constitute a case apart. But the dynamic analytic approach to religious movements demands a category correspond-ing to those groups which, though sectarian in more than one respect, have affected transformations in their early response towards the outside world. Originally revolutionary, this attitude may have become introverted later . . .

The *Utopian* sect is perhaps the most complex type. Its response to the outside world consists partly in withdrawing from it and partly in wishing to remake it to a better specification. It is more radical than the reformist sect, potentially less violent than the revolutionary sect and more constructive on a social level than the conversionist sect.

Bryan R. Wilson, 'A Typology of Sects', in *Archives des Sciences Sociales des Religions*, no. 16, 1963. Reprinted in R. Bocock and K. Thompson (eds), *Religion and Ideology*, Manchester, Manchester University Press, 1985, pp. 297–311.

SECULARIZATION

See also RELIGION

1 No human society can exist without legitimation in one form or another. If it is correct to speak of contemporary society as increasingly secularized (and we think that this is correct), one is thereby saying that the sociologically

crucial legitimations are to be found outside the area of institutionally specialized religion.

Peter Berger and Thomas Luckmann, 'Sociology of Religion and Sociology of Knowledge', *Sociology and Social Research*, vol. 47, 1963, pp. 417–27. Reprinted in R. Robertson (ed.), *Sociology of Religion*, Harmondsworth, Penguin, 1969, p. 68.

If we put aside the special usages of economics and the legal definition **2** derived from Westphalia, there appear to be six types of secularization concept in use today . . .

Decline of religion.
The previously accepted symbols, doctrines and institutions lose their prestige and influence. The culmination of secularization would be a religionless society . . .

Conformity with 'this world'.
The religious group or the religiously informed society turns its attention from the supernatural and becomes more and more interested in 'this world' . . . The culmination of secularization would be a society totally absorbed with the pragmatic tasks of the present and a religious group indistinguishable from the rest of society . . .

Disengagement of society from religion.
Society separates itself from the religious understanding which has previously informed it in order to constitute itself as an autonomous reality and consequently to limit religion to the sphere of private life. The culmination of this kind of secularization would be a religion of a purely inward character, influencing neither institutions nor corporate action, and a society in which religion made no appearance outside the sphere of the religious group . . .

Transposition of religious beliefs and institutions.
Knowledge, patterns of behavior and institutional arrangements which were once understood as grounded in divine power are transformed into phenomena of purely human creation and responsibility . . . The culmination of this kind of secularization process would be a totally anthropologized religion and a society which had taken over all the functions previously accruing to the religious institutions . . .

Desacralization of the world.
The world is gradually deprived of its sacred character as man and nature become the object of rational-causal explanation and manipulation. The culmination of secularization would be a completely 'rational' world society in which the phenomenon of the supernatural or even of 'mystery' would play no part . . .

Movement from a 'sacred' to a 'secular' society.

This is a general concept of social change, emphasizing multiple variables through several stages. According to Becker, its chief developer, the main variable is resistance or openness to change. Accordingly, the culmination of secularization would be a society in which all decisions are based on rational and utilitarian considerations and there is complete acceptance of change.

Larry Shiner, 'The Concept of Secularization in Empirical Research', *Journal for the Scientific Study of Religion*, vol. 6, 1967, pp. 207–20.

3   Secularization relates to the diminution in the social significance of religion. Its application covers such things as, the sequestration by political powers of the property and facilities of religious agencies; the shift from religious to secular control of various of the erstwhile activities and functions of religion; the decline in the proportion of their time, energy and resources which men devote to super-empirical concerns; the decay of religious institutions; the supplanting, in matters of behavior, of religious precepts by demands that accord with strictly technical criteria.

Bryan R. Wilson, *Religion in Sociological Perspective*, Oxford and New York, Oxford University Press, 1982, p. 149.

4   What has been proposed is a neo-Durkheimian reconceptualization of the processes previously designated by the concept of secularization, stressing Durkheim's notions of the binary opposition of the cultural principles of the sacred and profane, and the formation of symbolic community. The opposed cultural principles and processes of sacralization and profanization (including mundanization) should be seen as being in an ongoing dialectical relationship.

The 'sacred' is that which is socially transcendent and gives a sense of fundamental identity based on likeness (kinship), constructed and sustained by difference or opposition over and against: (1) the alien other (which may be another culture that threatens takeover or some other danger to the maintenance of its identity); (2) the mundane/profane i.e. the world of everyday routine, particularly economic activity and its rationality.

The community (*Gemeinschaft*) is based on symbolic unity – it is an imagined likeness with limits or boundaries that separate it from a different, alien other. It contrasts with the functionally-specific relations and instrumental rationalities characteristic of societal association (*Gesellschaft*). The contrast between the two social forms was illustrated by Weber's distinction between the nation, as a *Gemeinschaft*, and the state, as an example of large-scale *Gesellschaft*. Thus the legitimation needs of the state are frequently satisfied by cashing in on the surplus legitimacy accumulated through the discourses that have been combined in the cultural construction of the nation (including religious discourses).

Secularization, which has tended to mean decline of religion as an institution (laicization) as part of the modernization process of structural differentiation, is now largely superseded by this recast analytical framework (except in the case of newly-modernizing societies). This is theoretically necessary for the development of a sociology of culture dealing with the articulation of discourses and decoding of symbol systems in the circumstances of late or postmodernity. Concepts and frameworks developed to analyze the transition from traditional to modern society may no longer be adequate for the new tasks unless we are prepared to look at them afresh and undertake radical recasting.

Kenneth Thompson, 'Secularization and Sacralization', in J. C. Alexander and P. Sztompka (eds), *Rethinking Progress*, London and Boston, Unwin Hyman, 1990, p. 179.

SELF

See also COOLEY, MEAD

The self, as that which can be an object to itself, is essentially a social **1** structure, and it arises in social experience.

George Herbert Mead, *Mind, Self and Society* [1934], Chicago, University of Chicago Press, 1962, p. 140.

Each moral career, and behind this, each self, occurs within the confines of **2** an institutional system, whether a social establishment such as a mental hospital or a complex of personal and professional relationships. The self, then, can be seen as something that resides in the arrangements prevailing in a social system for its members. The self in this sense is not a property of the person to whom it is attributed, but dwells rather in the pattern of social control that is exerted in connection with the person by himself and those around him. This special kind of institutional arrangement does not so much support the self as constitute it.

Erving Goffman, *Asylums: Essays on the Social Situation of Mental Patients and Other Inmates*, New York, Doubleday, 1961, pp. 168–9.

SEMIOLOGY

Semiology aims to take in any system of signs, whatever their substance **1** and limits; images, gestures, musical sounds, objects, and the complex associations of all of these, which form the content of ritual, convention or public entertainment: these constitute, if not *languages*, at least systems of signification.

Roland Barthes, *Elements of Semiology*, London, Jonathan Cape, 1967, p. 9.

2   Semiology is the science of forms, since it studies significations apart from their content.
Roland Barthes, *Mythologies*, St Albans, Paladin, p. 111.

3   Barthes concentrates more on the mechanisms by which these ideas present themselves than on the structures of power and forms of change that they support. It is an attempt to 'go further than the pious show of unmasking', to provide an analytic method. Barthes identifies many forms of thought as they essentialise various social practices. Things as diverse as cooking and children's toys are submitted to an 'irrepressible tendency towards extreme realism'. Election photographs or an exhibition entitled 'The Family of Man' readily display an 'essential humanity' rather than differences. And the travel guide, *Guide bleu* writes a picturesque history of Spain which effortlessly integrates support for the Fascist regime. The social productivity of the world, the fact that it is constituted of complex relations which are in constant flux, disappears beneath a system of essences. The real is the immediately visible, and this visible does not appear to be a form of representation. Such is the work of myth.

The mechanism of myth is the way that habitual representations tangle themselves up in everyday objects and practices so that these ideological meanings come to seem natural, the common-sense reality of that object or practice. There are therefore two systems of meaning: the denotative and the connotative, the 'object-language' (the film, the toy, the meal, the car, inasmuch as they signify), and the myth which attaches itself to it, which takes advantage of the form of this denotative language to insinuate itself. In Barthes's famous example, there is a magazine cover, showing a black soldier saluting the French flag. This photo has one fully adequate denotative meaning ('Here's a black soldier saluting the French flag'), but this meaning is invaded by a second sense, which is precisely its intended sense: the connotative meaning which springs from a mixture of colonialist nationalism and militarism. It says – at the time of the Algerian war of independence – 'Colonialism must be right: there are negroes perfectly willing to defend it to the death'. The connotation leans on the denotation; there is a perpetual to-and-fro movement between them so that they appear as a natural unity. The connoted myth is successful exactly when it 'goes without saying', when it confirms an established position from doubt or attack, when it universalises history by saying 'That's the way it must be'.

In semiological terms, the whole of the denotative sign is used as the signifier by the connotative system. Whatever may be the form of an object or practice, as soon as it signifies, as soon as it is endowed with meaning, it submits to the differentiating system of language. It becomes a unity of concept and signifier: a sign. It then opens to the connotative process. The sign as a whole is taken up to be the articulator of a second concept, the ideological concept.

96

Rosalind Coward and John Ellis, *Language and Materialism: Developments in Semiology and the Theory of the Subject*, London, Routledge & Kegan Paul, 1977, pp. 27–8.

SEXUALITY AND SEXUAL IDENTITY

See also GENDER, DEVIANCE, FOUCAULT

Identity is not a destiny but a choice. But in a culture where homosexual desires, female or male, are still execrated and denied, the adoption of lesbian or gay identities inevitably constitutes a *political* choice. These identities are not expressions of secret essences. They are self-creations, but they are creations on ground not freely chosen but laid out by history. So homosexual identities illustrate the play of constraint and opportunity, necessity and freedom, power and pleasure. Sexual identities seem necessary in the contemporary world as starting-points for a politics around sexuality. But the form they take is not pre-determined. In the end, therefore, they are not so much about who we really are, what our sex dictates. They are about what we want to be and could be. But this means they are also about the morality of acts and the quality of relations. We live in a world of proliferating 'sexual identities' as specific desires (paedophile, sado-masochistic, bisexual) become the focus either for minute subdivisions of well-established notions (gayness or lesbianism) or spin off into wholly new ones. Can we therefore say that all identities are of equal value, and that minute subdivisions of desire, however apparently bizarre and esoteric, deserve their social recognition on the basis of the right to erotic difference and sexual identity?

Such questions have led to the development of what may be termed a 'relationship paradigm' as opposed to the traditional 'identity paradigm' as a way of thinking through some of the conceptual – and political – issues. If, as many advocates of gay politics have suggested, identity is a constraint, a limitation on the flux of possibilities and the exploration of desires, if it is only an historical acquisition, then surely its assertion should be historically junked or at least modified. The difficulty is to find a replacement that would equally satisfactorily provide a basis for personal coherence and social recognition. One possibility is to celebrate the flux, to indulge in a glorification of the 'polysexualities' to which, on a radical reading of the Freudian tradition, we are all heirs. The unfortunate difficulty with this is that most individuals do not feel 'polymorphously perverse'. On the contrary they feel their sexual desires are fairly narrowly organized, whatever use they make of those desires in real life. Moreover, a social identity is no less real for being historically formed. Sexual identities are no longer arbitrary divisions of the field of possibilities; they are encoded in a complex web of social practices – legal, pedagogic, medical, moral, and personal. They cannot be willed away.

The aim of the 'relationship paradigm', in contrast, is not to ignore questions of identity but to displace them, by stressing instead the need to examine relationships. If this is done we can look again both at our sexual history and our sexual presence. Historically, we need no longer look for the controversial emergence of identities. Instead we can see the complicated net of relationships through which sexuality is always expressed, changing over time. Looked at from a contemporary point of view, we see not the culmination of a process of identity development but the formation of new types of relationships, validating hitherto execrated sexualities, in complex communities of interest around sex.

Jeffrey Weeks, *Against Nature: Essays on History, Sexuality and Identity*, London, Rivers Oram Press, 1991, pp. 79–85. Extract in C. Lemert (ed.), *Social Theory*, Boulder, Colorado, and Oxford, Westview Press, 1993, pp. 635–6.

SIMULATION

See also BAUDRILLARD

A simulation is different from a fiction or lie in that it not only presents an absence as a presence, the imaginary as the real, it also undermines any contrast to the real, absorbing the real within itself. Instead of a 'real' economy of commodities that is somehow bypassed by an 'unreal' myriad of advertising images, Baudrillard now discerns only a hyperreality, a world of self-referential signs. He has moved from the TV ad which, however, never completely erases the commodity it solicits, to the TV newscast which creates the news if only to be able to narrate it, or the soap opera whose daily events are both referent and reality for many viewers.

Mark Poster, *Jean Baudrillard: Selected Works*, Cambridge, Polity Press, 1988, p. 6.

SOCIAL CHARACTER

It would be very surprising if variations in the basic conditions of reproduction, livelihood, and chances for survival, that is, in the supply of and demand for human beings, with all these imply for changes in the spacing of people, the size of markets, the role of children, the society's feeling of vitality or senescence, and many other intangibles, failed to influence character. My thesis is, in fact, that each of these three phases on the population curve appears to be occupied by a society that enforces conformity and molds social character in a definably different way.

The society of high growth potential develops in its typical members a social character whose conformity is insured by their tendency to follow tradition: these I shall term *tradition-directed* people and the society in which they live *a society dependent on tradition-direction.*

The society of transitional population growth develops in its typical members a social character whose conformity is insured by their tendency to acquire early in life an internalized set of goals. These I shall term *inner-directed* people and society in which they live *a society dependent on inner-direction.*

Finally, the society of incipient population decline develops in its typical members a social character whose conformity is insured by their tendency to be sensitized to the expectations and preferences of others. These I shall term *other-directed* people and the society in which they live *one dependent on other-direction* . . .

If we wanted to cast our social character types into social class molds, we could say that inner-direction is the typical character of the 'old' middle class – the banker, the tradesman, the small entrepreneur, the technically oriented engineer, etc. – while other-direction is becoming the typical character of the 'new' middle class – the bureaucrat, the salaried employee in business, etc. . . .

What is common to all other-directed people is that their contemporaries are the source of direction for the individual – either those known to him or those with whom he is indirectly acquainted, through friends or through the mass media. This source is of course 'internalized' in the sense that dependence on it for guidance in life is implanted early. The goals toward which the other-directed person strives shift with that guidance: it is only the process of striving itself and the process of paying close attention to the signals from others that remain unaltered throughout life.
David Riesman, N. Glazer and R. Denney, *The Lonely Crowd: A Study of Changing American Character* [1950], New Haven, Connecticut, Yale University Press, 1969, pp. 8–22.

SOCIAL CONTROL

In the classical nineteenth-century sociological tradition, the concept **1** of social control was at the centre of the enterprise – both in relating sociology to political philosophy and in solving the emergent debates of sociology. The unit of analysis was the whole society, and the question posed was how to achieve a degree of organization and regulation consistent with certain moral principles, but without an excessive degree of purely coercive control. This was the great problem of 'social order' – posed most explicitly, of course, by Durkheim and his functionalist inheritors and understood in different ways by Weber and Marx. An examination of the continuities and discontinuities from this classical lineage is a rewarding exercise. What largely happened in the twentieth-century development of sociology in America was that the concept of social control lost its original connections with the classic macro-sociological questions of order, authority, power and social organization. It was not that the concept became unimportant. Indeed, in the first indigenous American sociological tradition – the Chicago School of the 1920s – the concept of social control was much more central than is usually recognized. In Park and Burgess's famous text, 'All social problems turn out finally to be problems of social control'. Social control should be ' ... the central fact and the central problem of sociology'. But the way this sociological task was interpreted gave the clue to how the concept of social control was later to be used. Sociology was to be ' ... a point of view and method for investigating the processes by which individuals are inducted to and induced to cooperate in some sort of permanent corporate existence we call society' (Park and Burgess). Whether functionalist or interactionist, this essential social psychological perspective on social control was to remain dominant. The emphasis was on the *process* of the individual's induction into society – that is, the problem of socialization.

Stanley Cohen and Andrew Scull (eds), *Social Control and the State*, Oxford, Blackwell, 1985, p. 5.

2   The functionalist perspective emphasizes the acquisition of norms and values and the social psychological experiences of individuals that lead to this acquisition as the most important feature of social relations in understanding crime. The conflict perspective emphasizes the institutional patterns – particularly the economic system – and how these patterns affect the distribution of criminality. The functionalists accept criminal law as a given – a standard reflective of the 'agreed upon values' of 'the society'; the conflict perspective assumes that the criminal law is problematic and must be studied to determine how it is shaped and who gets processed as a criminal.

William Chambliss, 'Functional and Conflict Theories of Crime', in W. Chambliss and M. Mankoff (eds), *Whose Law? What Order?*, New York, Wiley & Sons, 1979, p. 7.

3   It is not part of control theory that human beings are born wicked or evil – these are evaluative labels others may choose to attach to some individual's behaviour. Instead, people are perceived as being by nature morally neutral. They are born capable of engaging in an extremely wide diversity of acts. Thus, in moral innocence, their reasons or passions could lead them into all manner of behavioural experiments. Left alone, a human being would know no moral boundary save that which s/he might wish to impose ... Only to varying degrees do individuals, at least temporarily, surrender their option to engage in diverse behaviours (including many outside legal and moral codes). Their preparedness to make this surrender depends upon the *attachments* they form, the *commitments* they develop, and the *beliefs* they accept. These three elements – *attachment*, *commitment* and *beliefs* – can be conceptualized as the bonds which tie an individual to

the 'conventional order'. If they are not made, or are broken, then the individuals remain free or regain their freedom to engage in law-violating behaviour. However, freedom to do something does not necessarily mean that the option will be exercised. Individuals may or may not be *able* or *want* to take up that option. Control theory seeks to map out the conditions under which individuals who are free to break the law – because they are not socially bonded – transform themselves into people who are *able* to do so and who, because they perceive deviant behaviour to hold out the possibility of a net reward, *want* to do so.

Steven Box, *Deviance, Reality and Society*, London, Holt, Rinehart & Winston (2nd edn), 1981, pp. 122–3.

SOCIALIZATION

The infant – a weak, dependent, completely helpless thing – is 'aware' of only his inner tensions and biological needs, but not of what they are, much less how to allay or gratify them. Yet very shortly, to join others as a member of his society, he will have to master a complicated range of techniques, beliefs, and values. When this happens, we may say that he is socialized . . .

Role-taking, identification, and internalization produce and form the self; they also bring about socialization of the child.

Joseph Bensman and Bernard Rosenberg, *Mass, Class, and Bureaucracy: The Evolution of Contemporary Society*, Englewood Cliffs, New Jersey, Prentice-Hall, 1963. Extract in P. Rose (ed.), *The Study of Society*, New York, Random House, 1967, p. 135.

SOCIAL MOVEMENTS

Most attempts to define social movements make some reference to the following features:

1 at least occasional mass mobilization;
2 tendency towards a loose organizational structure;
3 spasmodic activity;
4 working at least in part outside established institutional frameworks;
5 bringing about social change (or perhaps preserving aspects of the social order) as a central aim.

Alan Scott, 'Political Culture and Social Movements', in J. Allen, P. Braham and P. Lewis (eds), *Political and Economic Forms of Modernity*, Cambridge, Polity Press, 1992, p. 132.

In complex societies social movements develop only in limited areas and for limited periods of time. When movements mobilize they reveal the other, complementary face of the submerged networks. The hidden networks become visible whenever collective actors confront or come into conflict with public policy. Thus, for example, it is difficult to understand the massive peace mobilizations of recent years unless the vitality of the submerged networks of women, young people, ecologists and alternative cultures is taken into account. These networks make possible such mobilizations and from time to time render them visible.

Latency and visibility are the two interrelated poles of collective action ... The latency and visibility of social movements point to the existence of two other paradoxes. First, collective conflicts are increasingly personal and revolve around the capacity of individuals to initiate action and to control the space, time and interpersonal relations that define their social existence. This paradox is already apparent. During the past decade collective action has displayed a tension between the need to publicly declare objectives and the need to practice directly and personally the innovations in daily life. This tension has produced some dramatic splits within groups.

There is a second paradox: if the basis of contemporary conflicts has shifted towards the production of meaning, then they seemingly have little to do with politics. Instead collective action concerns everyday life, personal relationships, and new conceptions of space and time. Thus collective actors are prone to disperse, fragmented and atomized, into networks which quickly disappear into sects, emotional support circles or therapy groups. While collective action continually faces disintegration, it also poses questions about the production of symbols which transcend politics. As such, collective action can never be wholly represented by political mediation, in decisions (or 'policies') which translate collective efforts into institutional changes. The forms of action I am referring to are at one and the same time prior to and beyond politics: they are pre-political because they are rooted in everyday life experiences; and meta-political because political forces can never represent them completely. Paradoxically, unless collective action is represented it becomes fragmented and dispersed; at the same time, because it is never fully capable of representation it reappears on new ground, with changed objectives and altered strategies.

Alberto Melucci, *Nomads of the Present*, London, Hutchinson Radius, 1989, pp. 70–3.

SOCIAL PROBLEMS

A social problem is a condition which is defined by a considerable number of persons as a deviation from some norm which they cherish. Every social problem thus consists of an objective condition and a subjective definition. The objective condition is a verifiable situation which can be checked as to existence and magnitude (proportions) by impartial and trained observers, e.g. the state of national defense, trends in the birth rate, unemployment, etc. The subjective definition is the awareness of certain individuals that the condition is a threat to certain cherished values.

Howard S. Becker, *Social Problems: A Modern Approach*, New York, Wiley, 1966, pp. 1–2.

SOCIAL STATUS

See also WEBER

A status, as distinct from the individual who may occupy it, is simply a **1** collection of rights and duties. Since these rights and duties can find expression only through the medium of individuals, it is extremely hard for us to maintain a distinction in our thinking between statuses and the people who hold them and exercise the rights and duties which constitute them . . .

Ralph Linton, *The Study of Man*, New York, Appleton-Century, 1936, p. 113.

By social status, we mean a man's general standing *vis-à-vis* the other **2** members of a society or some section of it.

T. H. Marshall, *Sociology at the Crossroads*, London, Heinemann, 1963, p. 181.

SOCIAL STRATIFICATION

See also WEBER

On the basis of modern sociological approach, it may perhaps be said that **1** Marx looked at the structure of capitalistic enterprise and generalized a social system from it, including the class structure and, to him, the inevitable conflicts involved in it. Conversely, the concept of the generalized social system is the basis of modern sociological thinking. Analysed in this framework, both capitalistic enterprise and social stratification are seen in the context of their role in such a social system. The organization of production and social stratification are, of course, both variable in these terms, though also functionally related to each other. For the functional basis of the phenomena of stratification, it is necessary to analyze the problem of integrating and ordering social relationships within a social system. Some set of norms governing relations of superiority and inferiority is an inherent need of every stable social system. There will be immense variation, but this is a constant point of reference. Such a patterning or ordering is the stratification system of the society.

Talcott Parsons, *Essays in Sociological Theory*, New York, Free Press, 1964, pp. 324–5.

Treating *Stratification* from the abstract structural point of view, we have **2** used *Position* as the key concept. On the societal side, we have defined *Station* as a recurrent combination of positions inhering in the same person, masses of persons with roughly the same station as *Strata*. These strata have different *Prestige* ranks in accordance with the prestige of the positions making up the station. The prestige of a given position depends upon the function which the activities associated with it perform and upon the scarcity of the means for performing this function.

Kingsley Davis, 'A Conceptual Analysis of Stratification', *American Sociological Review*, vol. 7, no. 3, 1942, p. 321.

SOCIETY

See also DURKHEIM

1 I do not believe that one may commence social-philosophical investigations from a more specific definition of society than that society exists there wherever several individuals stand in reciprocal relationship to one another. For if society is to be an autonomous object of an independent discipline then it can only be so by virtue of the fact that, out of the sum total of individual elements which constitute it, a new entity emerges; otherwise, all problems of social science would only be those of individual psychology. Yet unity from several elements is nothing other than interaction of the same reciprocally exercised forces of cohesion, attraction, perhaps even a certain repulsion.

Georg Simmel, 'Zur Methodik der Sozialwissenschaften', *Jahrbuch für Gesetzgebung, Verwaltung und Volkswirtschaft*, vol. 20, 1896, pp. 232–3; trans. and ed. D. Frisby and D. Sayer, *Society*, London, Tavistock, 1986, p. 58.

2 In defining a society, we may use a criterion which goes back at least to Aristotle. A society is a type of social system, in any universe of social systems, which attains the highest level of self-sufficiency as a system in relation to its environment ...

We may now sum up the ramifications of the self-sufficiency criterion we used in defining the concept of a society. A society must constitute a societal *community* that has an adequate level of integration or solidarity and a distinctive membership status. This does not preclude relations of control or symbiosis with population elements only partially integrated into the societal community, such as the Jews in the Diaspora, but there must be a core of more fully integrated members.

This community must be the 'bearer' of a cultural system sufficiently generalized and integrated to legitimize normative order. Such legitimation requires a system of constitutive symbolism which grounds the identity and solidarity of the community, as well as beliefs, rituals, and other cultural components which embody such symbolism. Cultural systems are usually broader than any one society and its community organization, although in areas containing many societies distinct cultural systems may indeed shade into one another. A society's self-sufficiency in this context, then, involves its institutionalizing a sufficient range of cultural components to meet its societal exigencies tolerably well. Of course, the relations among societies having the same or closely related cultural systems present special problems . . .

The element of collective organization imposes additional criteria of self-sufficiency. Self-sufficiency by no means requires that *all* the role-involvements of all members be carried on within the society. However, a society does have to provide a repertoire of role-opportunities sufficient for individuals to meet their fundamental personal exigencies at all stages of the life cycle without going outside the society, and for the society itself to meet its own exigencies. A celibate monastic order does not meet this criterion because it cannot recruit new members by birth without violating its fundamental norms.

Talcott Parsons, *Societies: Evolutionary and Comparative Perspectives*, Englewood Cliffs, New Jersey, Prentice-Hall, 1966, pp. 9, 17.

Society is a continuous chain of role expectancies and behavior resulting   **3** from role expectancies. To put it another way, society is a fairly stable net-work of social relationships based on relatively uniform and predictable behavior maintained between specific individuals in specified positions.

Joseph Bensman and Bernard Rosenberg, *Mass, Class, and Bureaucracy: The Evolution of Contemporary Society*, Englewood Cliffs, New Jersey, Prentice-Hall, 1963. Extract in P. Rose (ed.) *The Study of Society*, New York, Random House, 1967, p. 140.

SOCIOLOGY

See also COMTE, SPENCER, DURKHEIM

At the risk of shocking sociologists, I should be inclined to say that it is   **1** their job to render social or historical content more intelligible than it was in the experience of those who lived it. All sociology is a reconstruction that aspires to confer intelligibility on human existences which, like all human existences, are confused and obscure.

Raymond Aron, *Main Currents in Sociological Thought*, vol. 2, Harmondsworth, Penguin, 1970, p. 207.

To ask sociological questions, then, presupposes that one is interested in   **2** looking some distance beyond the commonly accepted or officially defined goals of human actions. It presupposes a certain awareness that human events have different levels of meaning, some of which are hidden from the consciousness of everyday life.

Peter L. Berger, *Invitation to Sociology*, New York, Doubleday, 1963; Harmondsworth, Penguin, 1966, p. 41.

3   We will not be far off if we see sociological thought as part of what Nietzsche called 'the art of mistrust'.
Ibid., p. 42.

4   We would contend, then, that there is a debunking motif inherent in socio-logical consciousness. The sociologist will be driven time and again, by the very logic of his discipline, to debunk the social systems he is studying ... The sociological frame of reference, with its built-in procedure of looking for levels of reality other than those given in the official interpretations of society, carries with it a logical imperative to unmask the pretensions and the propaganda by which men cloak their actions with each other. This unmasking imperative is one of the characteristics of sociology particularly at home in the temper of the modern era.
Ibid., p. 51.

5   The sociological imagination enables its possessor to understand the larger historical scene in terms of its meaning for the inner life and the external career of a variety of individuals.
C. Wright Mills, *The Sociological Imagination*, London and New York, Oxford University Press, 1959, p. 5.

6   The sociological imagination enables us to grasp history and biography and the relations between the two within society. That is its task and its promise.
Ibid., p. 6.

7   Perhaps the most fruitful distinction with which the sociological imagination works is between 'the personal troubles of milieu' and 'the public issues of social structure'. This distinction is an essential tool of the sociological imagination and a feature of all classic work in social science.

Troubles occur within the character of the individual and within the range of his immediate relations with others; they have to do with his self and with those limited areas of social life of which he is directly and personally aware. Accordingly, the statement and the resolution of troubles properly lie within the individual as a biographical entity and within the scope of his immediate milieu – the social setting that is directly open to his personal experience and to some extent his wilful activity. A trouble is a private matter: values cherished by an individual are felt by him to be threatened.

Issues have to do with matters that transcend these local environments of the individual and the range of his inner life. They have to do with the organization of many such milieux into the institutions of an historical society as a whole, with the ways in which various milieux overlap and interpenetrate to form the larger structure of social and historical life. An

issue is a public matter: some value cherished by publics is felt to be threatened. Often there is a debate about what that value really is and about what it is that really threatens it. This debate is often without focus if only because it is the very nature of an issue, unlike even widespread trouble, that it cannot very well be defined in terms of the immediate and everyday environments of ordinary men. An issue, in fact, often involves a crisis in institutional arrangements, and often too it involves what Marxists call 'contradictions' or 'antagonisms'.
Ibid., pp. 8–9.

What are the essential unit-ideas of sociology, those which, above any **8** others, give distinctiveness to sociology in its juxtaposition to the other social sciences? There are, I believe, five: *community, authority, status*, the *sacred*, and *alienation* . . . *Community* includes but goes beyond local community to encompass religion, work, family, and culture; it refers to social bonds characterized by emotional cohesion, depth, continuity, and fullness. *Authority* is the structure or the inner order of an association, whether this be political, religious, or cultural, and is given legitimacy by its roots in social function, tradition, or allegiance. *Status* is the individual's position in the hierarchy of prestige and influence that characterizes every community or association. The *sacred* includes the mores, the non-rational, the religious and ritualistic ways of behavior that are valued beyond whatever utility they may possess. *Alienation* is a historical perspective within which man is seen as estranged, anomic, and rootless when cut off from the ties of community and moral purpose.

Each of these ideas is commonly linked to a conceptual opposite, to a kind of antithesis, from which it derives much of its continuing meaning in the sociological tradition. Thus, opposed to the idea of community is the idea of society (*Gesellschaft*, in Tönnies' usage) in which reference is to the large-scale, impersonal, contractual ties that were proliferating in the modern age, often, as it seemed, at the expense of community. The conceptual opposite of authority in sociological thought is *power*, which is commonly identified with military or political force or with administrative bureaucracy and which, unlike the authority that arises directly from social function and association, raises the problem of legitimacy. Status has for its conceptual opposite in sociology not the popular idea of equality but the novel and sophisticated idea of class, at once more specialized and collective. The opposite idea of the sacred is the utilitarian, the profane (in Durkheim's momentous wording), or the *secular*. And, finally, alienation – considered at least as a sociological perspective – is best seen as an inversion of *progress* . . .

Community–society, authority–power, status–class, sacred–secular, alienation–progress: these are rich themes in nineteenth-century thought. Considered as linked antitheses, they form the very warp of the sociological tradition. Quite apart from their conceptual significance in sociology, they may be regarded as epitomizations of the conflict between tradition and modernism, between the old order, made moribund by the industrial and democratic revolutions, and the new order, its outlines still unclear and as often the cause of anxiety as of elation or hope.

Robert A. Nisbet, *The Sociological Tradition*, New York, Basic Books, 1966, pp. 6–7.

9 In the same way that the novelist will always be able to learn from a study and re-study of Dostoyevsky or James – be able to learn a sense of development and form, as well as to draw inspiration from the creative source – so the sociologist can forever learn from a re-reading of such men as Weber and Simmel.

It is this element that separates sociology from some of the physical sciences. There is, after all, a limit to what the young physicist can learn from even a Newton. Having once grasped the fundamental points of the *Principia*, he is not likely to draw very much as a physicist from re-readings (though he could as a historian of science). How different is the relation of the sociologist to a Simmel or Durkheim. Always there will be something to be gained from a direct reading; something that is informative, enlarging and creative. This is precisely like the contemporary artist's return to the study of medieval architecture, the Elizabethan sonnet or the paintings of Matisse. This is the essence of the history of art, and why the history of sociology is so different from the history of science.

That such men as Weber, Durkheim and Simmel fall in the scientific tradition is unquestioned. Their works, for all the deep artistic sensitivity and intuition, no more belong in the history of art than the works of Balzac or Dickens do in the history of social science. The conclusion we draw is not that science and art are without differences. There are real differences, as there are among the arts and among the sciences. No one asks a Picasso to verify one of his visions by repeating the process; and, conversely, we properly give short shrift to ideas in science that no one but the author can find supported by experience. The ideas of Durkheim may, as I have suggested, be dependent upon thought-processes like those of the artist, but none of them would have survived in sociology or become fruitful for others were it not for criteria and modes of communication that differ from those of art.

The conclusion, then, is not that science and art are, or should be, alike. It is the simpler but more fundamental conclusion that in both art and science the same type of creative imagination works. And everything that impedes or frustrates this imagination strikes at the source of the discipline itself.

Robert A. Nisbet, 'Sociology as an Art Form' [1962]; in R. A. Nisbet, *Tradition and Revolt*, New York, Random House, 1968, pp. 156–7.

10 There are, then, two sociologies: a sociology of social system and a sociology of social action. They are grounded in the diametrically opposed concerns with two central problems, those of order and control. And, at every level, they are in conflict. They posit antithetical views of human nature, of society and of the relationship between the social and the individual. The first asserts the paramount necessity, for the societal and individual well-being, of external constraint; hence the notion of a social system ontologically and methodologically prior to its participants. The notion of the second is that of autonomous man, able to realize his full potential and to create a truly human social order only when freed from external constraint. Society is thus the creation of its members; the product of their construction of meaning, and of the action and relationships through which they attempt to impose that meaning on their historical situations.

Alan Dawe, 'The Two Sociologies', *British Journal of Sociology*, vol. 21, 1970, pp. 207–18. Extract in K. Thompson and J. Tunstall (eds), *Sociological Perspectives*, Harmondsworth and New York, Penguin, 1971, pp. 550–1.

SOCIOLOGY OF KNOWLEDGE

The principal thesis of the sociology of knowledge is that there are modes **1** of thought which cannot be adequately understood as long as their social origins are obscured . . .

Strictly speaking it is incorrect to say that the single individual thinks. Rather it is more correct to insist that he participates in thinking further what other men have thought before him. He finds himself in an inherited situation with patterns of thought which are appropriate to this situation and attempts to elaborate further the inherited modes of response or to substitute others for them in order to deal more adequately with the new challenges which have arisen out of the shifts and changes of his situation.

Karl Mannheim, *Ideology and Utopia* [1929], New York, Harcourt Brace Jovanovich, 1936, pp. 1–2.

The task of the sociology of knowledge is the analysis of the social forms **2** of knowledge, of the processes by which individuals acquire this knowledge and, finally, of the institutional organization and social distribution of knowledge.

Peter Berger and Thomas Luckmann, 'Sociology of Religion and Sociology of Knowledge', *Sociology and Social Research*, vol. 47, 1963, pp. 417–27. Extract in R. Robertson (ed.), *Sociology of Religion*, Harmondsworth, Penguin, 1969, p. 69.

STATE

See also NATION, WEBER

The nation-state, which exists in a complex of other nation-states, is a set of **1** institutional forms of governance maintaining an administrative monopoly over a territory with demarcated boundaries (borders), its rule being sanctioned by law and direct control of the means of internal and external violence.

Anthony Giddens, *A Contemporary Critique of Historical Materialism*, London, Macmillan, vol. 1, 1981, p. 190.

2   The primary formal characteristics of the modern state are as follows: It possesses an administrative and legal order subject to change by legislation, to which the organized activities of the administrative staff, which are also controlled by regulations, are oriented. This system of order claims binding authority, not only over the members of the state, the citizens, most of whom have obtained membership by birth, but also to a very large extent over all action taking place in the area of its jurisdiction. It is thus a compulsory organization with a territorial basis. Furthermore, today, the use of force is regarded as legitimate only so far as it is either permitted by the state or prescribed by it ... The claim of the modern state to monopolize the use of force is as essential to it as its character of compulsory jurisdiction and of continuous operation.

Max Weber, *Economy and Society*, Berkeley, University of California Press, vol. 1, 1978, p. 56.

3   There are many significant differences between the theorists of *overloaded government* and those of *legitimation crisis* ... None the less, they also appear to share a common thread. First, governmental, or more generally state, power is the capacity for effective political action. As such, power is the facility of agents to act within institutions and collectivities, to apply the resources of these insitutions and collectivities to chosen ends, even while institutional arrangements narrow the scope of their activities. Secondly, the power of the democratic state depends ultimately on the acceptance of its authority (overload theorists) or on its legitimacy (legitimation theorists). Thirdly, state power (measured by the ability of the state to resolve the claims and difficulties it faces) is being progressively eroded. The liberal democratic state is increasingly hamstrung or ineffective (overload theorists) or short on rationality (legitimation crisis theorists). Fourthly, the capacity of the state to act decisively is being undermined because its authority or legitimacy is declining progressively. For overload theorists, the 'taut and strained' relationship between government and social groups can be explained by excessive demands related to, among other things, increased expectations and to decline in deference. Legitimation crisis theorists, in turn, focus on the way increased state intervention undermines traditionally unquestioned values and norms, and politicizes ever more issues, that is, opens them up to political debate and conflict.

Although the emphasis of Offe's and Habermas's work is more explicitly on legitimation, both overload and legitimation crisis theorists claim that state power is being eroded in the face of growing demands: in one case

these demands are regarded as 'excessive', in the other they are regarded as the virtually inevitable result of the contradictions within which the state in enmeshed.
David Held, *Models of Democracy*, Cambridge, Polity Press, 1987, pp. 236–7.

STATUS

See also WEBER

By social status, we mean a man's general standing *vis-à-vis* the other members of society or some section of it. 'General' is inserted to indicate that we refer to something more all-embracing than a specialized standing as an expert in something, such as the maintenance of motor-cars, though such expertise may contribute something to social status. Secondly, social status, like stratification, carries with it the idea of superior and inferior ... In other words, social status is the position accorded in terms of the social values current in the society.
T. H. Marshall, *Sociology at the Crossroads*, London, Heinemann, 1963, p. 181.

STRUCTURALISM

See also SEMIOLOGY, BARTHES, LÉVI-STRAUSS

Variations on the Saussurean model of language, which postulates that a **1** linguistic *signifier* only has meaning within a specific system of *significations*, served as the basic reference point for the different structuralist theories. They all extrapolated from the rules and/or relations of grammar and of speech to explore social phenomena in terms of linguistic oppositions and transformations.
Edith Kurzweil, 'Structuralism in France', in H. Etzkowitz and R. M. Glassman (eds), *The Renascence of Sociological Theory*, Itasca, Illinois, F. E. Peacock, 1991, p. 306.

I call the combination of a concept and a sound-image a *sign*, but in current **2** usage the term generally designates only a sound-image, a word, for example (*arbor*, etc.). One tends to forget that *arbor* is called a sign only because it carries the concept 'tree', with the result that the idea of the sensory part implies the idea of the whole.

Ambiguity would disappear if the three notions involved here were designated by three names, each suggesting and opposing the others. I propose to retain the word *sign* [*signe*] to designate the whole and to replace *concept* and *sound-image* respectively by *signified* [*signifié*] and *signifier* [*significant*]; the last two terms have the advantage of indicating

111

the opposition that separates them from each other and from the whole of which they are parts . . .

The bond between the signifier and the signified is arbitrary. Since I mean by sign the whole that results from the associating of the signifier with the signified, I can simply say: *the linguistic sign is arbitrary.*

The idea of 'sister' is not linked by any inner relationship to the succession of sounds *s-ö-r* which serves as its signifier in French; that it could be represented by just any other sequence is proved by the differences among languages and by the very existence of different languages . . .

One remark in passing: when semiology becomes organized as a science, the question will arise whether or not it properly includes modes of expression based on completely natural signs, such as pantomime. Supposing that the new science welcomes them, its main concern will still be the whole group of systems grounded on the arbitrariness of the sign. In fact, every means of expression used in society is based, in principle, on collective behavior or – what amounts to the same thing – on convention. Polite formulas, for instance, though often imbued with a certain natural expressiveness (as in the case of a Chinese who greets his emperor by bowing down to the ground nine times) are nonetheless fixed by rule; it is this rule and not the intrinsic value of the gestures that obliges me to use them. Signs that are wholly arbitrary realize better than the others the ideal of the semiological process; that is why language, the most complex and universal of all systems of expression, is also the most characteristic; in this sense linguistics can become the master-pattern for all branches of semiology although language is only one particular semiological system . . .

Language is a system of interdependent terms in which the value of each term results solely from the simultaneous presence of the others . . . even outside language all values are apparently governed by the same paradoxical principle. They are always composed:

1 of a *dissimilar* thing that can be exchanged for the things of which the value is to be determined; and
2 of *similar* things that can be compared with the thing of which the value is to be determined.

. . . concepts are purely differential and defined not by their positive content but negatively by their relations with the other terms of the system. Their most precise characteristic is in being what the others are not.

Ferdinand de Saussure, *Course in General Linguistics* trans. J. Culler, London, Peter Owen, 1974, pp. 67–117. Originally published in French in 1915.

STRUCTURE

1   A structure is a set of relatively stable patterned relationships of units. Since the unit of social system is the actor, social structure is a patterned system of the social relationships of actors. It is a distinctive feature of the structure of

systems of social actions, however, that in most relationships the actor does not participate as a total entity, but only by virtue of a given differentiated 'sector' of his total action. Such a sector, which is the unit of a system of social relationships, has come predominantly to be called a 'role'. Hence, the previous statement must be revised to say that social structure is a system of patterned relationships of actors in their capacity as playing roles relative to one another. Role is the concept which links the subsystem of the actor as a 'psychological' behaving entity to the distinctly *social* structure.
Talcott Parsons, *Essays in Sociological Theory* [1954], New York, Free Press, pbk edn 1964, p. 230.

The term 'social structure' has nothing to do with empirical reality, but with models which are built up after it. This should help one to clarify the difference between two concepts which are so close to each other that they have often been confused, namely, those of social structure and of social relations. It will be enough to state at this time that social relations consist of the raw materials out of which the models making up the social structure are built, while social structure can, by no means, be reduced to the ensemble of the social relations to be described in a given society. Therefore, social structure cannot claim a field of its own among others in the social studies. It is rather a method to be applied to any kind of social studies, similar to the structural analysis current in other disciplines.
Claude Lévi-Strauss, *Structural Anthropology* [1963]; trans. C. Jacobson and B. Grundfest Schoepf, New York, Doubleday Anchor, p. 271.

SURVEILLANCE

See also FOUCAULT

Michel Foucault turned the attention of social historians to the emergence of 'surveillance' or 'disciplinary power', to the development of the 'gaze technique of social control' which occurred at the beginnings of the modern era and rendered the latter a period of bodily drill and pernickety regimentation of each and every aspect of human behaviour. We have seen, however, that such power was not new; it was not born with the advent of modern times. It remained a paramount method of social control throughout the pre-modern period. What indeed happened in the early modern era was the bankruptcy of the traditional agents of surveillance power. Disciplinary control could not, therefore, be exercised matter-of-factly, as in the past. It had now become visible, a problem to be taken care of, something to be designed for, organized, managed and consciously attended to. A new, more powerful agent was needed to perform the task. The new agent was the state.
Zygmunt Bauman, *Legislators and Interpreters*, Cambridge, Polity Press, 1987, p. 42.

SYMBOL

See also CULTURE, RELIGION

1   [R]ather like 'culture', 'symbol' has been used to refer to a great variety of things, often a number of them at the same time.

In some hands it is used for anything which signifies something else to someone: dark clouds are the symbolic precursors of an on-coming rain. In others it is used only for explicitly conventional signs of one sort or another: a red flag is a symbol of danger, a white of surrender. In others it is confined to something which expresses in an oblique and figurative manner that which cannot be stated in a direct and literal one, so that there are symbols in poetry but not in science, and symbolic logic is misnamed. In yet others, however, it is used for any object, act, event, quality, or relation which serves as a vehicle for a conception – the conception is the symbol's 'meaning' – and that is the approach I shall follow here. The number 6, written, imagined, laid out as a row of stones, or even punched into the program tapes of a computer, is a symbol. But so also is the Cross, talked about, visualized, shaped worriedly in air or fondly fingered at the neck, the expanse of painted canvas called *Guernica* or the bit of painted stone called a churinga, the word 'reality', or even the morpheme '-ing'. They are all symbols, or at least symbolic elements, because they are intangible formulations of notions, abstractions from experience fixed in perceptible forms, concrete embodiments of ideas, attitudes, judgements, longings, or beliefs.
Clifford Geertz, 'Religion as a Cultural System' [1966], in C. Geertz, *The Interpretation of Cultures*, London, Hutchinson, 1975, p. 91.

2   A symbol only has meaning from its relation to other symbols in a pattern. The pattern gives the meaning. Therefore, no one item in the pattern can carry meaning by itself. Therefore even the human physiology which we all share in common does not afford symbols which we can all understand. A cross-cultural, pan-human pattern of symbols must be an impossibility. For one thing, each symbolic system develops autonomously according to its own rules. For another, cultural environments add their difference. For another, the social structures add a further range of variation. The more closely we inspect the conditions of human interaction, the more unrewarding if not ridiculous the quest for natural symbols appears. However, the intuition against such a learned negative is strong. This book attempts to reinstate the intuition by following the line of argument of the French sociologists of *L'Année sociologique*. For if it is true, as they asserted, that the social relations of men provide the prototype for the logical relations between things, then, whenever this prototype falls into a common pattern, there should be something common to be discerned in the system of symbols it uses. Where regularities in the system are found, we should expect to find

recurring, and always intelligible across cultures, the same natural systems of symbols. Society was not simply a model which classificatory thought followed; it was its own divisions which served as divisions for the system of classification. The first logical categories were social categories; the first classes of things were classes of men into which these things were integrated. It was because men were grouped and thought of themselves in the form of groups that in their ideas they grouped other things. The centre of the first scheme of nature is not the individual; it is society. The quest for natural symbols becomes by the force of this argument the quest for natural systems of symbolising. We will look for tendencies and correlations between the character of the symbolic system and that of the social system.

Mary Douglas, *Natural Symbols* [1970], New York, Vintage Books, 1973, pp. 11–12.

SYMBOLIC INTERACTION

See also MEAD

The term 'symbolic interaction' refers, of course, to the peculiar and distinctive character of interaction as it takes place between human beings. This peculiarity consists in the fact that human beings interpret or 'define' each other's actions instead of merely reacting to each other's actions. Their 'response' is not made directly to the actions of another but instead is based on the meaning which they attach to such actions. Thus, human interaction is mediated by the use of symbols, by interpretation, or by ascertaining the meaning of one another's actions. This mediation is equivalent to inserting a process of interpretation between stimulus and response in the case of human behavior.

Herbert Blumer, 'Society as Symbolic Interaction', in A. M. Rose (ed.), *Human Behavior and Social Processes: An Interactionist Approach*, Boston, Houghton Mifflin, 1962, p. 180.

TOTAL INSTITUTION

See also GOFFMAN

A total institution may be defined as a place of residence and work where a large number of like-situated individuals, cut off from the wider society for an appreciable period of time, together lead an enclosed, formally administered round of life. Prisons serve as a clear example, providing we appreciate that what is prison-like about prisons is found in institutions whose members have broken no laws.

Erving Goffman, *Asylums*, New York, Doubleday Anchor, 1961, p. xiii.

URBANISM

See also COMMUNITY, *GEMEINSCHAFT/GESELLSCHAFT*

1 The central problem of the sociologist of the city is to discover the forms of social action and organization that typically emerge in relatively permanent, compact settlements of large numbers of heterogeneous individuals. We must also infer that urbanism will assume its most characteristic and extreme form in the measure in which the conditions with which it is congruent are present. Thus the larger, the more densely populated, and the more heterogeneous a community, the more accentuated the characteristics associated with urbanism will be. It should be recognized, however, that social institutions and practices may be accepted and continued for reasons other than those that originally brought them into existence, and that accordingly the urban mode of life may be perpetuated under conditions quite foreign to those necessary for its origin.
Louis Wirth, 'Urbanism as a Way of Life', *American Journal of Sociology*, vol. 44, no. 1, 1938, p. 9.

2 Now the fundamental point is this: everything described by Wirth as 'urbanism' is in fact the cultural expression of capitalist industrialization, the emergence of the market economy and the process of rationalization of modern society.
Manuel Castells, 'Is There an Urban Sociology?', in C. G. Pickvance (trans. and ed.), *Urban Sociology: Critical Essays*, London, Methuen, 1976, p. 38. Essay first published in French in 1968.

3 Many investigators, after a ritualistic bow to the notion of totality which asserts that cities are not just statistical aggregates of things and activities, quickly reduce their problem (in the name of competence or tractability) to the analysis of things and activities. The insights gained from such investigations are not to be dismissed – in fact they are invaluable raw material out of which we may fashion a conception of urbanism. But their net import is that we learn to deal . . . with problems *in* the city rather than *of* the city. Urbanism has to be regarded as a set of social relationships which reflects the relationships established throughout society as a whole. Further, these relationships have to express the laws whereby urban phenomena are structured, regulated and constructed.
David Harvey, *Social Justice and the City*, London, Edward Arnold, 1973, pp. 303–4.

4 If ways of life do not coincide with settlement types and if these ways are functions of class and life cycle rather than of the ecological attributes of the settlement, a sociological definition of the city cannot be formulated. Concepts such as city and suburb allow us to distinguish settlement types

from each other physically and demographically, but the ecological processes and conditions which they synthesize have no direct or invariate consequence for ways of life. The sociologist cannot, therefore, speak of an urban or suburban way of life.

Herbert Gans, 'Urbanism and Suburbanism as Ways of Life', in A. M. Rose (ed.), *Human Behavior and Social Processes*, Boston, Houghton Mifflin, 1962, p. 643.

We must relate social behavior to the way in which the city assumes a **5** certain geography, a certain spatial form. We must recognize that once a spatial form is created it tends to institutionalize and, in some respects, to determine the future development of social process. We need, above all, to formulate concepts which will allow us to harmonize and integrate strategies to deal with the intricacies of social process and the elements of spatial form.

Manuel Castells, 'Theory and Ideology in Urban Sociology', in C. J. Pickvance (ed. and trans.), *Urban Sociology: Critical Essays*, London, Methuen, 1976, p. 27. Essay first published in French in 1969.

The counterpart of the mall-as-panopticon-prison is the housing-project- **6** as-strategic-hamlet ... The security-driven logic of urban enclavization finds its most popular expression in the frenetic efforts of Los Angeles's affluent neighborhoods to insulate home values and lifestyles.

Mike Davis, *City of Quartz: Excavating the Future in Los Angeles*, London and New York, Verso, 1990, p. 244.

VALUES

See also WEBER

This is an account of a myth created by and about a magnificent minotaur named Max – Max Weber, to be exact; his myth was that social science should and could be value-free. The lair of this minotaur, although reached only by a labyrinthian logic and visited by a few who never return, is still regarded by many sociologists as a holy place. In particular, as sociologists grow older they seem impelled to make a pilgrimage to it and to pay their respects to the problem of the relations between values and social science.

Considering the perils of the visit, their motives are somewhat perplexing. Perhaps their quest is the first sign of professional senility; perhaps it is the last sigh of youthful yearnings. And perhaps a concern with the value problems is just a way of trying to take back something that was, in youthful enthusiasm, given too hastily.

In any event, the myth of a value-free sociology has become a conquering one. Today, all the powers of sociology, from Parsons to Lundberg, have entered into a tacit alliance to bind us to the dogma that 'Thou shalt not commit a value judgement', especially as sociologists. Where is the introductory textbook, where the lecture course on principles, that does not affirm or imply this?

In the end, we cannot disprove the existence of minotaurs, who, after all, are thought to be sacred precisely because, being half-man and half-bull, they are so unlikely. The thing to see is that a belief in them is not so much untrue as it is absurd. Like Berkeley's argument for solipsism, Weber's brief for a value-free sociology is a tight one and, some say, logically unassailable; yet it, too, is absurd. Both arguments appeal to reason but ignore experience.

Alvin W. Gouldner, 'Anti-Minotaur: The Myth of a Value-free Sociology', *Social Problems*, vol. 9, no. 3, 1962, p. 199.

VOCABULARY OF MOTIVES

What is reason for one man is rationalization for another. The variable is the accepted vocabulary of motives, the ultimates of (justificatory) discourse, of each man's dominant group about whose opinion he cares.

C. Wright Mills, 'Situated Actions and Vocabularies of Motive', *American Sociological Review*, vol. 5, no. 6, 1940, pp. 904–13. Reprinted in C. Wright Mills, *Power, Politics and People*, New York, Oxford University Press, p. 448.

WORK AND ORGANIZATIONS

1 Labour from dawn to dusk can appear to be 'natural' in a farming community, especially in the harvest months: nature demands that the grain be harvested before the thunderstorms set in. And we may note similar 'natural' work-rhythms which attend other rural or industrial occupations: sheep must be attended at lambing time and guarded from predators; cows must be milked; the charcoal fire must be attended and not burn away through the turfs (and the charcoal burners must sleep beside it); once iron is in the making, the furnaces must not be allowed to fail. The notation of time which arises in such contexts has been described as task-orientation. It is perhaps the most effective orientation in peasant societies, and it remains important in village and domestic industries . . . Three points may be proposed about task-orientation. First, there is a sense in which it is more humanly comprehensible than timed labour. The peasant or labourer appears to attend upon what is an observed necessity. Second, a community in which task-orientation is common appears to show least demarcation between 'work' and 'life'. Social intercourse and labour are intermingled – the working-day lengthens or contracts according to the task – and there is no great sense of conflict between labour and 'passing the time of day'. Third, to men accustomed to labour timed by the clock, this attitude to labour appears to be wasteful and lacking in urgency. Such a clear

distinction supposes, of course, the independent peasant or craftsman as referent. But the question of task-orientation becomes greatly more complex at the point where labour is employed. The entire family economy of the small farmer may be task-orientated; but within it there may be a division of labour, and allocation of roles, and the discipline of an employer–employed relationship between the farmer and his children. Even here time is beginning to become money, the employer's money. As soon as actual hands are employed the shift from task-orientation to timed labour is marked . . . Those who are employed experience a distinction between their employer's time and their 'own' time. And the employer must *use* the time of his labour, and see it is not wasted: not the task but the value of time when reduced to money is dominant. Time is now currency: it is not passed but spent.

E. P. Thompson, 'Time, Work Discipline and Industrial Capitalism', *Past and Present*, vol. 38, 1967, pp. 60–1.

Economic power, in terms of control over physical aspects, is apparently **2** responding to a centripetal force, tending more and more to concentrate in the hands of a few corporate managements. At the same time, beneficial ownership is centrifugal, tending to divide and sub-divide, to split into even smaller units and to pass freely from hand to hand. In other words, ownership continually becomes more dispersed; the power formerly joined to it becomes increasingly concentrated; and the corporate system is thereby more securely established.

A. A. Berle and G. C. Means, *The Modern Corporation and Private Property* [1932], New York, Harcourt Brace Jovanovich, 1968, pp. 9–10.

The means of control applied by an organization can be classified into three **3** analytical categories: physical, material or symbolic. The use of a gun, a whip or a lock is physical since it affects the body; the threat to use physical sanctions is viewed as physical because the effect on the subject is similar in kind, though not in intensity, to the actual use. Control based on application of physical means is described as *coercive power*. Material rewards consist of goods and services. The granting of symbols (e.g. money) which allow one to acquire goods and services is classified as material because the effect on the recipient is similar to that of material means. The use of material means for control purposes constitutes *utilitarian power*. Pure symbols are those whose use does not constitute a physical threat or a claim on material rewards. These include normative symbols, those of prestige and esteem; and social symbols, those of love and acceptance. When physical contact is used to symbolize prestige, such contacts or objects are viewed as symbols because their effect on the recipient is similar to that of 'pure' symbols. The use of symbols for control purposes is referred to as *normative, normative-social* or *social power*. Normative power is exercised by those in higher ranks to control the lower ranks directly as when an officer gives a pep talk to his men. Normative-social power is used indirectly, as when the higher in

rank appeals to the peer group of a subordinate to control him (e.g. as a teacher will call on a class to ignore the distractions of an exhibitionist child). Social power is the power which peers exercise over one another.
Amitai Etzioni, *Modern Organisations*, New York, Prentice-Hall, 1964, p. 59.

4   In mechanistic systems the problems and tasks which face the concern as a whole are, typically, broken down into specialisms. Each individual carries out his assigned task as something apart from the overall purpose of the company as a whole. 'Somebody at the top' is responsible for seeing that his work is relevant to that of others. The technical methods, duties, and powers attached to each post are precisely defined, and a high value is placed on precision and demarcation. Interaction within the working organisation follows vertical lines – i.e., between superiors and subordinates . . .

Organismic systems are adapted to unstable conditions, when new and unfamiliar problems and requirements continually arise which cannot be broken down and distributed among specialist roles within a hierarchy. Jobs lose much of their formal definition. The definitive and enduring demarcation of functions, and even methods and powers, have to be constantly redefined through interaction with others participating in common tasks or in the solution of common problems. Each individual has to do his job with knowledge of overall purpose and situation of the company as a whole. Interaction runs laterally as much as vertically, and communication between people of different rank tends to resemble 'lateral' consultation rather than 'vertical' command. Omniscience can no longer be imputed to the boss at the top.
T. Burns, 'Industry in a New Age', *New Society*, 31 January 1963, pp. 17–20.

5   The less the expertise, the more direct the surveillance, and the more obtrusive the controls. The more the expertise, the more unobtrusive the control. The best situation of all, although they do not come cheap, is to hire professionals, for someone else has socialized them and even unobtrusive controls are hardly needed. The professional, the prima donna of organization theory, is really the ultimate eunuch – capable of doing everything well in the harem except that which he should not do, and in this case that is to mess around with the goals of the organization, or the assumptions that determine to what ends he will use his professional skills.
Charles Perrow, quoted in G. Salaman and K. Thompson, *Control and Ideology in Organizations*, Milton Keynes, Open University Press, 1980, p. 13.

6   The new forms of power that are developing in modern society are closely connected with the great efficiency of indirect mechanisms of organizational control. Slave drivers have gone out of fashion not because they were so cruel but because they were so inefficient. Men can be controlled much more efficiently by tying their economic needs and interests to their performance on behalf of employers. Calling this wage slavery is a

half-truth, which correctly indicates that workers dependent on their wages can be exploited as slaves can be, and which conveniently ignores the basic differences between economic exploitation and slavery. The efforts of men can be controlled still far more efficiently than through wages alone by mobilizing their professional commitments to the work they can do best and like to do most and by putting these highly motivated energies and skills at the disposal of organizations.

Peter M. Blau and R. A. Schoenherr, *The Structure of Organizations*, New York, Basic Books, 1971, p. 352.

In our sociological analysis as well as our political thinking, it is time that **7** we 'push men finally out', to place proper emphasis on the study of social structure in sociology, and to recognize the power of organizations as the main threat to liberty in modern society. The enemy is not an exploitative capitalist or an imperialist general or a narrow-minded bureaucrat. It is no man. It is the efficient structure of modern organizations which enables the giant ones and their combinations to dominate our lives, our fortunes, and our honour.

Ibid., p. 357.

WORLD-SYSTEM

We have defined a world-system as one in which there is extensive division of labor. This division is not merely functional – that is, occupational – but geographical. That is to say, the range of economic tasks is not evenly distributed throughout the world-system. In part this is a consequence of ecological considerations, to be sure. But for the most part, it is a function of the social organization of work, one which magnifies and legitimizes the ability of some groups within the system to exploit the labor of others, that is, to receive a larger share of the surplus.

While, in an empire, the political structure tends to link culture with occupation, in a world-economy the political structure tends to link culture with spatial location. The reason is that in a world-economy the first point of political pressure available to groups is the local (national) state structure. Cultural homogenization tends to serve the interests of the key groups and the pressures build up to create cultural-national identities.

This is particularly the case in the advantaged areas of the world-economy – what we have called the core-states. In such states, the creation of a strong state machinery coupled with a national culture, a phenomenon often referred to as integration, serves both as a mechanism to protect disparities that have arisen within the world-system, and as an ideological mask and justification for the maintenance of these disparities.

World-economies then are divided into core-states and peripheral areas. I do not say peripheral *states* because one characteristic of peripheral areas is that the indigenous state is weak, ranging from its non-existence (that is, a colonial situation) to one with a low degree of autonomy (that is, a neo-colonial situation).

There are also semiperipheral areas which are in between the core and the periphery on a series of dimensions, such as complexity of economic activities, strength of the state machinery, cultural integrity, etc. . . .

The division of a world-economy involves a hierarchy of occupational tasks, in which tasks requiring higher levels of skill and greater capitalization are reserved for higher-ranking areas. Since a capitalist world-economy essentially rewards accumulated capital, including human capital, at a higher rate than 'raw' labor power, the geographical maldistribution of these occupational skills involves a strong trend toward self-maintenance. The forces of the marketplace reinforce them rather than undermine them. And the absence of a central political mechanism for the world economy makes it very difficult to intrude counteracting forces to the maldistribution of rewards.

Immanuel Wallerstein, *The Modern World-System: Capitalist Agriculture and the Origins of the European World-Economy in the Sixteenth Century*, New York, Academic Press, 1976, pp. 229–33.

Part 2

KEY SOCIOLOGICAL THINKERS

BAUDRILLARD, JEAN (1929–)

Consumption

In fact we can conceive of consumption as a characteristic mode of industrial   **1**
civilization on the condition that we separate it fundamentally from its
current meaning as a process of satisfaction of needs. Consumption is not a
passive mode of assimilation (*absorption*) and appropriation which we
can oppose to an active mode of production, in order to bring to bear naive
concepts of action (and alienation). From the outset, we must clearly state
that consumption is an active mode of relations (not only to objects, but to
the collectivity and to the world), a systematic mode of activity and a global
response on which our whole cultural system is founded. We must clearly
state that material goods are not the objects of consumption: they are merely
the objects of need and satisfaction. We have all at times purchased, possessed, enjoyed, and spent, and yet not 'consumed' ... Consumption is
neither a material practice, nor a phenomenology of 'affluence'. It is not
defined by the food we eat, the clothes we wear, the car we drive, nor by the
visual and oral substance of images and messages, but in the organization
of all this as signifying substance. Consumption is the virtual totality of
all objects and messages presently constituted in a more or less coherent
discourse. Consumption, in so far as it is meaningful, is a systematic act of
the manipulation of signs.
Le Système des objets, Paris, Gallimard, 1968, pp. 255–83. Trans. J. Mourrain in
Mark Poster (ed.), *Jean Baudrillard: Selected Writings*, Cambridge, Polity Press,
1988, pp. 21–2.

Simulation, simulacra and the hyperreal: Disneyland

Disneyland is a perfect model of all the entangled orders of simulation.   **2**
To begin with it is a play of illusions and phantasms: pirates, the frontier,
future world, etc. This imaginary world is supposed to be what makes the
operation successful. But, what draws the crowds is undoubtedly much
more the microcosm, the miniaturized and *religious* revelling in real
America, in its delights and drawbacks ... The objective profile of the
United States, then, may be traced throughout Disneyland, even down to
the morphology of individuals and the crowd. All its values are exalted
here, in miniature and comic-strip form. Embalmed and pacified. Whence
the possibility of an ideological analysis of Disneyland: digest of the
American way of life, panegyric to American values, idealized transposition
of a contradictory reality. To be sure. But this conceals something else, and
that 'ideological' blanket exactly serves to cover over a *third-order simulation*: Disneyland is there to conceal the fact that it is the 'real' country, all of
'real' America, which *is* Disneyland (just as prisons are there to conceal the

125

fact that it is the social in its entirety, in its banal omnipresence, which is carceral). Disneyland is presented as imaginary in order to make us believe that the rest is real, when in fact all of Los Angeles and the America surrounding it are no longer real, but of the order of the hyperreal and of simulation. It is no longer a question of a false representation of reality (ideology), but of concealing the fact that the real is no longer real, and thus of saving the reality principle.

Simulacres et simulation, Paris, Galilée, 1981. Trans. P. Foss, P. Patton and P. Beitchman, as *Simulations*, New York, Semiotext(e), 1983, p. 25.

3 Seduction is that which extracts meaning from discourse and detracts it from its truth. It would thus be the opposite of the psychoanalytic distinction between manifest and latent discourse. For latent discourse diverts manifest discourse not *from* its truth but *towards* it and makes it say what it did not wish to say . . . In seduction, conversely, it is somehow the manifest discourse, the most 'superficial' aspect of discourse, which acts upon the underlying prohibition (conscious or unconscious) in order to nullify it and to substitute for it the charms and traps of appearances.

De la séduction, Paris, Éditions Galilée, 1979, p. 75. Trans. J. Mourrain in Mark Poster (ed.), *Jean Baudrillard: Selected Writings*, Cambridge, Polity Press, 1988, p. 149.

BERGER, PETER L. (1929–)

1 The fundamental dialectic process of society consists of three moments, or steps. These are externalization, objectivation, and internalization. Only if these three moments are understood together can an empirically adequate view of society be maintained. Externalization is the ongoing outpouring of human beings into the world, both in the physical and the mental activity of men. Objectivation is the attainment by the products of this activity (again both physical and mental) of a reality that confronts its original producers as a facticity external to and other than themselves. Internalization is the reappropriation by men of this same reality, transforming it once again from structures of the objective world into structures of the subjective consciousness. It is through externalization that society is a human product. It is through objectivation that society becomes *sui generis*. It is through internalization that man is a product of society.

The Social Reality of Religion, London, Faber & Faber, 1969, pp. 3–4. Published in America as *The Sacred Canopy*, New York, Doubleday, 1967.

2 It is important to keep in mind that the objectivity of the institutional world, however massive it may appear to the individual, is a humanly produced, constructed objectivity.

Peter L. Berger and Thomas Luckmann, *The Social Construction of Reality*, Harmondsworth, Penguin, 1967, p. 78.

Society is a human product. Society is an objective reality. Man is a social **3**
product.
Ibid., p. 78.

The paradox is that man is capable of producing a world that he then **4**
experiences as something other than a human product.
Ibid., p. 57.

All social life is precarious. All societies are constructions in the face of **5**
chaos.
Ibid., p. 96.

He who has the bigger stick has the better chance of imposing his definitions. **6**
Ibid., p. 101.

BOURDIEU, PIERRE (1930–)

Structures, *habitus*, practices

Objectivism constitutes the social world as a spectacle offered to an observer **1**
who takes up a 'point of view' on the action and who, putting into the object
the principles of his relation to the object, proceeds as if it were intended
solely for knowledge and as if all the interactions within it were purely
symbolic exchanges. This viewpoint is the one taken from high positions in
the social structure, from which the social world is seen as a representation
(as the word is used in idealist philosophy, but also as in painting) or a
performance (in the theatrical or musical sense), and practices are seen as
no more than the acting-out of roles, the playing of scores or the implementation of plans. The theory of practice as practice insists, contrary to positivist
materialism, that the objects of knowledge are constructed, not passively
recorded, and, contrary to intellectualist idealism, that the principle of
this construction is the system of structured, structuring dispositions, the
habitus, which is constituted in practice and is always oriented towards
practical functions. It is possible to step down from the sovereign viewpoint
from which objectivist idealism orders the world, as Marx demands in the
Theses on Feuerbach, but without having to abandon to it the 'activist aspect'
of apprehension of the world by reducing knowledge to a mere reordering.
To do this, one has to situate oneself *within* 'real activity as such', that is, in
the practical relation to the world, the preoccupied, active presence in the
world through which the world imposes its presence, with its urgencies, its
things to be done and said, things made to be said, which directly govern
words and deeds without ever unfolding as a spectacle. One has to escape
from the realism of the structure, to which objectivism, a necessary stage in
breaking with primary experience and constructing the objective relationships, necessarily leads when it hypostatizes these relations by treating them

as realities already constituted outside of the history of the group – without falling back into subjectivism, which is quite incapable of giving an account of the necessity of the social world. To do this, one has to return to practice, the site of the dialectic of the *opus operatum* and the *modus operandi*; of the objectified products and the incorporated products of historical practices; of structures and *habitus* . . .

The conditions associated with a particular class of conditions of existence produce *habitus*, systems of durable, transposable dispositions, structured structures predisposed to function as structuring structures, that is, as principles which generate and organize practices and representations that can be objectively adapted to their outcomes without presupposing a conscious aiming at ends or an express mastery of the operations necessary in order to attain them. Objectively 'regulated' and 'regular' without being in any way the product of obedience to rules, they can be collectively orchestrated without being the product of the organizing action of a conductor . . .

If a very close correlation is regularly observed between the scientifically constructed objective probabilities (for example, the chances of access to a particular good) and agents' subjective aspirations ('motivations' and 'needs'), this is not because agents consciously adjust their aspirations to an exact evaluation of their chances of success, like a gambler organizing his stakes on the basis of perfect information about his chances of winning. In reality, the dispositions durably inculcated by the possibilities and impossibilities, freedoms and necessities, opportunities and prohibitions inscribed in the objective conditions (which science apprehends through statistical regularities such as probabilities objectively attached to a group or class) generate dispositions objectively compatible with these conditions and in a sense pre-adapted to their demands . . . Unlike scientific estimations, which are corrected after each experiment according to rigorous rules of calculation, the anticipations of the *habitus*, practical hypotheses based on past experience, give disproportionate weight to early experiences. Through the economic and domestic economy and family relations, or more precisely, through the specifically familial manifestations of this external necessity (forms of the division of labour between the sexes, household objects, modes of consumption, parent–child relations, etc.), the structures characterizing a determinate class of conditions of existence produce the structures of the *habitus*, which in their turn are the basis of the perception and appreciation of all subsequent experiences.

The Logic of Practice, trans. Richard Nice, Stanford, Stanford University Press, 1990, pp. 52–8. First published in French in 1974.

2   The disposition to make use of the school and the predispositions to succeed in it depend, as we have seen, on the objective chances of using it and succeeding in it that are attached to the different social classes, these dispositions and predispositions in turn constituting one of the most important

factors in the perpetuation of the structure of eductional chances as an objectively graspable manifestation of the relationship between the educational system and the structure of class relations.

Pierre Bourdieu and J. C. Passeron, *Reproduction in Education, Society and Culture*, trans. R. Nice, London, Sage, 1977, p. 204.

Taste is the practical operator of the transmutation of things into distinct **3** and distinctive signs, of continuous distributions into discontinuous oppositions; it raises the differences inscribed in the physical order of bodies to the symbolic order of significant distinctions. It transforms objectively classified practices, in which a class condition signifies itself (through taste), into classifying practices, that is, into a symbolic expression of class position.

Distinction: Social Critique of the Judgement of Taste, Cambridge, Massachusetts, Harvard University Press, 1984, p. 175. First published in French in 1979.

The endless changes in fashion result from the objective orchestration **4** between, on the one hand, the logic of struggles internal to the field of production, which are organized in terms of old/new, itself linked, through the oppositions expensive/(relatively) cheap and classical/practical (or rearguard/avant-garde), to the opposition old/young . . . and, on the other hand, the logic of the struggles internal to the field of the dominant and dominated fractions, or, more precisely, the established and the challengers.

Ibid., p. 233.

COMTE, AUGUSTE (1798–1857)

Science and sociology

From science comes prevision; from prevision comes action [*Savoir pour* **1** *prévoir et prévoir pour pouvoir*].

The Positive Philosophy of Auguste Comte (3 vols), translated and condensed by Harriet Martineau, 1896, vol. 1. First published in six volumes in French, 1830–42. And in Kenneth Thompson (ed.), *Auguste Comte: The Foundation of Sociology*, London, Thomas Nelson, and New York, Halsted/Wiley, 1975, p. 51.

No real observation of any kind of phenomena is possible, except in so far **2** as it is first directed, and finally interpreted, by some theory: and it was this logical need which, in the infancy of human reason, occasioned the rise of theological philosophy, as we shall see in the course of our historical survey. The positive philosophy does not dissolve this obligation, but, on the contrary, extends and fulfils it more and more, the further the relations of phenomena are multiplied and perfected by it. Hence it is clear that, scientifically speaking, all isolated, empirical observation is idle, and even radically uncertain; that science can use only those observations which are connected, at least hypothetically, with some law; that it is such a connection

which makes the chief difference between scientific and popular observation, embracing the same facts, but contemplating them from different points of view: and that observations empirically conducted can at most supply provisional materials, which must usually undergo an ulterior revision. The rational method of observation becomes more necessary in proportion to the complexity of the phenomena, amidst which the observer would not know what he ought to look at in the facts before his eyes, but for the guidance of a preparatory theory; and thus it is that by the connection of foregoing facts we learn to see the facts that follow.
Positive Philosophy, vol. 2; and in Thompson, op. cit., pp. 102–3.

3   I am not blind to the vast difficulty which this requisition imposes on the institution of positive sociology, obliging us to create at once, so to speak, observations and laws, on account of their indispensable connection, placing us in a sort of vicious circle, from which we can issue only by employing in the first instance materials which are badly elaborated, and doctrines which are ill-conceived.
Positive Philosophy, vol. 2.

Human progress and the law of the three stages

4   If we regard the course of human development from the highest scientific point of view, we shall perceive that it consists in educing more and more, the characteristic faculties of humanity, in comparison with those of animality; and especially with those which man has in common with the whole organic kingdom . . .

Civilization develops to an enormous degree, the actions of man upon his environment: and thus, it may seem, at first, to concentrate our attentions upon the cares of material existence, the support and improvement of which appear to be the chief object of most social occupations. A closer examination will show, however, that this development gives the advantage to the highest human faculties, both by the security which sets free our attention from physical wants, and by the direct and steady excitement which it administers to the intellectual functions, and even the social feelings.
Positive Philosophy, vol. 2; in Thompson, op. cit., pp. 153–4.

5   Each of our leading conceptions, each branch of our knowledge, passes successively through three different theoretical conditions: the Theological, or fictitious; the Metaphysical, or abstract; and the Scientific, or positive . . .
In the theological state, the human mind, seeking the essential nature of beings, the first and final causes (the origin and purpose) of all effects . . . supposes all phenomena to be produced by the immediate action of supernatural beings. In the metaphysical state . . . the mind supposes . . . abstract forces, veritable entities (that is, personified abstractions) . . . capable of

130

producing all phenomena ... In the final, the positive state, the mind has given over the vain search after Abstract notions, the origin and destination of the universe, and the causes of phenomena, and applies itself to the study of their laws – that is, their invariable relations of succession and resemblance.
Positive Philosophy, vol. 1; in Thompson, op. cit., pp. 39–40.

The progress of the individual mind is not only an illustration, but an **6** indirect evidence of that of the general mind. The point of departure of the individual and of the race being the same, the phases of the mind of a man correspond to the epochs of the mind of the race. Now, each of us is aware, if he looks back upon his own history, that he was a theologian in his childhood, a metaphysician in his youth and a natural philosopher in his manhood.
Positive Philosophy, vol. 1; in Thompson, op. cit., p. 41.

It cannot be necessary to prove to anybody who reads this work that Ideas **7** govern the world, or throw it into chaos: in other words, that all social mechanism rests upon Opinions.
Positive Philosophy, vol. 1; in Thompson, op. cit., p. 48.

During the whole of our survey of the sciences, I have endeavoured to keep **8** in view the great fact that all the three states, theological, metaphysical and positive, may and do exist at the same time in the same mind in regard to different sciences. I must once more recall this consideration, and insist upon it; because in the forgetfulness of it lies the only real objection that can be brought against the grand law of the three states. It must be steadily kept in view that the same mind may be in the positive state with regard to the most simple and general sciences; in the metaphysical with regard to the more complex and special; and in the theological with regard to social science.
Positive Philosophy, vol. 2; in Thompson, op. cit., p. 163.

To complete my long and difficult demonstration, I have only now to show **9** that material development, as a whole, must follow a course, not only analogous, but perfectly correspondent with that of intellectual development, which, as we have seen, governs every other.

All political investigation of a rational kind proves the primitive tendency of mankind, in a general way, to a military life; and to its final issue in an industrial life. No enlightened mind disputes the continuous decline of the military spirit, and the gradual ascendancy of the industrial. We see now, under various forms, and more and more indisputably, even in the very heart of armies, the repugnance of modern society to a military life. We see that compulsory recruiting becomes more and more necessary, and that there is less and less voluntary persistence in that mode of life.
Positive Philosophy, vol. 2; in Thompson, op. cit., p. 166.

10 *Hierarchy of the Sciences*:
We have before us five fundamental sciences in successive dependence, Astronomy, Physics, Chemistry, Physiology and finally Social Physics. The first considers the most general, simple, abstract and remote phenomena known to us, and those which affect all other without being affected by them. The last considers the most particular, compound, concrete phenomena, and those which are the most interesting to man. Between these two, the degrees of speciality, of complexity and individuality are in regular proportion to the place of the respective sciences in the scale exhibited.
Positive Philosophy, vol. 1.

Social statics and dynamics

11 The statical study of sociology consists in the investigation of the laws of action and reaction of the different parts of the social system, apart, for the occasion, from the fundamental movement which is always gradually modifying them ... The true general spirit of social dynamics then consists in conceiving of each of these consecutive social states as the necessary result of the preceding, and the indispensable mover of the following, according to the axiom of Leibniz, *the present is big with the future*. In this view, the object of science is to discover the laws which govern this continuity, and the aggregate of which determines the course of human development. In short, social dynamics studies the laws of succession, while social statics inquires into those of coexistence.
Positive Philosophy, vol. 2; in Thompson, op. cit., pp. 90–4.

12 Thus, then, we see what is the function of social science. Without extolling or condemning political facts, science regards them as subjects of observation: it contemplates each phenomenon in its harmony with co-existing phenomena, and in its connections with the foregoing and the following state of human development: it endeavours to discover, from both points of view, the general relations which connect all social phenomena: and each of them is *explained*, in the scientific sense of the word, when it has been connected with the whole of the existing situation, and the whole of the preceding movement.
Positive Philosophy, vol. 2; Thompson, op. cit., p. 100.

13 The chief phenomenon in sociology ... that is, the gradual and continuous influence of generations upon each other – would be disguised or unnoticed, for want of the necessary key – historical analysis ...
    Still, history has more of a literary and descriptive than of a scientific character. It does not yet establish a rational filiation in the series of social events so as to admit (as in other sciences, and allowing for its greater complexity) of any degree of systematic prevision of their future succession.
Positive Philosophy, vol. 2; in Thompson, op. cit., p. 19.

There can be no scientific study of society either in its conditions or its **14** movements, if it is separated into portions, and its divisions are studied apart.
Positive Philosophy, vol. 2.

There are three methods ... Observation, Experiment and Comparison **15** ... No real observation of any kind of phenomena is possible, except in as far as it is first directed, and finally interpreted, by some theory ...
Positive Philosophy, vol. 2; in Thompson, op. cit., p. 101f.

We cannot, of course, fully appreciate a phenomenon which is for ever **16** proceeding before our eyes, and in which we bear a part; but if we withdraw ourselves in thought from the social system, and contemplate it from afar, can we conceive of a more marvellous spectacle, in the whole range of natural phenomena, than the regular and constant convergence of an innumerable multitude of human beings, each possessing a distinct and, in a certain degree, independent existence, and yet incessantly disposed, amidst all their discordance of talent and character, to concur in many ways in the same general development, without concert, and even consciousness on the part of most of them, who believe that they are merely following their personal impulses? This is the scientific picture of the phenomenon: and no temporary disturbances can prevent its being, under all circumstances, essentially true ...
Positive Philosophy, vol. 2.

As every system must be composed of elements of the same nature with **17** itself, the scientific spirit forbids us to regard society as composed of individuals. The true social unit is certainly the family, reduced, if necessary, to the elementary couple which forms its base.
Positive Philosophy, vol. 2.

Division of labour and specialization

If we have been accustomed to deplore the spectacle among the artisan class **18** of a workman occupied during his whole life in nothing else but making knife-handles or pins' heads, we may find something quite as lamentable in the intellectual class, in the exclusive employment of a human brain in resolving some equations, or in classifying insects. The moral effect is, unhappily, analogous in the two cases. It occasions a miserable indifference about the general course of human affairs, as long as there are equations to resolve and pins to manufacture. This is an extreme case of human automatism; but the frequency, and the growing frequency, of the evil gives a real scientific importance to the case, as indicating the general tendency, and warning us to restrain it.
Positive Philosophy, vol. 2; Thompson, p. 124.

COOLEY, CHARLES HORTON (1864–1929)

1   The Self and Social Interaction:
     Each to each a looking-glass
     Reflects the other that doth pass.

As we see our face, figure, and dress in the glass, and are interested in them because they are ours, and pleased or otherwise with them according as they do or do not answer to what we should like them to be, so in imagination we perceive in another's mind some thought of our appearance, manners, aims, deeds, character, friends, and so on, and are variously affected by it.
Human Nature and the Social Order, New York, Schocken, 1964, p. 184.

2   Society is an interweaving and interworking of mental selves. I imagine your mind, and especially what your mind thinks about my mind, and what your mind thinks about what my mind thinks about your mind. I dress my mind before yours and expect that you will dress yours before mine. Whoever cannot or will not perform these feats is not properly in the game.
Life and the Student, New York, Alfred A. Knopf, 1927, pp. 200–1.

3   By primary groups I mean those characterized by intimate face-to-face association and co-operation. They are primary in several senses but chiefly in that they are fundamental in forming the social nature and ideals of individuals. The result of intimate association, psychologically, is a certain fusion of individualities in a common whole, so that one's very self, for many purposes at least, is the common life and purpose of the group. Perhaps the simplest way of describing this wholeness is by saying that it is a 'we'.
Social Organization, New York, Schocken, 1962, p. 23.

DURKHEIM, ÉMILE (1858–1917)

Sociology and the rules of sociological method

1   We think it a fertile idea that social life must be explained, not by the conceptions of it created by those who participate in it, but by profound causes which escape awareness; and we also think that these causes must principally be sought in the way in which associated individuals are grouped.
Review of Antonio Labriola, 'Essais sur la conception matérialiste de l'histoire' [1897]; in M. Traugott (ed. and trans.), *Émile Durkheim on Institutional Analysis*, Chicago, University of Chicago Press, 1978, p. 127.

2   There exists a social consciousness of which individual consciousnesses are, at least in part, only an emanation. How many ideas or sentiments are there which we obtain completely on our own? Very few. Each of us speaks a language which he has not himself created: we find it ready-made.

134

Review of A. Schäffle, *Bau und Leben der sozialen Körpers* (published in French 1885); in M. Traugott (ed. and trans.), *Émile Durkheim on Institutional Analysis*, Chicago, University of Chicago Press, 1978, p. 102.

Instead of stopping at the exclusive consideration of events that lie at the surface of social life, there has arisen the need for studying the less obvious points at the base of it – internal causes and impersonal, hidden forces that move individuals and collectivities. **3**
'Sociology' (published in French 1900). Trans. J. D. Folkman in *Essays on Sociology and Philosophy*, ed. Kurt H. Wolff, New York, Harper Torchbooks, 1964, p. 381.

Without distorting the meaning of this expression, we can, in fact, call all beliefs and all modes of behaviour instituted by the collectivity 'institutions'; sociology can then be defined as the science of institutions, their genesis and their functioning. **4**
The Rules of Sociological Method (first published in French in 1895); in Kenneth Thompson (ed. and trans.), *Readings from Émile Durkheim*, London, Routledge, 1985, p. 67.

The first and fundamental rule is to consider social facts as things. **5**
Ibid., p. 72.

But in reality there is in every society a specific group of phenomena which are distinguished by characteristics that are quite separate from those studied by the other natural sciences. When I undertake my duties as a brother, husband, or citizen and fulfil the commitments that I have entered into, I perform obligations which are defined outside myself and my actions, in law and custom . . . **6**
    Here, then, is a category of facts with very special characteristics: they consist of ways of acting, thinking and feeling that are external to the individual and are endowed with a coercive power by virtue of which they exercise control over him.
Ibid., pp. 68–9.

We thus arrive at the point where we can formulate precisely the field of sociology. It includes only one specific group of phenomena. A social fact is recognized by the power of external coercion which it exercises, or is capable of exercising, over individuals; and the presence of this power is in turn recognizable by the existence of some specific sanction, or by the resistance that it offers to any individual action that would violate it. **7**
Ibid., p. 71.

A social fact is every way of acting, whether fixed or not, which is capable of exercising an external constraint on the individual; or, which is general throughout a given society, whilst having an existence of its own, independent of its individual manifestations. **8**
Ibid., p. 72.

9 Crime consists of an action which offends certain collective sentiments that are particularly strong and clear-cut.
Ibid., p. 80.

10 Crime is necessary; it is linked to the fundamental conditions of all social life and, because of that, is useful; for those conditions to which it is bound are themselves indispensable to the normal evolution of morality and law.
Ibid., p. 81.

11 When one undertakes to explain a social phenomenon, one must study separately the efficient cause which produces it and the function it fulfils . . . For example, the social reaction which constitutes punishment is due to the intensity of the collective sentiments that the crime offends. On the other hand, its useful function is to maintain these sentiments at the same degree of intensity, for they would soon diminish if the offences committed against them went unpunished.
Ibid., pp. 84–5.

12 The determining cause of a social fact must be sought among antecedent social facts preceding it and not among the states of the individual consciousness . . . The function of a social fact must always to be sought in its relationship to some social end.
Ibid., pp. 86.

The division of labour in society

13 This work originated with the question about the relationship between individual personality and social solidarity. How can it be that the individual, while becoming more autonomous, depends more heavily on society? How can he be at the same time both more individual and more socially integrated? It is undeniable that these two movements, contradictory though they may appear, develop along parallel lines. That was the problem we raised: it seemed that what resolved this apparent dichotomy was a change in social solidarity brought about by the ever-increasing development of the division of labour.
The Division of Labour in Society (first published in French in 1893), in Kenneth Thompson (ed. and trans.), *Readings from Émile Durkheim*, London, Routledge, 1985, p. 33.

14 Since law reproduces the principal forms of social solidarity, we have only to classify the different types of law in order to discover which are the different, corresponding types of social solidarity . . . There are two kinds. The first consists essentially of imposing some suffering, or at least some disadvantage, upon the offender . . . The second kind of sanction does not necessarily involve suffering on the part of the offender, but consists only of restoring the previous state of affairs, of re-establishing relationships

that have been disturbed to their normal state ... We must therefore divide juridical rules into two major classes, depending on whether they have organized repressive sanctions or purely restitutive sanctions. The first class includes all penal law; the second, civil law, commercial law, procedural law, administrative and constitutional law, after allowing for the penal rule that may be found in them.
Ibid., pp. 38–9.

The totality of beliefs and sentiments common to average members of the **15** same society forms a particular system with a life of its own life; one might call it the *collective* or *common consciousness*.
Ibid., p. 39.

We can say that an act is criminal when it offends strong and defined states **16** of the collective consciousness ... In other words, we must not say that an action offends the common consciousness because it is criminal, but rather that it is criminal because it shocks the common consciousness. We do not condemn it because it is a crime, but it is a crime because we condemn it.
Ibid., p. 40.

Thus, we can say, without being paradoxical, that punishment is above all **17** designed to act upon law-abiding people. For, since it serves to heal wounds inflicted upon the collective sentiments, it can only fulfil this role where such sentiments exist and to the extent that they are active.
Ibid., p. 45.

If there is one truth that history has settled beyond doubt, it is that religion **18** embraces an ever-diminishing part of social life.
Ibid., p. 49.

Social life derives from a dual source, the similarity of consciousness and **19** the social division of labour. In the first case the individual is socialized because, in the absence of any real individuality, he is united with others with whom he shares a common likeness, becoming part of the same collective type; in the second case, because, while having an appearance and personal activity which distinguish him from others, he is dependent on them to the extent that he is distinguished from them, and consequently upon the society which results from this combination.
Ibid., pp. 49–50.

The division of labour develops, therefore, to the extent that there are **20** more individuals in sufficient contact to be able to act and react upon one another. If we can agree to call this relation and the active commerce that results 'dynamic or moral density', it can be said that the progress of the division of labour is in direct ratio to the moral or dynamic density of society.
Ibid., pp. 50–1.

21 The division of labour can only be produced within a pre-existing society. That is to say, not merely must individuals be materially linked, but it is also necessary for there to be moral links between them ... Hence, the claim that the division of labour constitutes the fundamental fact of all social life is wrong.
Ibid., p. 53.

22 If the division of labour does not produce solidarity, it is because the relationships between the organs are not regulated, they are in a state of anomie.
Ibid., p. 56.

23 But it is not enough that rules exist, for sometimes these very rules are the cause of evil. This is what happens in class-wars. The institution of classes or castes constitutes one organization of the division of labour, one that is strictly regulated. Yet it is often a source of dissension. When the lower classes are not, or no longer satisfied with the role allotted to them through custom or law, they aspire to functions forbidden to them, and try to dispossess those who exercise these functions. From this arise civil wars, which are due to the way in which work is distributed.
Ibid., p. 56.

24 In order for the division of labour to engender solidarity, it is not, therefore, sufficient that each person has his task: this task must also suit him ... In effect, if the institution of classes or castes sometimes gives rise to painful wrangling, instead of producing solidarity, this is because the distribution of social functions on which the solidarity is based, does not correspond, or rather no longer responds to the distribution of talent.
Ibid., p. 56.

25 If one class in society is obliged to take any price for its services in order to survive, while another can abstain from such action thanks to the resources that it has at its disposal, which are not the result of any social superiority, the second has an unjust legal advantage over the first. In other words, there cannot be rich and poor from birth without there being unjust contracts.
Ibid., p. 57.

26 But if the division of labour produces solidarity, it is not only because it makes each individual an 'exchangist', as the economists say; it is because it creates between men a whole system of rights and duties which bind them together in an enduring way.
Ibid., p. 57.

27 But it is not enough that rules exist. They must also be just, and for that to be so, the external conditions for competition must be equal.
Ibid., p. 57.

Suicide

The term suicide is applied to every case of death which results directly or **28**
indirectly from a positive or negative act, carried out by the victim himself,
knowing that it will produce this result.
Suicide (first published in French in 1897), in Kenneth Thompson (ed. and trans.),
Readings from Émile Durkheim, London, Routledge, 1985, p. 95.

If, instead of seeing suicides only as isolated, individual events that need to **29**
be examined separately, one considers all suicides committed in a particular society during a specific time period as a whole, it is evident that the
total thus obtained is not simply a sum of independent units, a collective
total, but constitutes in itself a new fact *sui generis*, which has its own unity
and individuality, and therefore, its own pre-eminently social nature.
Ibid., p. 95.

Everywhere, without exception, Protestants evidence many more suicides **30**
than members of other denominations. The propensity of Jews to commit
suicide is always less than that of Protestants; in general terms, though to
a lesser degree, it is also lower than that of Catholics.
Ibid., p. 100.

If religion protects man against the desire to kill himself, it is not because it **31**
preaches respect for his person based on arguments *sui generis*, but because
it is a society. What constitutes this society is the existence of a certain number
of beliefs and practices common to all the faithful which are traditional and
therefore obligatory. The more numerous and strong these collective states
are, the more strongly integrated is the religious community, and the greater
its preservative value.
Ibid., p. 102.

In France, married but childless women commit suicide half again as often **32**
as unmarried women of the same age. We have already noted that generally
the wife benefits less from family life than the husband. Now we can see
the cause of this; taken by itself, conjugal life is harmful to the woman and
aggravates her tendency to suicide. If, nevertheless, most wives have
appeared to enjoy a favourable coefficient of preservation, this is because
childless households are the exception and consequently the presence of
children remedies and reduces the bad effects of marriage in most cases.
Ibid., p. 105.

Suicide varies inversely with the degree of integration of the social groups **33**
to which the individual belongs.
Ibid., p. 106.

So if we agree to call this state 'egoism', where the individual ego asserts itself **34**
to excess in the face of the social ego, and at its expense, we can call the
particular type of suicide that results from excessive individualism 'egoistic'.
Ibid., p. 106.

35 If, as we have just seen, excessive individualism leads to suicide, insufficient individualism produces the same effects. When man is detached from society, he can easily kill himself, and this is also the case when he is too strongly integrated in society.
Ibid., pp. 106–7.

36 Having designated as 'egoism' the condition in which the ego pursues its own life and is obedient only to itself, the designation 'altruism' adequately expresses the opposite condition in which the ego is not its own property. It is blended with something other than itself, and the goal of conduct is external to itself, that is, in one of the groups in which it participates. Thus we call the suicide caused by intense altruism 'altruistic suicide'.
Ibid., p. 107.

37 Human nature in itself cannot set variable limits to our needs. Consequently, in so far as it is left to the individual alone, these needs are unlimited. Without reference to any external regulating influence our capacity for sensation is a bottomless abyss that nothing can satisfy.
Ibid., p. 109.

38 Anomie, therefore, is a regular and specific factor in causing suicide in our modern societies. It is one of the sources feeding the annual totals. This is a new type that must be distinguished from the others. It differs from them in that it does not depend on the way in which individuals are attached to society, but on the way in which they are regulated by society. Egoistic suicide stems from the fact that men no longer see a reason for living; altruistic suicide comes from the fact that this reason appears to them to lie outside life itself; the third kind of suicide, whose existence we have just established, comes from the fact that their activity is unregulated and they suffer as a consequence. Because of its origin, we shall call this last type 'anomic suicide'.
Ibid., p. 112.

39 There is a type of suicide that is the opposite of anomic suicide, just as egoistic and altruistic suicide are opposites. This one results from excessive regulation; the type committed by people whose future is mercilessly blocked, whose passions are violently suppressed by an oppressive discipline . . . we might call this 'fatalistic suicide'.
Ibid., p. 114.

Religion and knowledge

40 There is no religion that is not a cosmology at the same time that it is a speculation upon divine things. If philosophy and the sciences were born of religion, it is because religion began by taking the place of science and philosophy.

The Elementary Forms of the Religious Life, trans. J. W. Swain, London, Allen & Unwin, 1915; New York, Free Press, 1965 (pbk edn), p. 21. First published in French in 1912.

At the roots of all our judgements there are a certain number of essential **41** ideas which dominate all our intellectual life; they are what philosophers since Aristotle have called the categories of the understanding: ideas of time, space, class, number, cause, substance, personality, etc. . . . Now when primitive religious beliefs are systematically analysed, the principal categories are naturally found. They are born in religion and of religion; they are the product of religious thought . . .

    . . . religion is something eminently social. Religious representations are collective representations which express collective realities; the rites are a manner of acting which take rise in the midst of the assembled groups and which are destined to excite, maintain or recreate certain mental states in these groups.
Ibid., p. 21–2.

We cannot conceive of time, except on condition of distinguishing its different **42** moments . . . The divisions into days, weeks, months, years, etc., correspond to the periodical recurrence of rites, feasts, and public ceremonies. A calendar expresses the rhythm of the collective activities, while at the same time its function is to assure their regularity . . . It is the same thing with space . . . There are societies in Australia and North America where space is conceived in the form of an immense circle, because the camp has a circular form; and this spatial circle is divided up exactly like the tribal circle, and is in its image.
Ibid., p. 22–4.

All known religious beliefs, whether simple or complex, present one common **43** characteristic: they presuppose classification of all things, real and ideal, of which men think, into two classes or opposed groups, generally designated by two distinct terms which are translated well enough by the words *profane* and *sacred*.
Ibid., p. 52.

A religion is a unified system of beliefs and practices relative to sacred things, **44** that is to say, things set apart and forbidden – beliefs and practices which unite into one single moral community called a Church, all those who adhere to them.
Ibid., p. 62.

We have shown how the clan, by the manner in which it acts upon its **45** members, awakens within them the idea of external forces which dominate them and exalt them; but we must still demand how it happens that these forces are thought of under the form of totems, that is to say, in the shape of an animal or plant. It is because the animal or plant has given its name to the clan and serves as its emblem.
Ibid., p. 251.

46 Before all else, it [religion] is a system of ideas with which the individuals represent to themselves the society of which they are members, and the obscure but intimate relations which they have with it.
Ibid., p. 257.

47 The practices of the cult, whatever they may be, are something more than movements without importance and gestures without efficiency. By the mere fact that their apparent function is to strengthen the bonds attaching the believer to his god, they at the same time really strengthen the bonds attaching the individual to the society of which he is a member, since the god is only a figurative expression of the society.
Ibid., pp. 257–8.

48 Religious force is only the sentiment inspired by the group in its members, but projected outside of the consciousnesses that experience them, and objectified. To be objectified, they are fixed upon some object which thus becomes sacred; but any object might fulfil this function.

... when a sacred thing is subdivided, each of its parts remains equal to the thing itself ... Since the part makes us think of the whole, it evokes the same sentiments as the whole. A mere fragment of the flag represents the fatherland just as well as the flag itself: so it is sacred in the same way and to the same degree.
Ibid., pp. 261–2.

49 Therefore it is necessary to avoid seeing in this theory of religion a simple restatement of historical materialism: that would be misunderstanding our thought to an extreme degree. In showing that religion is something essentially social, we do not mean to say that it confines itself to translating into another language the material forms of society and its immediate vital necessities.
Ibid., p. 471.

50 Thus there is something eternal in religion which is destined to survive all the particular symbols in which religious thought has successively enveloped itself. There can be no society which does not feel the need of upholding and reaffirming at regular intervals the collective sentiments and the collective ideas which make its unity and its personality.
Ibid., p. 475.

51 Not only is individualism not anarchical, but it henceforth is the only system of beliefs which can ensure the moral unity of the country. We often hear it said today that religion alone can produce this harmony. This proposition, which modern prophets believe they must develop in mystic tones, is essentially a simple truism about which everyone can agree. For we know today that a religion does not necessarily imply symbols and rites, properly speaking, or temples and priests. This whole exterior apparatus is only the superficial part. Essentially, it is nothing other than a body of collective beliefs and practices endowed with a certain authority. As soon as a goal is pursued by an entire people, it acquires, in consequence of this unanimous adherence, a sort of moral supremacy which raises it far above private aims and thus gives it a religious character. From another viewpoint, it is apparent that a society cannot be coherent if there does not exist among its members a certain intellectual and moral community. However, after recalling once again this sociological truism, we have not gotten very far. For if it is true that religion is, in a sense, indispensable, it is no less certain that religions change – that the religion of yesterday could not be the religion of tomorrow. What is important is to say what the religion of today should be. Now everything converges in the belief that this religion of humanity, of which the individualistic ethic is the rational expression, is the only one possible.

'Individualism and the Intellectuals' (first published in French in 1898), trans. M. Traugott, in *Émile Durkheim on Morality and Society*, ed. Robert N. Bellah, Chicago and London, University of Chicago Press, 1973, pp. 50–1.

The first logical categories were social categories; the first classes of things **52** were classes of men, into which these things were integrated. It was because men were grouped, and thought of themselves in the form of groups, that in their ideas they grouped other things, and in the beginning the two modes of groupings were merged to the point of being indistinct.

Émile Durkheim and Marcel Mauss, *Primitive Classification*, trans. R. Needham, London, Cohen & West, 1963. First published in French in 1903.

Politics

Socialist theory, in fact, like classical economic theory holds that economic **53** life is equipped to organize itself and to function in an orderly way and in harmony, without any moral authority intervening; this, however, depends on a radical change in the laws of property, so that things cease to be in the exclusive ownership of individuals or families and instead, are transferred to the hands of the society. Once this were done, the State would do no more than keep accurate statistics of the wealth produced over given periods and distribute this wealth amongst the associate members according to an agreed formula. Now, both these theories do no more than raise a *de facto* state of affairs which is unhealthy, to the level of a *de jure* state of affairs. It is true, indeed, that economic life has this character at the present day, but it is impossible for it to preserve this, even at the price of a thoroughgoing change in the structure of property. It is not possible for a social function to exist without moral discipline. Otherwise, nothing remains but individual appetites, and since they are by nature boundless and insatiable, if there is nothing to control them they will not be able to control themselves.

Professional Ethics and Civic Morals, trans. C. Brookfield, London, Routledge &

Kegan Paul, 1957, p. 10. First published posthumously in French as *Leçons de sociologie* in 1950.

54 Science is a study bearing on a delimited portion of reality which it aims at knowing and, if possible, understanding. To describe and explain what is and what has been – this is its only job. Speculation about the future is not its affair, although it may seek as its final objective to render this possible. Socialism, on the contrary, is entirely oriented towards the future. It is above all a plan for the reconstruction of societies, a program for a collective life which does not exist as yet or in the way it is dreamed of, and which is proposed to men as worthy of their preference. It is an ideal. It concerns itself much less with what is or was than what ought to be. Undoubtedly, even under its most utopian forms it never disdained the support of facts, and has even, in more recent times, increasingly affected a certain scientific turn of phrase. It is indisputable that it has rendered social science more services perhaps than it received from it. For it has aroused reflection, it has stimulated scientific activity, it has instigated research, posed problems, so that in more than one way its history blends with the very history of sociology. Yet, how can one fail to note the enormous disparity between the rare and meager data it borrows from science and the extent of the practical conclusions that it draws, and which are, nevertheless, the heart of the system.
Socialism and Saint-Simon, trans. C. Sattler, London, Collier-Macmillan, 1962, p. 39. First published posthumously in French as *Le Socialisme* in 1928.

55 The only attitude that science permits in the face of these problems is reservation and circumspection, and socialism can hardly maintain this without lying to itself. And, in fact, socialism has not maintained this attitude. Not even the strongest work – the most systematic, the richest in ideas – that this school has produced: Marx's *Capital*. What statistical data, what historical comparisons, what studies would be indispensable to solve any of the innumerable questions that are dealt with there!
Ibid., pp. 40–1.

Moral education

56 Education must help the child understand at an early point that, beyond certain contrived boundaries that constitute the historical framework of justice, there are limits based on the nature of things, that is to say, in the nature of each of us. This has nothing to do with insidiously inculcating a spirit of resignation in the child, or curbing his legitimate ambitions; or preventing him from seeing the conditions existing around him. Such proposals would contradict the very principles of our social system. But he must be made to understand that the way to be happy is to set proximate and realizable goals, corresponding to the nature of each person and not attempt to reach objectives by straining neurotically and unhappily toward infinitely distant and consequently inaccessible goals.

Moral Education, trans. E. K. Wilson and H. Schnurer, New York, Free Press, 1961, p. 49. First published posthumously in French in 1925.

FOUCAULT, MICHEL (1926–84)

Knowledge

This book first arose out of a passage in Borges, out of the laughter that **1** shattered as I read the passage, all the familiar landmarks of thought – *our* thought, the thought that bears the stamp of our age and our geography – breaking up all the ordered surfaces and all the planes with which we are accustomed to tame the wild profusion of existing things and continuing long afterwards to disturb and threaten with collapse our age-old distinction between the Same and the Other. This passage quotes 'a certain Chinese encyclopaedia' in which it is written that 'animals are divided into: (a) belonging to the Emperor, (b) embalmed, (c) tame, (d) sucking pigs, (e) sirens, (f) fabulous, (g) stray dogs, (h) included in the present classification, (i) frenzied, (j) innumerable, (k) drawn with a very fine camelhair brush, (l) et cetera, (m) having just broken the water pitcher, (n) that from a very long way off look like flies'. In the wonderment of this taxonomy, the thing we apprehend in one great leap, the thing that, by means of the fable, is demonstrated as the exotic charm of another system of thought, is the limitation of our own, the stark impossibility of thinking *that*. But what is it impossible to think, and what kind of impossibility are we faced with here?

The Order of Things, trans. A. Sheridan, London, Tavistock, and New York, Pantheon, 1970, p. xv. First published in French as *Les mots et les choses* in 1966.

I am not concerned, therefore, to describe the progress of knowledge **2** towards an objectivity in which today's science can finally be recognized; what I am attempting to bring to light is the epistemological field, the *episteme* in which knowledge, apart from all criteria having reference to its rational value or to its objective forms, grounds its positivity and thereby manifests a history which is not that of its growing perfection, but rather that of its conditions of possibility; in this account, what should appear are those configurations within the *space* of knowledge which have given rise to the diverse forms of empirical science. Such an enterprise is not so much a history, in the traditional meaning of that word, as an 'archaeology'.

Ibid., p. xxii.

What I would like to do, however, is to reveal a *positive unconscious* of **3** knowledge: a level that eludes the consciousness of the scientist and yet is part of scientific discourse, instead of disputing its validity and seeking to diminish its scientific nature.

Ibid., p. xi.

4   Marxism exists in the nineteenth-century thought like a fish in water: that is, it is unable to breathe anywhere else. Though it is in opposition to the 'bourgeois' theories of economics and though this opposition leads it to use the project of a radical reversal of History as a weapon against them, that conflict and that project nevertheless have as their condition of possibility, not the reworking of all History, but an event that archaeology can situate with precision and that prescribes simultaneously, and according to the same mode, both nineteenth-century bourgeois economics and nineteenth-century revolutionary economics. The controversies may have stirred up a few waves and caused a few surface ripples; but they are no more than storms in a children's paddling pool.
Ibid., pp. 261–2.

5   In other words, the archaeological description of discourses is deployed in the dimension of a general history; it seeks to discover that whole domain of institutions, economic processes and social relations on which a discursive formation can be articulated; it tries to show how the autonomy of discourse and its specificity nevertheless do not give it the status of pure ideality and total historical independence; what it wishes to uncover is the particular level in which history can give place to definite types of discourse, which have their own types of historicity and which are related to a whole set of various historicities.
The Archaeology of Knowledge, trans. A. Sheridan, London, Tavistock, and New York, Pantheon, 1972, pp. 163–5. First published in French in 1969.

Madness and the asylum

6   The asylum was substituted for the lazar house, in the geography of haunted places as in the landscape of the moral universe. The old rites of excommunication were revived, but in the world of production and commerce . . . It is not immaterial that madmen were included in the proscription of idleness. From its origin, they would have their place beside the poor, deserving or not, and the idle, voluntary or not. Like them, they would be subject to the rules of forced labour . . . In the workshops in which they were interned, they distinguished themselves by their inability to work and to follow the rhythms of collective life. The necessity, discovered in the eighteenth century, to provide a special regime for the insane, and the great crisis of confinement that shortly preceded the Revolution, are linked to the experience of madness available in the universal necessity of labour. Men did not wait until the seventeenth century to 'shut up' the mad, but it was in this period that they began to 'confine' or 'intern' them, along with an entire population with whom their kinship was recognized. Until the Renaissance, the sensibility of madness was linked to the presence of imaginary transcendences. In the Classical age, for the first time, madness was perceived

146

through a condemnation of idleness and in a social immanence guaranteed by the community of labour. This community acquired an ethical power of segregation, which permitted it to eject, as into another world, all forms of social uselessness. It was in this *other world*, encircled by the sacred powers of labour, that madness would assume the status we now attribute to it. If there is, in Classical madness, something which refers elsewhere, and to *other things*, it is no longer because the madman comes from the world of the irrational and bears its stigmata; rather, it is because he crosses the frontiers of bourgeois order of his own accord and alienates himself outside the sacred limits of its ethic.

Madness and Civilization, trans. R. Howard, New York, Pantheon, 1965; London, Tavistock, 1967, pp. 57–8. First published in French in 1972 as *Histoire de la folie*.

Power

Power relations (with the struggles that traverse them or the institutions that   **7**
maintain them) do not only play with respect to knowledge a facilitating or obstructive role; they are not content merely to encourage or to stimulate it, to distort or to limit it; power and knowledge are not linked together solely by the play of interests or ideologies; the problem is not therefore that of determining how power subjugates knowledge and makes it serve its ends, or how it imprints its mark on knowledge, imposes on it ideological content and limits. No body of knowledge can be formed without a system of communications, records, accumulation and displacement which is in itself a form of power and which is linked, in its existence and functioning, to the other forms of power. Conversely, no power can be exercised without the extraction, appropriation, distribution or retention of knowledge. On this level, there is not knowledge on the one side and society on the other, or science and the state, but only the fundamental forms of knowledge/ power . . .

'Théories et institutions pénales', *Annuaire du Collège de France, 1971–72*, Paris, 1971; in *Michel Foucault: The Will to Truth*, trans. and ed. A. Sheridan, London, Tavistock, 1980, p. 131.

The judges of normality are present everywhere. We are in the society   **8**
of the teacher-judge, the doctor-judge, the educator-judge, the 'social-worker'-judge; it is on them that the universal reign of the normative is based; and each individual, wherever he may find himself, subjects to it his body, his gestures, his behaviour, his aptitudes, his achievements. The carceral network, in its compact or disseminated forms, with its systems of insertion, distribution, surveillance, observation, has been the greatest support, in modern society, of the normalizing power. The carceral texture of society assures both the real capture of the body and its perpetual observation; it is, by its very nature, the apparatus of punishment that

conforms most completely to the new economy of power and the instrument for the formation of knowledge that this very economy needs. Its panoptic functioning enables it to play this double role. By virtue of its methods of fixing, dividing, recording, it has been one of the simplest, crudest, also most concrete, but perhaps most indispensable conditions for the developments of this immense activity of examination that has objectified human behaviour . . . I am not saying that the human sciences emerged from the prison. But, if they have been able to be formed and to produce so many profound changes in the episteme, it is because they have been conveyed by a specific and new modality of power: a certain policy of the body, a certain way of rendering the accumulation of men docile and useful. This policy required the involvement of definite relations of knowledge in relations of power; it called for a technique of overlapping subjection and objectification; it brought with it new procedures of individualization. The carceral network constituted one of the armatures of this power-knowledge that has made the human sciences historically possible. Knowable man (soul, individuality, consciousness, conduct, whatever it is called) is the object-effect of this analytical investment, of this domination-observation.

Discipline and Punish, trans. A. Sheridan, New York, Pantheon, and London, Allen Lane, 1977, pp. 304–5. First published in French as *Surveiller et punir* in 1975.

9　Power is everywhere: not because it embraces everything, but because it comes from everywhere . . . One should probably be a nominalist in this matter: power is not an institution, nor a structure, nor a possession. It is the name we give to a complex strategic situation in a particular society.

The History of Sexuality, trans. R. Hurley, vol. 1, New York, Pantheon, 1978; London, Allen Lane, 1979, p. 93. First published in French as *La Volonté de savoir* in 1976.

10　When I think of the mechanics of power, I think of its capillary form of existence, of the extent to which power seeps into the very grain of individuals, reaches right into their bodies, permeates their gestures, their posture, what they say, how they learn to live and work with other people.

M. Foucault and J.-L. Brochier, 'Entretien sur la prison: le livre et sa méthode' [1975]; trans. C. Gordon, 'Prison Talk', *Radical Philosophy*, no. 16, Spring 1977, p. 28.

11　We must cease at once and for all to describe the effects of power in negative terms: it 'excludes', it 'represses', it 'censors', it 'abstracts', it 'masks', it 'conceals'. In fact power produces; it produces reality; it produces domains of objects and rituals of truth. The individual and the knowledge that may be gained of him belong to this production.

Discipline and Punish, trans. A. Sheridan, New York, Pantheon, and London, Allen Lane, 1977, p. 194. First published in French as *Surveiller et punir* in 1975.

Power/knowledge

Truth isn't outside power, or lacking in power . . . Each society has its regime **12** of truth, its 'general politics' of truth: that is, the types of discourse which it accepts and makes function as true; the mechanisms and instances which enable one to distinguish 'true' and 'false' statements; the means by which each is sanctioned; and the techniques and procedures accorded value in the acquisition of truth; the status of those who are charged with saying what counts as true.

Power/Knowledge: Selected Interviews and Other Writings, 1972–1977, New York, Pantheon, 1980, p. 131.

Sexuality

Sex was driven out of hiding and forced to lead a discursive existence. From **13** the singular imperialism that compels everyone to transform his sexuality into a permanent discourse, to the multiple mechanisms which, in the areas of economy, pedagogy, medicine and justice, incite, extract, distribute and institutionalize sexual discourse, our civilization has demanded and organized an immense prolixity. Perhaps no other type of society has ever accumulated – and in such a relatively short time – such a quantity of discourse on sex. It may well be that we talk about sex more than anything else . . . that where sex is concerned, the most long-winded, the most impatient of societies is our own.

The History of Sexuality, trans. R. Hurley, New York, Pantheon, 1978; London, Allen Lane, 1979, p. 33. First published in French as *La Volonté de savoir* in 1976.

The confession has spread its effects far and wide. It plays a part in law, **14** medicine, education, family relationships and sexual relations, in ordinary, everyday matters and in the most solemn rites; one confesses one's crimes, one confesses one's sins, one confesses one's thoughts and desires, one confesses to one's past and to one's dreams, one confesses to one's child-hood, one confesses one's illnesses and troubles; one sets about telling, with the greatest precision, what is most difficult to tell; one confesses in public and in private, to one's parents, to one's teachers, to one's doctor, to those one loves; one confesses to oneself, in pleasure and in pain, things that it would be impossible to tell anyone else, the things people write books about. One confesses – or one is forced to confess . . . Western man has become a confessing animal.

Ibid., p. 59.

Sexuality is the name that may be given to a set of interlocking historical **15** mechanisms; not some reality below the surface on which it is difficult to get a hold, but a great surface network on which the stimulation of bodies, the intensification of pleasures, the incitement to discourse, the formation of sciences, the strengthening of controls and resistances are linked together in accordance with a few great strategies of knowledge and power. Ibid., pp. 105–6.

16 Sexual behaviour is not, as is too often assumed, a superimposition of, on the one hand, desires which derive from natural instincts, and, on the other hand, of permissive or restrictive laws which tell us what we should or shouldn't do. Sexual behaviour is more than that. It is also the consciousness one has of what one is doing, what one makes of the experience, and the value one attaches to it.
'An Interview with Michel Foucault', in *Salmagundi*, 1982–3, nos. 58–61, pp. 10–11.

FREUD, SIGMUND (1856–1939)

The psychical apparatus and the theory of instincts

1 We have arrived at our knowledge of this psychical apparatus by studying the individual development of human beings. To the oldest of these psychical provinces or agencies we give the name of *id*. It contains everything that is inherited, that is present at birth, that is laid down in the constitution – above all, therefore, the instincts, which originate from the somatic organization and which find a first psychical expression here (in the id) in forms unknown to us.

Under the influence of the real external world around us, one portion of the id has undergone a special development. From what was originally a cortical layer, equipped with the organs for receiving stimuli and with arrangements for acting as a protective shield against stimuli, a special organization has arisen which henceforward acts as an intermediary between the id and the external world. To this region of our mind we have given the name of *ego*.

Here are the principal characteristics of the ego. In consequence of the pre-established connection between sense perception and muscular action, the ego has voluntary movement at its command. It has the task of self-preservation. As regards external events, it performs that task by becoming aware of stimuli, by storing up experiences about them (in the memory), by avoiding excessively strong stimuli (through flight), by dealing with moderate stimuli (through adaptation) and finally by learning to bring expedient changes in the external world to its own advantage (through activity). As regards internal events, in relation to the id, it performs that task by gaining control over the demands of the instincts, by deciding whether they are to be allowed satisfaction, by postponing their satisfaction to times and circumstances favourable in the external world or by suppressing their excitations entirely. It is guided in its activity by consideration of the tensions produced by the stimuli, whether these tensions are present in it or introduced into it. The raising of these tensions is in general felt as *unpleasure* and their lowering as *pleasure*. It is probable, however, that what is felt as pleasure or unpleasure is not the *absolute* height of this tension but something in the rhythm of the changes in them. The ego strives after pleasure and seeks to avoid unpleasure. An increase in unpleasure that is expected and foreseen is met by a signal of anxiety; the occasion of such an increase, whether it threatens from without or within, is known as a danger. From time to time the ego gives up its connection with the external world and withdraws into the state of sleep, in which it makes far-reaching changes in its organization. It is to be inferred from the state of sleep that this organization consists in a particular distribution of mental energy.

The long period of childhood, during which the growing human being lives in dependence on his parents, leaves behind it as a precipitate the formation in his ego of a special agency in which this parental influence is prolonged. It has received the name of *super-ego*. In so far as this super-ego is differentiated from the ego or is opposed to it, it constitutes a third power which the ego must take into account.

An action by the ego is as it should be if it satisfies simultaneously the demands of the id, of the super-ego and of reality – that is to say, if it is able to reconcile their demands with one another. The details of the relation between the ego and the super-ego become completely intelligible when they are traced back to the child's attitude to its parents. This parental influence of course includes in its operation not only the personalities of the actual parents but also the family, racial and national traditions handed on through them, as well as the demands of the immediate social *milieu* which they represent. In the same way, the super-ego, in the course of an individual's development, receives contributions from later successors and substitutes of his parents, such as teachers and models in public life of admired social ideals. It will be observed that, for all their fundamental difference, the id and the super-ego have one thing in common: they represent the influence of the past – the id the influence of heredity, the super-ego the influence, essentially, of what is taken over from other people – whereas the ego is principally determined by the individual's own experience, that is by accidental and contemporary events . . .

An Outline of Psycho-Analysis, ed. and trans. J. Strachey, standard edn, vol. 23, New York, Norton, 1949, pp. 13–21; London, Hogarth Press, rev. edn 1969, pp. 2–4. (This extract and the next are from one of Freud's last statements of his psychoanalytic theory.)

The theory of the instincts

After long hesitancies and vacillations we have decided to assume the **2** existence of only two basic instincts, *Eros* and the *destructive instinct*. (The contrast between the instincts of self-preservation and the preservation of the species, as well as the contrast between ego-love and object-love, fall within Eros.) The aim of the first of these basic instincts is to establish ever greater unities and to preserve them thus – in short, to bind together; the aim of the second is, on the contrary, to undo connections and to destroy things. In the case of the destructive instinct we may suppose that its final aim is to lead what is living into an inorganic state. For this reason we also call it the *death instinct*.

Ibid., p. 25 and 1949 edn, p. 21.

Dream-work and interpretation

3 We find our way to the understanding ('interpretation') of a dream by assuming that what we recollect as the dream after we have woken up is not the true dream-process but only a *facade* behind which that process lies concealed. Here we have our distinction between the *manifest* content of a dream and the *latent* dream-thoughts. The process which produces the former out of the latter is described as the *dream-work*. The study of the dream-work teaches us by an excellent example the way in which unconscious material from the id (originally unconscious and repressed unconscious alike) forces its way into the ego, becomes preconscious and, as a result of the ego's opposition, undergoes the changes which we know as *dream-distortion*. There are no features of a dream which cannot be explained in this way.

It is best to begin by pointing out that the formation of a dream can be provoked in two different ways. Either, on the one hand, an instinctual impulse which is ordinarily suppressed (an unconscious wish) finds enough strength during sleep to make itself felt by the ego, or, on the other hand, an urge left over from waking life, a preconscious train of thought with all the conflicting impulses attached to it, finds reinforcement during sleep from an unconscious element. In short, dreams may arise either from the id or from the ego. The mechanism of dream-formation is in both cases the same and so also is the necessary dynamic precondition. The ego gives evidence of its original derivation from the id by occasionally ceasing its functions and allowing a reversion to an earlier state of things. This is logically brought about by its breaking off its relations with the external world and withdrawing its cathexes from the sense organs. We are justified in saying that there arises at birth an instinct to return to the intra-uterine life that has been abandoned – an instinct to sleep. Sleep is a return of this kind to the womb. Since the waking ego governs motility, that function is paralysed in sleep, and accordingly a good part of the inhibitions imposed on the unconscious id become superfluous. The withdrawal or reduction of these 'anticathexes' thus allows the id what is now a harmless amount of liberty.

The evidence of the share taken by the unconscious id in the formation of dreams is abundant and convincing. (a) Memory is far more comprehensive in dreams than in waking life. Dreams bring up recollections which the dreamer had forgotten, which are inaccessible to him when he is awake. (b) Dreams make an unrestricted use of linguistic symbols, the meaning of which is for the most part unknown to the dreamer. Our experience, however, enables us to confirm their sense. They probably originate from earlier phases in the development of speech. (c) Memory very often reproduces in dreams impressions from the dreamer's early childhood of which we can definitely assert not only that they had been forgotten but that they had become unconscious owing to repression. That explains the help – usually indispensable – given us by dreams in the attempts we make during the analytic treatment of neuroses to reconstruct the dreamer's early life. (d) Furthermore, dreams bring to light material which cannot have originated either from the dreamer's adult life or from his forgotten childhood. We are obliged to regard it as part of the *archaic heritage* which a child brings with him into the world, before any experience of his own, influenced by the experiences of his ancestors. We find the counterpart of this phylogenetic material in the earliest human legends and in surviving customs. Thus dreams constitute a source of human prehistory which is not to be despised.

Ibid., pp. 22–4 and 1949 edn, pp. 38–9.

Oedipus, the child

In my experience, which is already extensive, the chief part in the mental lives **4** of all children who later become psychoneurotics is played by their parents. Being in love with the one parent and hating the other are among the essential constituents of the stock of psychical impulses which is formed at that time and which is of such importance in determining the symptoms of the later neurosis. It is not my belief, however, that psychoneurotics differ sharply in this respect from other human beings who remain normal – that they are able, that is, to create something absolutely new and peculiar to themselves. It is far more probable – and this is confirmed by occasional observations on normal children – that they are only distinguished by exhibiting on a magnified scale feelings of love and hatred to their parents which occur less obviously and less intensely in the minds of most children . . .

It is the fate of all of us, perhaps, to direct our first sexual impulse towards our mother and our first hatred and our first murderous wish against our father. Our dreams convince us that this is so. King Oedipus, who slew his father Laïus and married his mother Jocasta, merely shows us the fulfilment of our own childhood wishes. But, more fortunate than he, we have meanwhile succeeded, in so far as we have not become psychoneurotics, in detaching our sexual impulses from our mothers and in forgetting our jealousy of our fathers.

The Interpretation of Dreams, ed. and trans. J. Strachey, New York, Avon Books, 1965, pp. 294–301. First published in German in 1900.

The return of the repressed in social life

5   As a consequence of a certain experience there arises an instinctual demand which claims satisfaction. The Ego forgoes this satisfaction, either because it is paralysed by the excessiveness of the demand or because it recognizes in it a danger. The first of these reasons is the original one; both end in the avoidance of a dangerous situation. The Ego guards against this danger by repression. The excitation becomes inhibited in one way or another; the incitement, with the observations and perceptions belonging to it, is forgotten. This, however, does not bring the process to an end; either the instinct has kept its strength, or it will regain it, or it is reawakened by a new situation. It renews its claim and – since the way to normal satisfaction is barred by what we may call the scar tissue of repression – it gains at some weak point new access to a so-called substitutive satisfaction which now appears as a symptom, without the acquiescence and also without the comprehension of the Ego. All phenomena of symptom-formation can be fairly described as 'the return of the repressed'. The distinctive character of them, however, lies in the extensive distortion the returning elements have undergone, compared with their original form . . .

The psychoanalyses of individuals have taught us that their earliest impressions, received at a time when they were hardly able to talk, manifest themselves later in an obsessive fashion, although these impressions themselves are not consciously remembered. We feel that the same must hold good for the earliest experiences of mankind. One result of this is the emergence of the conception of one great God. It must be recognized as a memory – a distorted one, it is true, but nevertheless a memory. It has an obsessive quality; it simply must be believed. As far as its distortion goes, it must be called a delusion; in so far as it brings to light something from the past, it must be called truth. The psychiatric delusion also contains a particle of truth; the patient's conviction issues from this and extends to the whole delusional fabrication surrounding it.

. . . In 1912 I tried in my book *Totem and Taboo* to reconstruct the ancient situation from which all these effects issued. In that book I made use of certain theoretical reflections of Charles Darwin, J. J. Atkinson, and especially Robertson Smith, and combined them with findings and suggestions from psychoanalytic practice. From Darwin I borrowed the hypothesis that men originally lived in small hordes; each of the hordes stood under the rule of an older male, who governed by brute force, appropriated all the females, and belaboured or killed all the young males, including his own sons. From Atkinson I received the suggestion that this patriarchal system came to an end through the rebellion of the sons, who united against the father, overpowered him, and together consumed his body. Following Robertson Smith's totem theory, I suggested that this horde, previously ruled by the father, was followed by a totemistic brother clan. In order to be able to live in peace with one another the victorious brothers renounced the women for whose sake they had killed the father, and agreed to practice exogamy. The power of the father was broken and the families were regulated by matriarchy. The ambivalence of the sons toward the father remained in force during the whole further development. Instead of the father a certain animal was declared the totem; it stood for their ancestor and protecting spirit, and no one was allowed to hurt or kill it. Once a year, however, the whole clan assembled for a feast at which the otherwise revered totem was torn to pieces and eaten. No one was permitted to abstain from this feast; it was the solemn repetition of the father-murder, in which social order, moral laws, and religion had had their beginnings. The correspondence of the totem feast (according to Robertson Smith's description) with the Christian Communion has struck many authors before me.

Moses and Monotheism, trans. K. Jones, New York, Vintage, 1939, pp. 160–9. First published in German in 1937–9.

Civilization and its discontents

The analogy between the process of civilization and the path of individual **6** development may be extended in an important respect. It can be asserted that the community, too, evolves a super-ego under whose influence cultural development proceeds . . . The super-ego of an epoch of civilization has an origin similar to that of an individual. It is based on the impression left behind by the personalities of great leaders – men of overwhelming force of mind or men in whom one of the human impulses has found its strongest and purest, and therefore often its most one-sided expression. In many instances the analogy goes still further, in that during their lifetime these figures were – often enough, if not always – mocked and maltreated by others and even despatched in a cruel fashion. In the same way, indeed, the primal father did not attain divinity until long after he met his death by violence. The most arresting example of this fateful conjunction is to be seen in the figure of Jesus Christ – if, indeed, that figure is not part of mythology, which called it into being from an obscure memory of that primal event. Another point of agreement between the cultural and the individual super-ego is that the former, just like the latter, sets up strict ideal demands, disobedience to which is visited with 'fear of conscience'. Here indeed, we come across the remarkable circumstance that the mental processes concerned are actually more familiar to us and more accessible to consciousness as they are seen in the group than they can be in the individual man . . .

The cultural super-ego has developed its ideals and set up its demands. Among the latter, those which deal with the relations of human beings to one another are comprised under the heading of ethics. People have at all times set the greatest value on ethics, as though they expected that it in particular would produce especially important results. And it does in fact deal with a subject which can easily be recognized as the sorest spot in every civilization. Ethics is thus to be regarded as a therapeutic attempt – as an endeavour to achieve, by means of a command of the super-ego, something which has so far not been achieved by means of any other cultural activities. As we already know, the problem before us is how to get rid of the greatest hindrance to civilization – namely, the constitutional inclination of human beings to be aggressive to one another; and for that very reason we are especially interested in what is probably the most recent of the cultural commands of the super-ego, the commandment to love one's neighbour as oneself. In our research into, and therapy of, a neurosis, we are led to make two reproaches against the super-ego of the individual. In the severity of its commands and prohibitions it troubles itself too little about the happiness of the ego, in that it takes insufficient account of the resistances against obeying them – of the instinctual strength of the id (in the first place), and of the difficulties presented by the real external environment (in the second). Consequently we are often obliged, for therapeutic purposes, to oppose the super-ego, and we endeavour to lower its demands. Exactly the same objections can be made against the ethical demands of the cultural super-ego . . .

If the development of civilization has such a far-reaching similarity to the development of the individual and if it employs the same methods, may we not be justified in reaching the diagnosis that, under the influence of cultural urges, some civilizations, or some epochs of civilization – possibly the whole of mankind – have become 'neurotic'?

Civilization and Its Discontents, ed. and trans. J. Strachey, New York, Norton, 1961, pp. 88–92; London, Hogarth Press, 1969, pp. 78–81. First published in German in 1930.

GARFINKEL, HAROLD (1917–)

1   In doing sociology, lay and professional, every reference to the 'real world', even where the reference is to physical or biological events, is a reference to the organized activities of everyday life. Thereby, in contrast to certain versions of Durkheim that teach that the objective reality of social facts is sociology's fundamental principle, the lesson is taken instead, and used as a study policy, that the objective reality of social facts as an ongoing accomplishment of the concerted activities of daily life, with the ordinary, artful ways of that accomplishment being by members known, used, and taken for granted, is, for members doing sociology, a fundamental phenomenon. Because, and in the ways it is practical sociology's fundamental phenomenon, it is the prevailing topic of ethnomethodological study. Ethnomethodological studies analyze everyday activities as members' methods for making those same activities visibly-rational-and-reportable-for-all-practical-purposes, i.e., 'accountable', as organizations of commonplace everyday activities. The reflexivity of that phenomenon is a singular feature of practical actions, of practical circumstances, of common sense knowledge of social structures, and of practical sociological reasoning. By permitting us to locate and examine their occurrence the reflexivity of that phenomenon establishes their study.

Studies in Ethnomethodology, Englewood Cliffs, New Jersey, Prentice-Hall, 1967, p. vii.

Procedurally it is my preference to start with familiar scenes and ask what **2** can be done to make trouble. The operations that one would have to perform in order to multiply the senseless features of perceived environments; to produce and sustain bewilderment, consternation, and confusion; to produce the socially structured affects of anxiety, shame, guilt, and indignation; and to produce disorganized interaction should tell us something about how the structures of everyday activities are ordinarily and routinely produced and maintained.

Ibid., pp. 37–8.

GEERTZ, CLIFFORD (1926–)

Ethnography and thick description

In anthropology, or anyway social anthropology, what the practitioners do **1** is ethnography. And it is understanding what ethnography is, or more exactly *what doing ethnography is*, that a start can be made toward grasping what anthropological analysis amounts to as a form of knowledge. This, it must immediately be said, is not a matter of methods. From one point of view, that of the textbook, doing ethnography is establishing rapport, selecting informants, transcribing texts, taking genealogies, mapping fields, keeping a diary, and so on. But it is not these things, techniques and received procedures, that define the enterprise. What defines it is the kind of intellectual effort it is: an elaborate venture in, to borrow a notion from Gilbert Ryle, 'thick description'.

. . . Consider, he says, two boys rapidly contracting the eyelids of their right eyes. In one, this is an involuntary twitch; in the other, a conspiratorial signal to a friend. The two movements are, as movements, identical; from an I-am-a-camera, 'phenomenalistic' observation of them alone, one could not tell which was twitch or wink. Yet the difference, however unphotographable, between a twitch and a wink is vast; as anyone unfortunate enough to have had the first taken for the second knows. The winker is communicating, and indeed communicating in a quite precise and special way: (1) deliberately, (2) to someone in particular, (3) to impart a particular

157

message, (4) according to a socially established code, and (5) without cognizance of the rest of the company. As Ryle points out, the winker has not done two things, contracted his eyelids and winked, while the twitcher has done only one, contracted his eyelids. Contracting your eyelids on purpose when there exists a public code in which so doing counts as a conspiratorial signal is winking. That's all there is to it: a speck of behavior, a fleck of culture, and – *voilà!* – a gesture ...

But the point is that between what Ryle calls the 'thin description' of what the rehearser (parodist, winker, twitcher ...) is doing ('rapidly contracting his right eyelids') and the 'thick description' of what he is doing ('practicing a burlesque of a friend faking a wink to deceive an innocent into thinking a conspiracy is in motion') lies the object of ethnography: a stratified hierarchy of meaningful structures in terms of which twitches, winks, fake-winks, parodies, rehearsals of parodies are produced, perceived, and interpreted, and without which they would not (not even the zero-form twitches, which, as a cultural category, are as much nonwinks as winks are nontwitches) in fact exist, no matter what anyone did or didn't do with his eyelids ...

Doing ethnography is like trying to read (in the sense of 'construct a reading of') a manuscript – foreign, faded, full of ellipses, incoherencies, suspicious emendations, and tendentious commentaries, but written not in conventionalized graphs of sound but in transient examples of shaped behavior.

'Thick Description: Toward an Interpretive Theory of Culture', in C. Geertz, *The Interpretation of Cultures*, New York, Basic Books, 1973; London, Hutchinson, 1975, pp. 5–10.

Culture as control mechanism

2 The establishment of a common language in the social sciences is not a matter of mere coordination of terminologies or, worse yet, of coining artificial new ones; nor is it a matter of imposing a single set of categories upon the area as a whole. It is a matter of integrating different types of theories and concepts in such a way that one can formulate meaningful propositions embodying findings now sequestered in separate fields of study.

In attempting to launch such an integration from the anthropological side and to reach, thereby, a more exact image of man, I want to propose two ideas. The first of these is that culture is best seen not as complexes of concrete behavior patterns – customs, usages, traditions, habit clusters – as has, by and large, been the case up to now, but as a set of control mechanisms – plans, recipes, rules, instructions (what computer engineers call 'programs') – for the governing of behavior. The second idea is that man is precisely the animal most desperately dependent upon such extragenetic, outside-the-skin control mechanisms, such cultural programs, for ordering his behavior . . .

The 'control mechanism' view of culture begins with the assumption that human thought is basically both social and public – that its natural habitat is the house yard, the marketplace, and the town square. Thinking consists not of 'happenings in the head' (though happenings there and elsewhere are necessary for it to occur) but of a traffic in what have been called, by G. H. Mead and others, significant symbols – anything, in fact, that is disengaged from its mere actuality and used to impose meaning upon experience. From the point of view of any particular individual, such symbols are largely given.

'The Impact of the Concept of Culture on the Concept of Man', in J. Platt (ed.), *New Views of the Nature of Man*, Chicago, University of Chicago Press, 1966, pp. 93–118.

Religion

As we are to deal with meaning, let us begin with a paradigm: viz., that **3** sacred symbols function to synthesize a people's ethos – the tone, character, and quality of their life, its moral and aesthetic style and mood – and their world view – the picture they have of the way things in sheer actuality are, their most comprehensive ideas of order. In religious belief and practice a group's ethos is rendered intellectually reasonable by being shown to represent a way of life ideally adapted to the actual state of affairs the world view describes, while the world view is rendered emotionally convincing by being presented as an image of an actual state of affairs peculiarly well-arranged to accommodate such a way of life. This confrontation and mutual confirmation has two fundamental effects. On the one hand, it objectivizes moral and aesthetic preferences by depicting them as the imposed conditions of life implicit in a world with a particular structure, as mere common sense given the unalterable shape of reality. On the other, it supports these received beliefs about the world's body by invoking deeply felt moral and aesthetic sentiments as experiential evidence for their truth. Religious symbols formulate a basic congruence between a particular style of life and a specific (if, most often, implicit) metaphysic, and in so doing sustain each with the borrowed authority of the other.

'Religion as a Cultural System', in M. Banton (ed.), *Anthropological Approaches to the Study of Religion*, London, Tavistock, 1966. Extract in R. Bocock and K. Thompson (eds), *Religion and Ideology*, Manchester, Manchester University Press, 1985, p. 67.

GIDDENS, ANTHONY (1938–)

Here are some new 'rules of sociological method' . . . Section A concerns **1** the 'subject-matter of sociology': the production and reproduction of society; Section B, the boundaries of agency, and the modes in which processes of production and reproduction may be examined; Section C, the modes in which social life is observed and characterizations of social activity established; Section D, the formulation of concepts within the meaning-frames of social science as metalanguages.

A

ONE: Sociology is not concerned with a 'pre-given' universe of objects, but with one which is constituted or produced by the active doings of subjects . . .

TWO: The production and reproduction of society thus has to be treated as a skilled performance on the part of its members, not as merely a mechanical series of processes . . .

B

ONE: The realm of human agency is bounded. Men produce society, but they do so as historically located actors, and not under conditions of their own choosing . . .

TWO: Structures must not be conceptualized as simply placing constraints upon human agency, but as enabling . . .

THREE: Processes of structuration involve an interplay of meanings, norms and power . . .

C

ONE: The sociological observer cannot make social life available as a 'phenomenon' for observation independently of drawing upon his knowledge of it as a resource whereby he constitutes it as a 'topic for investigation' . . .

TWO: Immersion in a form of life is the necessary and only means whereby an observer is able to generate such characterizations . . .

D

ONE: Sociological concepts thus obey what I call a double hermeneutic: (1) Any generalized theoretical scheme in the natural or social sciences is in a certain sense a form of life in itself, the concepts of which have to be mastered as a mode of practical activity generating specific types of description . . . (2) Sociology, however, deals with a universe which is already constituted within frames of meaning by social actors themselves, and reinterprets these within its own theoretical schemes, mediating ordinary and technical language . . .

TWO: In sum, the primary tasks of sociological analysis are the following: (1) The hermeneutic explication and mediation of divergent forms of life within metalanguages of social science; (2) Explication of the production and reproduction of society as the accomplished outcome of human agency.

New Rules of Sociological Method, London, Hutchinson, 1976, pp. 159–62.

Structure, as recursively organized sets of rules and resources, is out of **2** time and space, save in its instantiations and co-ordination as memory traces, and is marked by an 'absence of the subject'. The social systems in which structure is recursively implicated, on the contrary, comprise the situated activities of human agents, reproduced across time and space. Analysing the structuration of social systems means studying the modes in which such systems, grounded in the knowledgeable activities of situated actors who draw upon rules and resources in the diversity of action contexts, are produced and reproduced in interaction. Critical to the idea of structuration is the theorem of the duality of structure ... The constitution of agents and structures are not two independently given sets of phenomena, a dualism, but represent a duality. According to the notion of the duality of structure, the structural properties of social systems are both medium and outcome of the practices they recursively organize. Structure is not 'external' to individuals ... Structure is not to be equated with constraint but is always both constraining and enabling.
The Constitution of Society: Outline of the Theory of Structuration, Cambridge, Polity, 1984, p. 25.

I have long contended that the neglect of what any causal survey of history **3** shows to be an overwhelmingly obvious and chronic trait of human affairs – recourse to violence and war – is one of the most extraordinary blank spots in social theory in the twentieth century.
The Nation-State and Violence, vol. 2 of *A Contemporary Critique of Historical Materialism*, Cambridge, Polity Press, 1985, p. 177.

Various main features of European state development were shaped in a **4** decisive way by the contingent outcomes of military confrontations and wars. Nothing shows more clearly how implausible it is to regard the emergence of modern societies as the result of some sort of evolutionary scheme that inexorably led from the alluvial dirt of Sumer to the factory shop-floor of latter-day Europe.
Ibid., p. 112.

Among the industrialized societies at least, capitalism is by now a very **5** different phenomenon from what it was in the nineteenth century and labour movements have played a prime role in changing it. In most of the capitalist countries, we now have to speak of the existence of 'welfare capitalism', a system in which the labour movement has achieved a considerable stake and in which economic (social) citizenship rights brook large.
Ibid., p. 325.

I continue to maintain, as I expressed it in *A Contemporary Critique of* **6** *Historical Materialism*, that there are three main axes of exploitative relationships in modern systems besides that of class: exploitation associated with the use of political power, including military domination; with relationships

between ethnic groups; and that associated with gender relationships. Gender divisions and ethnic schisms are more deeply engraved in human social organization, and human psychology, than are the other forms of exploitative domination. Class relationships are associated with one of the main institutional orderings of modernity, *capitalistic institutions. Industrialism*, another major institutional clustering of modernity, concerns above all the exploitative relationships between human beings and nature, rather than social relationships as such. Exploitative relationships on the political level here group together *governmental power* and *control of the means of violence . . .*
'A Reply to My Critics', in D. Held and J. B. Thompson (eds), *Social Theory and Modern Societies: Anthony Giddens and His Critics*, Cambridge, Cambridge University Press, 1989, p. 265.

7 Sex is not driven underground in modern civilization. On the contrary, it comes to be continually discussed and investigated. It has become part of 'a great sermon', replacing the more ancient tradition of theological preaching. Statements about sexual repression and the sermon of transcendence mutually reinforce one another; the struggle for sexual liberation is part of the self-same apparatus of power that it denounces. Has any other social order, Foucault asks rhetorically, been so persistently and pervasively preoccupied with sex?
The Transformation of Intimacy: Sexuality, Love and Eroticism in Modern Societies, Cambridge, Polity Press, 1992, p. 19.

8 Foucault's interpretation of the development of the self in modern societies should also be placed in question in a rather basic way. Instead of seeing the self as constructed by a specific 'technology', we should recognize that self-identity becomes particularly problematic in modern social life, particularly in the very recent era. Fundamental features of a society of high reflexivity are the 'open' character of self-identity and the reflexive nature of the body. For women struggling to break free from pre-existing gender roles, the question 'Who am I?' – which Betty Friedan labelled 'the problem that has no name' – comes to the surface with particular intensity. Much the same is true for homosexuals, male and female, who contest dominant heterosexual stereotypes. The question is one of sexual identity, but not only this. The self is for everyone a reflexive project – a more or less continuous interrogation of past, present and future. It is a project carried on amid a profusion of reflexive resources: therapy and self-help manuals of all kinds, television programmes and magazine articles.
Ibid., p. 30.

9 We should reformulate the question of order as a problem of how it comes about that social systems 'bind' time and space. The problem of order is here seen as one of *time–space distanciation* – the conditions under which time and space are organized so as to connect presences and absences.
The Consequences of Modernity, Cambridge, Polity Press, 1991, p. 14.

By disembedding I mean the 'lifting out' of social relations from local **10** contexts of interaction and their restructuring across indefinite spans of time–space.
Ibid., p. 21.

The pivotal position of sociology in the reflexivity of modernity comes **11** from its role as the most generalized type of reflection upon modern social life.
Ibid., p. 41.

The discourse of sociology and the concepts, theories, and findings of the **12** other social sciences continually 'circulate in and out' of what it is that they are about. In so doing they reflexively restructure their subject matter, which itself has learned to think sociologically. *Modernity is itself deeply and intrinsically sociological.*
Ibid., p. 43.

The undue reliance which sociologists have placed upon the idea of 'society', **13** where this means a bounded system, should be replaced by a starting point that concentrates upon analysing how social life is ordered across time and space – the problem of time–space distanciation. The conceptual framework of time–space distanciation directs our attention to the complex relations between *local involvements* (circumstances of co-presence) and *interaction across distance* (the connections of presence and absence). In the modern era, the level of time–space distanciation is much higher than in any previous period, and the relations between local and distant social forms and events become correspondingly 'stretched'. Globalisation refers essentially to that stretching process, in so far as the modes of connection between different social contexts or regions become networked across the earth's surface as a whole.

Globalisation can thus be defined as the intensification of worldwide social relations which link distant localities in such a way that local happenings are shaped by events occurring many miles away and vice versa.
Ibid., pp. 63–4.

GOFFMAN, ERVING (1922–82)

On face work

Every person lives in a world of social encounters, involving him either in **1** face-to-face or mediated contact with other participants. In each of these contacts, he tends to act out what is sometimes called a *line* – that is, a pattern of verbal and nonverbal acts by which he expresses his view of the situation and through this his evaluation of the participants, especially himself. Regardless of whether a person intends to take a line, he will find that he has done so in effect. The other participants will assume that he has more or less wilfully taken a stand, so that if he is to deal with their response to him he must take into consideration the impression they have possibly formed of him.

The term *face* may be defined as the positive social value a person effectively claims for himself by the line others assume he has taken during a particular contact. Face is an image of self delineated in terms of approved social attributes – albeit an image that others may share, as when a person makes a good showing for his profession or religion by making a good showing of himself.

Interaction Ritual [1955], Garden City, New York, Anchor Books, 1967, p. 5.

2   Universal human nature is not a very human thing. By acquiring it, the person becomes a kind of construct, built up not from inner psychic propensities but from moral rules that are impressed upon him from without. These rules, when followed, determine the evaluation he will make of himself and of his fellow-participants in the encounter, the distribution of his feelings, and the kinds of practices he will employ to maintain a specified and obligatory kind of ritual equilibrium. The general capacity to be bound by moral rules may well belong to the individual, but the particular set of rules which transforms him into a human being derives from requirements established in the ritual organization of social encounters. And if a particular person or group or society seems to have a unique character all its own, it is because its standard set of human-nature elements is pitched and combined in a particular way.

Ibid., p. 45.

The presentation of self in everyday life

3   Throughout Western society there seems to be one informal or backstage language of behavior, and another language of behavior for occasions when a performance is being presented. The backstage language consists of reciprocal first-naming, co-operative decision-making, profanity, open sexual remarks, elaborate griping, smoking, rough informal dress, 'sloppy' sitting and standing posture, use of dialect or sub-standard speech, mumbling and shouting, playful aggressivity and 'kidding', inconsiderateness for the other in minor but potentially symbolic acts, minor physical self-involvements, such as humming, whistling, chewing, nibbling, belching and flatulence. The frontstage of behavior language can be taken as the absence (and in some sense the opposite) of this. In general, then, backstage conduct is one which allows minor acts which might easily be taken as symbolic of intimacy and disrespect for others present and the region, while front region conduct is one which disallows such potentially offensive behavior.

The Presentation of Self in Everyday Life, Garden City, New York, Anchor, 1958, p. 2.

I have suggested that any social establishment may be studied profitably **4**
from the point of view of impression management. Within the walls of
a social establishment we find a team of performers who co-operate to
present to an audience a given definition of the situation. This will include
the conception of own team and of audience and assumptions concerning
the ethos that is to be maintained by rules of politeness and decorum. We
often find a division into back region, where the performance of a routine is
prepared and front region, where the performance is presented. Access to
these regions is controlled in order to prevent the audience from seeing
backstage and to prevent outsiders from coming into a performance that is
not addressed to them. Among members of the team we find that familiarity
prevails, solidarity is likely to develop, and that secrets that could give the
show away are shared and kept. A tacit agreement is maintained between
performers and audience to act as if a given degree of opposition and of
accord existed between them. Typically, but not always, agreement is
stressed and opposition is underplayed. The resulting working consensus
tends to be contradicted by the attitude toward the audience which the performers express in the absence of the audience and by carefully controlled
communication out of character conveyed by the performers while the
audience is present.
Ibid., p. 238.

It seems to me that the dramaturgical approach may constitute a fifth **5**
perspective, to be added to the technical, political, structural, and cultural
perspectives. The dramaturgical perspective, like each of the other four, can
be employed as the end-point of analysis, as a final way of ordering facts.
This would lead us to describe the techniques of impression management
employed in a given establishment, the principal problems of impression
management in the establishment, and the identity and interrelationships of
the several performance teams which operate in the establishment. But, as
with the facts utilized in each of the other perspectives, the facts specifically
pertaining to impression management also play a part in the matters that
are a concern in all the other perspectives.
Ibid., pp. 240–1.

Total institutions – asylums

A basic social arrangement in modern society is that the individual tends to **6**
sleep, play, and work in different places, with different co-participants,
under different authorities, and without an overall rational plan. The
central feature of total institutions can be described as a breakdown of the
barriers ordinarily separating these three spheres of life. First, all aspects of
life are conducted in the same place and under the same single authority.
Second, each phase of the member's daily activity is carried on in the

immediate company of a large batch of others, all of whom are treated alike and required to do the same thing together. Third, all phases of the day's activities are tightly scheduled, with one activity leading at a prearranged time onto the next, the whole sequence of activities being imposed from above by a system of explicitly formal rules and a body of officials. Finally, the various enforced activities are brought together into a single rational plan purportedly designed to fulfil the official aims of the institution.
Asylums, Harmondsworth, Penguin, 1968, p. 17.

On cooling the mark out

7   In cases of criminal fraud, victims find they must suddenly adapt themselves to the loss of sources of security and status which they had taken for granted. A consideration of this adaptation can lead us to an understanding of some relations in our society between involvements and the selves that are involved.

In the argot of the criminal world, the term 'mark' refers to any individual who is a victim or prospective victim of certain forms of planned illegal exploitation. The mark is the sucker – the person who is taken in . . .

Sometimes, however, a mark is not quite prepared to accept his loss as a gain in experience and to say and do nothing about his venture. He may feel moved to complain to the police or to chase after the operators . . . In order to avoid this adverse publicity, an additional phase is sometimes added at the end of the play. It is called 'cooling the mark out'. After the blowoff has occurred, one of the operators stays with the mark and makes an effort to keep the anger of the mark within manageable and sensible proportions . . .

Although the term 'mark' is commonly applied to a person who is given short-lived expectations by operators who have intentionally misrepresented the facts, a less restricted definition is desirable in analyzing the larger social scene. An expectation may finally prove false, even though it has been possible to sustain it for a long time and even though the operators acted in good faith. So, too, the disappointment of reasonable expectations, as well as misguided ones, creates a need for consolation. Persons who participate in what is recognized as a confidence game are found in only a few social settings, but persons who have to be cooled out are found in many. Cooling the mark out is one theme in a very basic social theory . . .

For the mark, cooling represents a process of adjustment to an impossible situation – a situation arising from having defined himself in a way which the social facts come to contradict. The mark must therefore be supplied with a new set of apologies for himself, a new framework in which to see himself and judge himself. A process of redefining the self along defensible lines must be instigated and carried along; since the mark himself is frequently in too weakened a condition to do this, the cooler must initially do it for him.

One general way of handling the problem of cooling the mark out is to give the task to someone whose status relative to the mark will serve to ease the situation in some way ...

A second general solution to the problem of cooling the mark out consists of offering him a status which differs from the one he has lost or failed to gain but which provides at least something or somebody for him to become ...

A related way of handling the mark is to offer him another chance to qualify for the role at which he has failed ...

Another standard method of cooling the mark out – one which is frequently employed in conjunction with other methods – is to allow the mark to explode, to break down, to cause a scene, to give full vent to his reactions and feelings, to 'blow his top' ...

A related procedure for cooling the mark out is found in what is called stalling ...

As another procedure, there is the possibility that the operator and the mark enter into a tacit understanding according to which the mark agrees to act as if he were leaving of his own accord, and the operator agrees to preserve the illusion that this is the case. It is a form of bribery. In this way the mark may fail in his own eyes but prevent others from discovering the failure.

'On Cooling the Mark Out: Some Aspects of Adaptation to Failure', *Psychiatry: Journal for the Study of Interpersonal Relations*, vol. 15, no. 4 (November), 1952, pp. 451–63.

The nature of deference and demeanor

In all societies, rules of conduct tend to be organized into codes which **8** guarantee that everyone acts appropriately and receives his dues. In our society the code which governs substantive rules and substantive expressions comprises our law, morality and ethics, while the code which governs ceremonial rules and ceremonial expressions is incorporated in what we call etiquette ...

Ceremonial activity seems to contain certain basic components ... two of these components [are] deference and demeanor ...

By deference I shall refer to that component of activity which functions as a symbolic means by which appreciation is regularly conveyed *to* a recipient *of* this recipient, or of something of which this recipient is taken as a symbol, extension or agent ... Such ceremonial activity is perhaps seen most clearly in the little salutations, compliments and apologies which punctuate social intercourse, and may be referred to as 'status rituals' or 'interpersonal rituals' ... I use the term 'ritual' because this activity, however informal and secular, represents a way in which the individual must guard and design the symbolic implications of his acts while in the immediate presence of an object that has a special value for him ...

Deference can take many forms, of which I shall consider only two broad groupings, avoidance rituals and presentational rituals.

Avoidance rituals, as a term, may be employed to refer to those forms of deference which lead the actor to keep at a distance from the other recipient and not violate what Simmel has called the 'ideal sphere' that lies around the recipient . . . .

A second type, termed *presentational rituals*, encompasses acts through which the individual makes specific attestations to recipients concerning how he regards them and how he will treat them in the on-coming interaction. Rules regarding these ritual practices involve specific prescriptions, not specific proscriptions; while avoidance rituals specify what is not to be done, presentational rituals specify what is to be done . . .

By demeanor I shall refer to that element of the individual's ceremonial behavior typically conveyed through deportment, dress and bearing, which serves to express to those in his immediate presence that he is a person of certain desirable or undesirable qualities. In our society, the 'well' or 'properly' demeaned individual displays such attributes as: discretion and sincerity; modesty in claims regarding self; sportsmanship; command of speech and physical movements; self-control over his emotions, his appetites and his desires; poise under pressure and so forth . . .

The Meadian notion that the individual takes toward himself the attitude others take to him seems very much an oversimplification. Rather, the individual must rely on others to complete the picture of him of which he himself is allowed to paint only certain parts. Each individual is responsible for the demeanor image of himself and the deference image of others, so that for a complete man to be expressed, individuals must hold hands in a chain of ceremony, each giving deferentially with proper demeanor to the one on the right what will be received deferentially from the one on the left. While it may be true that the individual has a unique self all his own, evidence of this possession is thoroughly a product of joint ceremonial labor, the part expressed through the individual's demeanor being no more significant than the part conveyed by others through their deferential behavior toward him.
'The Nature of Deference and Demeanor', *American Anthropologist*, vol. 58, 1956, pp. 47–85.

HABERMAS, JÜRGEN (1929–)

Emancipatory knowledge

1   The glory of the sciences is their unswerving application of their methods without reflecting on knowledge-constitutive interests. From knowing not what they do methodologically, they are much surer of their discipline, that is of methodical progress within an unproblematic framework. False consciousness has a protective function. For the sciences lack the means of dealing

with the risks that appear once the connection of knowledge and human interest has been comprehended on the level of self-reflection ... As soon as the objectivist illusion is turned into an affirmative *Weltanschauung*, methodologically unconscious necessity is perverted to the dubious virtue of a scientific profession of faith. Objectivism in no way prevents the sciences from intervening in the conduct of life, as Husserl thought it did. They are integrated into it in any case. But they do not themselves develop their practical efficacy in the direction of a growing rationality of action.

Instead, the positivist self-understanding of the nomological sciences lends countenance to the substitution of technology for enlightened action. It directs the utilization of scientific information from an illusory viewpoint, namely that the practical mastery of history can be reduced to technical control of objectified processes. The objectivist self-understanding of the *hermeneutic sciences* is of no lesser consequence. It defends sterilized knowledge against the reflected appropriation of active traditions and locks up history in a museum. Guided by the objectivist attitude of theory as the image of facts, the nomological and hermeneutic sciences reinforce each other with regard to their practical consequences. The latter displace our connection with tradition into the realm of the arbitrary, while the former, on the levelled-off basis of the repression of history, squeeze the conduct of life into the behavioral system of instrumental action. The dimension in which acting subjects could arrive rationally at agreement about goals and purposes is surrendered to the obscure area of mere decision among reified value systems and irrational beliefs. When this dimension, abandoned by all men of good will, is subjected to reflection that relates to history objectivistically, as did the philosophical tradition, then positivism triumphs at the highest level of thought, as with Comte. This happens when critique uncritically abdicates its own connection with the emancipatory knowledge-constitutive interest in favour of pure theory. This sort of high-flown critique projects the undecided process of the evolution of the human species onto the level of a philosophy of history that dogmatically issues instructions for action. A delusive philosophy of history, however, is only the obverse of deluded decisionism. Bureaucratically prescribed partisanship goes only too well with contemplatively misunderstood value freedom.

These practical consequences of a restricted, scientistic consciousness of the science can be countered by a critique that destroys the illusion of objectivism ... The insight that the truth of statements is linked in the last analysis to the intention of the good and true life can be preserved today only on the ruins of ontology.

Knowledge and Human Interests, trans. J. J. Shapiro, Boston, Beacon Press, 1971, pp. 315–17. First published in German in 1968.

Theory of communicative competence

2   If one thus analyzes the structure which we generate and describe by pure dialogue-constitutive universals, one arrives at a number of symmetrical relations for the ideal speech situation. Pure intersubjectivity is determined by a symmetrical relation between I and You (We and You), I and He (We and They). An unlimited interchangeability of dialogue roles demands that no side be privileged in the performance of these roles; pure intersubjectivity exists only where there is complete symmetry in the distribution of assertion and disputation, revelation and hiding, prescription and following among the partners of communication. As long as these symmetries exist, communication will not be hindered by constraints arising from its own structure: (1) In the case of unrestricted discussion (in which no prejudiced opinion can continually avoid being made thematic and being criticized) it is possible to develop strategies for reaching unconstrained consensus; (2) based on the mutuality of unimpaired self-representation (which includes the acknowledgement of the self-representation of the Other as well), it is possible to achieve subtle nearness along with inviolable distance among the partners and that means communication under conditions of extreme individuation; (3) in the case of full complementation of expectations (which exclude one-sided obliging norms), the claim of universal understanding exists as well as the necessity of universalized norms. These three symmetries represent, by the way, a linguistic conceptualization for that which we traditionally apprehend as the ideas of truth, freedom, and justice.

The speech situation, which is determined by pure intersubjectivity, is an idealization. The mastery of dialogue-constitutive universals is not synonymous to the capability of actually establishing the ideal speech situation. But communicative competence does mean the mastery of the means of construction necessary for the establishment of an ideal speech situation. No matter how the intersubjectivity of mutual understanding may be deformed, the design of an ideal speech situation is necessarily implied with the structure of potential speech; for every speech, even that of intentional deception, is oriented towards the idea of truth. This idea can only be analyzed with regard to a consensus achieved in unrestrained and universal discourse. Insofar as we master the means for the construction of an ideal speech situation, we can conceive the ideas of truth, freedom, and justice – which interpret each other – only as ideas of course. For on the strength of communicative competence we can by no means really produce the ideal speech situation independent of the empirical structure of the social system to which we belong; we can only anticipate this situation.

'Toward a Theory of Communicative Competence', in Hans Peter Dreitzel (ed.), *Recent Sociology No. 2: Patterns of Communicative Behavior*, New York, Macmillan, 1970, pp. 143–4.

LÉVI-STRAUSS, CLAUDE (1908–)

The structural study of myth

Mythology confronts the student with a situation which at first sight **1**
appears contradictory. On the one hand it would seem that in the course
of a myth anything is likely to happen. There is no logic, no continuity. Any
characteristic can be attributed to any subject; every conceivable relation
can be found. With myth, everything becomes possible. But on the other
hand, this apparent arbitrariness is belied by the astounding similarity
between myths collected in widely different regions. Therefore the problem:
If the content of a myth is contingent, how are we to explain the fact that
myths throughout the world are so similar?

It is precisely this awareness of a basic antinomy pertaining to the nature
of myth that may lead us toward its solution. For the contradiction which
we face is very similar to that which in earlier times brought considerable
worry to the first philosophers concerned with linguistic problems ...
Whatever emendations the original formulation may now call for, everybody will agree that the Saussurean principle of the arbitrary character of
linguistic signs was a prerequisite for the accession of linguistics to the
scientific level ...

There is a very good reason why myth cannot simply be treated as
language if its specific problems are to be solved; myth *is* language: to be
known, myth has to be told; it is a part of human speech. In order to preserve
its specificity we must be able to show that it is both the same thing as
language, and also something different from it. Here too, the past experience of linguistics may help us. For language itself can be analyzed into
things which are at the same time similar and yet different. This is precisely
what is expressed in Saussure's distinction between *langue* and *parole*, one
being the structural side of language, the other the statistical aspect of it,
langue belonging to a reversible time, *parole* being non-reversible ...

Whatever our ignorance of the language and the culture of the people
where it originated, a myth is still felt as a myth by any reader anywhere
in the world. Its substance does not lie in its style, its original music, or its
syntax, but in the story which it tells. Myth is language, functioning on an
especially high level where meaning succeeds practically at 'taking off'
from the linguistic ground on which it keeps on rolling.

To sum up the discussion at this point, we have so far made the following
claims: (1) If there is a meaning to be found in mythology, it cannot reside
in the isolated elements which enter into the composition of a myth, but
only in the way those elements are combined. (2) Although myth belongs
to the same category as language, being as a matter of fact, only part of it,
language in myth exhibits specific properties. (3) Those properties are only
to be found above the ordinary linguistic level, that is, they exhibit more

complex features than those which are to be found in any other kind of linguistic expression . . .

The true constituent units of a myth are not the isolated relations but *bundles of such relations*, and it is only as bundles that these relations can be put to use and combined so as to produce a meaning.

'The Structural Study of Myth' [1958], in C. Lévi-Strauss, *Structural Anthropology*, trans. C. Jacobson and B. G. Schoepf, New York, Basic Books, 1963; London, Allen Lane, 1968, pp. 208–11.

The savage mind

2   There still exists among ourselves an activity which on the technical plane gives us quite a good understanding of what a science we prefer to call 'prior' rather than 'primitive', could have been on the plane of speculation. This is what is commonly called 'bricolage' in French. In its old sense the verb 'bricoler' applied to ball games and billiards, to hunting, shooting and riding. It was however always used with reference to some extraneous movements: a ball rebounding, a dog straying or a horse swerving from its direct course to avoid an obstacle. And in our own time the 'bricoleur' is still someone who works with his hands and uses devious means compared to those of a craftsman. The characteristic feature of mythical thought is that it expresses itself by means of a heterogeneous repertoire which, even if extensive, is nevertheless limited. It has to use this repertoire, however, whatever the task in hand because it has nothing else at its disposal. Mythical thought is therefore a kind of intellectual 'bricolage' – which explains the relation which can be perceived between the two . . .

The 'bricoleur' is adept at performing a large number of diverse tasks; but, unlike the engineer, he does not subordinate each of them to the availability of raw material and tools conceived and procured for the purpose of the project. His universe of instruments is closed and the rules of his game are always to make do with 'whatever is at hand', that is to say with a set of tools and materials which is always finite and is also heterogeneous because what it contains bears no relation to the currect project, or indeed to any particular project, but is the contingent result of all the occasions there have been to renew or enrich the stock or to maintain it with the remains of previous constructions or destructions . . .

The elements which the 'bricoleur' collects and uses are 'pre-constrained' like the constitutive units of myth, the possible combinations of which are restricted by the fact that they are drawn from the language where they already possess a sense which sets a limit on their freedom of manoeuvre.

The Savage Mind, London, Weidenfeld & Nicolson, 1962, pp. 16–19. Published in French in 1962.

The raw and the cooked

First of all, when considered from the formal point of view, myths which **3**
seem very different but all deal with the origin of man's mortality transmit
the same message and can only be distinguished from one another by the
code they use. Second, all the codes are similar in type; they use contrasts
between tangible qualities, which are thus raised to the point of having a
logical existence. Third, since man possesses five senses, there are five basic
codes, which shows that all the empirical possibilities have been systematically explored and used. Fourth, one of the codes occupies a privileged
position; this is the one connected with eating habits, the gustatory code,
whose message is more often transmitted by the others than it is used to
translate theirs, since it is through myths explaining the origin of fire, and
thus of cooking, that we gain access to myths about man's loss of immortality;
among the Apinaye, for instance, the origin of mortality is only one episode
of the myth relating to the origin of fire. We thus begin to understand the
truly essential place occupied by cooking in native thought: not only does
cooking mark the transition from nature to culture, but through it and by
means of it, the human state can be defined with all its attributes, even those
that, like mortality, might seem to be the most unquestionably natural.
The Raw and the Cooked, trans. J. and D. Weightman, New York, Harper & Row,
1969, p. 164. First published in French in 1964.

LUHMANN, NIKLAS (1927–)

I cannot for many reasons share the faith Jürgen Habermas places in the
opportunities afforded by resorting to a paradigm of intersubjective understanding. It is above all difficult to conceive of how a sufficiently complex
theory of society resulting from an intersubjective understanding could be
generated from the discourses of everyday life. Instead, it would seem to me
to make more sense to utilize certain of the theoretical resources that have
already been quite extensively elaborated in the course of interdisciplinary
research on a cybernetics of self-referential orders, on general systems
theory, on autopoiesis and on information and communication . . .

This approach at the same time allows us to establish premises on which
a theory of society could be based. It is possible, using this methodology, to
treat society as a social system that consists solely of communications and
therefore as a system that can only reproduce communications by means
of communications. This also includes communications by the society
about itself (in particular, theories of society). All other conditions for the
evolution of society and its day to day functioning, including life and human
consciousness, belong to the *environment* of this system.

In current debates it has been this unusual design for a theory that has
met with the greatest resistance, owing no doubt to the continued presence

of a tradition of humanism. But from the standpoint of systems theory, 'environment' is by no means an area to be considered of secondary importance; on the contrary, it is the single most important condition for systems formation ...

What this theoretical perspective does have in common with Foucault's work is a clearly post-humanistic perspective ... But, whereas Foucault would speak in terms of the power of discourse over our suffering bodies, systems theory analyses a relationship between system and environment. Indeed, systems theory additionally makes it possible to create a complex theoretical apparatus that can describe the non-random character of variations in social relations, if not actually explain the individual characteristics of the latter of these. In other words, it does not have to leave the genesis of the particular discourses and their subsequent disappearance unexplained. The dominant semantics of a given period becomes plausible only by virtue of its compatibility with the social structure – not in the sense of a mere 'reflection', and by no means in the sense of a relationship of the superstructure. Compatibility is the more elaborate concept. It also embraces the problems of evolutionary, transitional states in which the losses in plausibility experienced by the old order that is passing have to be compensated for and new figures of meaning tested for their suitability to the changed conditions.

The present work deals with only a minute facet of this enormous theoretical programme and is informed by two hypotheses:

1 that the transition from traditional societies to modern society can be conceived of as the transition from a primarily stratified form of differentiation of the social system to one which is primarily functional;
2 that this transformation occurs primarily by means of the differentiation of various symbolically generalized media of communication.

This change destroyed the traditional order of life, which had been based primarily on stratified family households, religious cosmology and morals, i.e. on multifunctional institutions. These were replaced by a primary orientation toward such systems as the economy, politics, science, intimacy, law, art, etc., which thus all acquired a high degree of systemic autonomy, and yet precisely because of this became all the more interdependent.
Love as Passion: The Codification of Intimacy, trans. J. Gaines and D. L. Jones, Cambridge, Polity Press, 1986, pp. 3–5.

MARX, KARL (1818–83)

1 The first premise of all human history is, of course, the existence of living human individuals. Thus the first fact to be established is the physical organization of these individuals and their consequent relation to the rest of nature. Of course, we cannot here go either into the actual physical nature of man, or into the natural conditions in which man finds himself

174

– geological, orohydrographical, climatic, and so on. The writing of history must always set out from these natural bases and their modification in the course of history through the action of man.

Men can be distinguished from animals by consciousness, by religion or anything else you like. They themselves begin to distinguish themselves from animals as soon as they begin to *produce* their means of subsistence, a step which is conditioned by their physical organization. By producing their means of subsistence men are indirectly producing their actual material life.

The way in which men produce their means of subsistence depends first of all on the nature of the actual means they find in existence and have to reproduce. This mode of production must not be considered simply as being the reproduction of the physical existence of the individuals. Rather it is a definite form of activity of these individuals, a definite form of expressing their life, a definite *mode of life* on their part. As individuals express their life, so they are. What they are, therefore, coincides with their production, both with *what* they produce and with *how* they produce. The nature of individuals thus depends on the material conditions determining their production.

Karl Marx and Friedrich Engels, *The German Ideology* [1845–6]; New York, International Publishers, 1963 (pbk edn), p. 7.

Legal relations as well as forms of the State could neither be understood **2** by themselves, nor explained by the so-called general progress of the human mind, but rather have their roots in the material conditions of life, which are summed up by Hegel – under the name *civil society*, and that the anatomy of civil society is to be sought in political economy.

Preface to *A Contribution to the Critique of Political Economy* [1859]; trans. T. B. Bottomore in *Karl Marx: Selected Writings in Sociology and Social Philosophy*, ed. T. B. Bottomore and M. Rubel, Harmondsworth, Penguin, 1963, p. 67.

It is not the consciousness of men that determines their being, but, on the **3** contrary, their social being determines their consciousness.

Ibid., p. 67.

In broad outline we can designate the Asiatic, the ancient, the feudal, and **4** the modern bourgeois modes of production as progressive epochs in the economic formation of society.

Ibid., p. 68.

The real nature of man is the totality of social relations. **5**

Theses on Feuerbach [1845]; in *Karl Marx: Selected Writings . . .*, op. cit., p. 83.

The philosophers have only *interpreted* the world in different ways; the **6** point is to change it.

Ibid., p. 84.

7 Hegel remarks somewhere that all great, world-historical facts and personages occur, as it were, twice. He has forgotten to add: the first time as tragedy, the second as farce.
The Eighteenth Brumaire of Louis Bonaparte [1852]; Moscow, Progress Publishers, 1954, p. 10.

8 Men make their own history, but they do not make it just as they please; they do not make it under circumstances chosen by themselves, but under circumstances directly found, given and transmitted from the past. The tradition of all the dead generations weighs like a nightmare on the brain of the living. And just when they seem engaged in revolutionising themselves and things, in creating something entirely new, precisely in such epochs of revolutionary crisis they anxiously conjure up the spirits of the past to their service and borrow from them names, battle slogans and costumes in order to present the new scene of world history in this time-honoured disguise and this borrowed language.
Ibid., p. 10.

9 Society does not consist of individuals, but expresses the sum of inter-relations, the relations within which these individuals stand.
Foundations [Grundrisse] of the Critique of Political Economy [1857–8]; trans. M. Nicolaus in *The Marx–Engels Reader*, ed. Robert C. Tucker, 2nd edn, New York, W. W. Norton, 1978, p. 247.

The fetishism of commodities

10 A commodity is therefore a mysterious thing, simply because in it the social character of men's labour appears to them as an objective character stamped upon the product of that labour; because the relation of the producers to the sum total of their own labour is presented to them as a social relation, existing not between themselves, but between the products of their labour. This is the reason why the products of labour become com-modities, social things whose qualities are at the same time perceptible and imperceptible by the senses. In the same way the light from an object is perceived by us not as the subjective excitation of our optic nerve, but as the objective form of something outside the eye itself. But, in the act of seeing, there is at all events, an actual passage of light from one thing to another, from the external object to the eye. There is a physical relation between physical things. But it is different with commodities. There, the existence of the things qua commodities, and the value-relation between the products of labour which stamps them as commodities, have absolutely no connexion with their physical properties and with the material relations arising therefrom. There is a definite social relation between men, that assumes, in their eyes, the fantastic form of a relation between things. In order, therefore, to find an analogy, we must have recourse to the

mist-enveloped regions of the religious world. In that world the productions of the human brain appear as independent beings endowed with life, and entering into relations both with one another and the human race. So it is in the world of commodities with the products of men's hands. This I call the Fetishism which attaches itself to the products of labour, so soon as they are produced as commodities, and which is therefore inseparable from the production of commodities.

Capital, vol. 1 [1867]; trans. S. Moore and E. Aveling in *The Marx–Engels Reader*, ed. R. C. Tucker, 2nd edn, New York, W. W. Norton, 1978, pp. 320–1.

Modes of production

In the social production which men carry on they enter into definite relations **11** that are indispensable and independent of their will; these relations of production correspond to a definite state of development of their material powers of production. The totality of these relations of production constitutes the economic structure of society – the real foundation on which legal and political superstructures arise and to which definite forms of social consciousness correspond. The mode of production of material life determines the general character of the social, political and spiritual processes of life. It is not the consciousness of men that determines their being, but, on the contrary, their social being determines their consciousness.

Preface to *A Contribution to the Critique of Political Economy* [1859]; in *Karl Marx: Selected Writings . . .*, op. cit., p. 67.

Classes

And now as to myself, no credit is due to me for discovering the existence **12** of classes in modern society or the struggle between them. Long before me bourgeois historians had described the historical development of this class struggle and bourgeois economists the economic anatomy of the classes. What I did that was new was to prove: (1) that the existence of classes is only bound up with particular historical phases in the development of production, (2) that the class struggle necessarily leads to the dictatorship of the proletariat, (3) that this dictatorship itself only constitutes the transition to the abolition of all classes and to a classless society.

Letter to Joseph Weydemeyer, 5 March 1852; in *The Marx–Engels Reader*, op. cit., p. 220.

The lower strata of the middle class – the small tradespeople, shopkeepers, **13** and retired tradesmen generally, the handicraftsmen and peasants – all these sink gradually into the proletariat, partly because their diminutive capital does not suffice for the scale on which modern industry is carried on, and is swamped in the competition with the larger capitalists, partly because their specialized skill is rendered worthless by new methods of production. Thus the proletariat is recruited from all classes of the population.

Communist Manifesto [1848]; Moscow, Foreign Languages Publishing House, 1959, p. 55.

14 What [Ricardo] forgets to mention is the continual increase in numbers of the middle classes ... situated midway between the workers on the one side and the capitalists and landowners on the other. These middle classes rest with all their weight upon the working class and at the same time increase the social security and power of the upper class.

Theories of Surplus Value [1905–10], vol. 2; in *Karl Marx: Selected Writings ...*, op. cit., p. 198.

15 The owners of mere labour-power, the owners of capital, and the landowners, whose respective sources of income are wages, profit, and rent of land, or in other words, wage-labourers, capitalists, and landowners, form the three great classes of modern society based on the capitalist mode of production.

Capital [1893–4], vol. 3; ibid., p. 186.

16 Society as a whole is more and more splitting up into two great hostile camps, into two great classes directly facing each other – bourgeoisie and proletariat.

Communist Manifesto [1848]; Moscow, Foreign Languages Publishing House, 1959, p. 46.

17 The executive of the modern State is but a committee for managing the common affairs of the whole bourgeoisie.

Communist Manifesto [1848]; ibid., p. 48.

18 The history of all hitherto existing society is the history of class struggles. Freeman and slave, patrician and plebeian, lord and serf, guild-master and journeyman, in a word, oppressor and oppressed, stood in constant opposition to one another, carried on an uninterrupted, now hidden, now open fight, a fight that each time ended either in a revolutionary reconstitution of society at large, or in the common ruin of the contending classes.

Communist Manifesto [1848]; ibid., pp. 45–6.

Modes of production and social stages

19 The social relations within which individuals produce, the social relations of production, are altered, transformed, with the change and development of the material means of production, of the forces of production. The relations of production in their totality constitute what is called the social relations, society, and, moreover, a society at a definite stage of historical development, a society with a unique and distinctive character. Ancient society, feudal society, bourgeois (or capitalist) society, are such totalities

of relations of production, each of which denotes a particular stage of development in the history of mankind.
Wage Labour and Capital [1849]; in *Karl Marx: Selected Writings* . . . op. cit., p. 156.

Unless material production itself is understood in its specific historical **20** form, it is impossible to grasp the characteristics of the intellectual production which corresponds to it or the reciprocal action between the two.
Theories of Surplus Value [1905–10]; ibid., pp. 96–7.

The same men who establish social relations in conformity with their **21** material power of production also produce principles, laws and categories in conformity with their social relations. Thus, these ideas, these categories, are no more eternal than the relations which they express. They are *historical and transient products.*
The Poverty of Philosophy [1847]; ibid., pp. 108–9.

For as soon as the division of labour begins, each man has a particular, **22** exclusive sphere of activity, which is forced upon him and from which he cannot escape. He is a hunter, a fisherman, a shepherd, or a critical critic, and must remain so if he does not want to lose his means of livelihood; whereas in a communist society, where nobody has one exclusive sphere of activity, but each can become accomplished in any branch he wishes, production as a whole is regulated by society, thus making it possible for me to do one thing today and another tomorrow, to hunt in the morning, fish in the afternoon, rear cattle in the evening, criticize after dinner, in accordance with my inclination, without ever becoming hunter, fisherman, shepherd, or critic.
The German Ideology [1845–6]; New York, International Publishers, 1963 (pbk edn), p. 22.

Even when I carry out *scientific work* – an activity which I can seldom **23** conduct in direct association with other men – I perform a *social*, because *human*, act. It is not only the material of my activity – like the language itself which the thinker uses – which is given to me as a social product. My *own* existence *is* a social activity. For this reason, what I myself produce, I produce for society and with the consciousness of acting like a social being.
Economic and Philosophical Manuscripts [1844]; in *Karl Marx: Selected Writings* . . ., op. cit., p. 91.

It is above all necessary to avoid postulating 'society' once more as an **24** abstraction confronting the individual. The individual is a *social being.*
Ibid., pp. 91–2.

Religion

Man makes religion, religion does not make man. In other words, religion **25** is the self-consciousness and self-feeling of man who has either not yet found himself or has already lost himself again. But man is no abstract being squatting outside the world. Man is the world of man, the state, society. This state, this society, produce religion, a reversed world-consciousness, because they are a reversed world. Religion is the general theory of that world, its encyclopaedic compendium, its logic in a popular form, its spiritualistic *point d'honneur*, its enthusiasm, its moral sanction, its solemn completion, its universal ground for consolation and justification. It is the fantastic realization of the human essence because the human essence has no true reality. The struggle against religion is therefore immediately the fight against the other world, of which religion is the spiritual aroma. Religious distress is at the same time the expression of real distress and the protest against real distress. Religion is the sigh of the oppressed creature, the heart of a heartless world, just as it is the spirit of a spiritless situation. It is the opium of the people.

Contribution to the Critique of Hegel's Philosophy of Right [1844]; in K. Marx and F. Engels, *On Religion*, Moscow, Foreign Languages Publishing House, n.d., pp. 41–2.

MEAD, GEORGE HERBERT (1863–1931)

The self and social interaction

1 The self is something which has a development; it is not initially there at birth but arises in the process of social experience and activity, that is, develops in the given individual as a result of his relations to that process as a whole and to other individuals within that process.
Mind, Self and Society [1934], Chicago, University of Chicago Press, 1967 (pbk edn), p. 135.

2 The self, as that which can be an object to itself, is essentially a social structure and it arises in social experience.
Ibid., p. 140.

3 The individual experiences himself as such, not directly, but only indirectly, from the particular standpoints of other individual members of the same social group or from the generalized standpoint of the social group as a whole to which he belongs. For he enters his own experience as a self or individual, not directly or immediately, not by becoming a subject to himself, but only in so far as he first becomes an object to himself just as other individuals are objects to him or are in his experience; and he becomes an object to himself only by taking the attitudes of other individuals toward himself within a social environment or context of experience and behaviour to which both he and they are involved.
Ibid., p. 138.

4 The organized community or social group which gives to the individual his unity of self can be called 'the generalized other'.
Ibid., p. 154.

There is a definite unity, then, which is introduced into the organization of **5**
other selves when we reach such a stage as that of the game, as against
the situation of play where there is a simple succession of one role after
another, a situation which is, of course, characteristic of the child's own
personality. The child is one thing at one time and another at another, and
what he is at one moment does not determine what he is at another. That
is both the charm of childhood as well as its inadequacy.
Ibid., p. 159.

The 'I' is the response of the organism to the attitudes of the others; the **6**
'me' is the organized set of attitudes of others which one himself assumes.
The attitudes of the others constitute the organized 'me', and then one
reacts toward that as an 'I'.
Ibid., p. 175.

Gestures become significant symbols when they implicitly arouse in an **7**
individual making them the same responses which they explicitly arouse,
or are supposed to arouse, in other individuals, the individuals to whom
they are addressed . . .
Ibid., p. 47.

MERTON, ROBERT K. (1910–)

Middle-range theories

. . . *theories of the middle range:* theories that lie between the minor but **1**
necessary working hypotheses that evolve in abundance during day-to-day
research and the all-inclusive systematic efforts to develop a unified theory
that will explain all the observed uniformities of social behavior, social
organization and social change.

Middle-range theory is principally used in sociology to guide empirical
inquiry. It is intermediate to general theories of social systems which are
too remote from particular classes of social behavior, organization and
change to account for what is observed and to those detailed orderly
descriptions of particulars that are not generalized at all.
Social Theory and Social Structure, New York, Free Press, 1949; enlarged edition
1968, p. 39.

Functions and dysfunctions

Functions are those observed consequences which make for the adaptation **2**
or adjustment of a given system; and *dysfunctions*, those observed consequences which lessen the adaptation or adjustment of the system. There is
also the empirical possibility of *nonfunctional* consequences, which are
simply irrelevant to the system under consideration . . .

Manifest functions are those objective consequences contributing to the adjustment or adaptation of the system which are intended and recognized by participants in the system;

Latent functions, correlatively, being those which are neither intended nor recognized.
Ibid., p. 105.

3   The functionalist approach therefore abandons the position, held by various individualistic theories, that different rates of deviant behavior in diverse groups and social strata are the accidental result of varying proportions of pathological personalities found in these groups and strata. It attempts instead to determine how the social and cultural structure generates pressure for socially deviant behavior upon people variously located in that structure . . . The key concept bridging the gap between statics and dynamics in functional theory is that of strain, tension, contradiction, or discrepancy between the component elements of social and cultural structure. Such strains may be dysfunctional for the social system in its then existing form; they may also be instrumental in leading to changes in that system.
Ibid., pp. 175–6.

Puritanism, pietism and science

4   It is the thesis of this study that the Puritan ethic, as an ideal-typical expression of the value-attitudes basic to ascetic Protestantism generally, so canalized the interests of seventeenth-century Englishmen as to constitute one important *element* in the enhanced cultivation of science. The deep-rooted religious *interests* of the day demanded in their forceful implications the systematic, rational, and empirical study of Nature for the glorification of God in His works and for the control of the corrupt world.
Ibid., pp. 628–9.

PARSONS, TALCOTT (1902–79)

The structure of social action

1   For convenience of reference this conceptual scheme will be called the theory of action . . . The basic unit may be called the 'unit act'. Just as the units of a mechanical system in the classical sense, particles, can be defined only in terms of their properties, mass, velocity, location in space, direction of motion, etc., so the units of action systems also have certain basic properties without which it is not possible to conceive of the unit as 'existing' . . . an 'act' involves logically the following: (1) It implies an agent, an 'actor'. (2) For purposes of definition the act must have an 'end', a future state of affairs toward which the process of action is oriented. (3) It must

be initiated in a 'situation' of which the trends of development differ in one or more important respects from the state of affairs to which the action is oriented, the end. This situation is in turn analysable into two elements: those over which the actor has no control, that is which he cannot alter, or prevent from being altered, in conformity with his end, and those over which he has such control. The former may be termed the 'conditions' of action, the latter the 'means'. Finally (4) there is inherent in the conception of this unit, in its analytical uses, a certain mode of relationship between these elements. That is, in the choice of alternative means to the end, in so far as the situation allows alternatives, there is a 'normative' orientation of action.

The Structure of Social Action [1937]; New York, Free Press, 1968 (pbk edn), vol. 1, p. 44.

It has been seen that the solution of the power question, as well as of a **2** plurality of other complex features of social action systems, involves a common reference to the fact of integration of individuals with reference to a common value system, manifested in the legitimacy of institutional norms, in the common ultimate ends of action, in ritual and in various modes of expression. All these phenomena may be referred back to a single general emergent property of social action systems which may be called 'common-value integration'. This is a clearly marked emergent property distinguishable from both the economic and the political. If this property is designated the sociological, sociology may then be defined as 'the science which attempts to develop an analytical theory of social action systems in so far as these systems can be understood in terms of the property of common-value integration.

Ibid., vol. 2, p. 768.

The social system

Reduced to the simplest possible terms, then, a social system consists in a **3** plurality of individual actors interacting with each other in a situation which has at least a physical or environmental aspect, actors who are motivated in terms of a tendency to the 'optimization of gratification' and whose relation to their situations, including each other, is defined and mediated in terms of a system of culturally structured and shared symbols. Thus conceived, a social system is only one of three aspects of the structuring of a completely concrete system of social action. The other two are the personality systems of the individual actors and the cultural system which is built into their action.

The Social System [1951], New York, Free Press, 1964 (pbk edn), pp. 5–6.

For the convenience of the reader these five concept pairs, which will be **4** called the *pattern variables* of role-definition, may be schematically outlined as follows:

183

I.　The Gratification–Discipline Dilemma
Affectivity vs. Affective Neutrality

II　The Private vs. Collective Interest Dilemma
Self-Orientation vs. Collectivity-Orientation

III　The Choice between Types of Value-Orientation Standard
Universalism vs. Particularism

IV　The Choice between 'Modalities' of the Social Object
Achievement vs. Ascription

V　The Definition of Scope of Interest in the Object
Specificity vs. Diffuseness.

Ibid., pp. 66–7.

5 Structured deviant behavior tendencies, which are not successfully coped with by the control mechanisms of the social system, constitute one of the principal sources of change in the structure of the social system.
Ibid., p. 321.

6 Sociological theory, then, is for us *that aspect of the theory of social systems which is concerned with the phenomena of the institutionalization of patterns of value-orientation in the social system,* with the conditions of that institutionalization, and of changes in the patterns, with conditions of conformity with and deviance from a set of such patterns and with motivational processes in so far as they are involved in all of these.
Ibid., p. 552.

7 Our most general proposition is that total societies *tend* to differentiate into sub-systems (social structures) which are specialized in each of the four primary functions. Where concrete structures cannot be identified, as is often the case, it is still possible to isolate types of processes which are thus specialized. The economy is the primary sub-system specialized in relation to the *adaptive* function of a society. If this proposition is correct, three other cognate sub-systems in a differentiated society should correspond to the other three functional problems. The sub-system goal of each of the three should be defined as a primary *contribution* to the appropriate functional need of the total society. For instance, the goal of the economy is the production of income which is at the disposal of the society. In these terms, the other three societal sub-systems cognate with the economy are: (1) a goal-attainment sub-system, (2) an integrative sub-system, and (3) a pattern-maintenance and tension-management sub-system – all three of which possess the characteristics of social systems. Let us discuss each in turn. The goal-attainment sub-system focuses on the political (in a broader sense) functions in a society ... the goal of the polity is to maximize the capacity of the society to attain its system goals, i.e., collective goals ... The integrative sub-system of the society relates the cultural value-patterns to

184

the motivational structures of individual actors in order that the larger social system can function without undue internal conflict and other failures of co-ordination ... The pattern-maintenance and tension-management sub-system stands relative to the society as the land complex stands relative to the economy. At the societal level, this sub-system focuses on the institutionalized culture, which in turn centres on patterns of value orientations.

Talcott Parsons and Neil J. Smelser, *Economy and Society* [1956]; New York, Free Press, 1965 (pbk edn), pp. 46–9.

Action systems and social systems

We consider social systems to be constituents of the more general system of action, the other primary constituents being cultural systems, personality systems, and behavioral organisms; all four are abstractly defined relative to the concrete behavior of social interaction. We treat the three subsystems of actions other than the social system as constituents of its environment. This usage is somewhat unfamiliar, especially for the case of personalities of individuals. It is justified fully elsewhere, but to understand what follows it is essential to keep in mind that neither social nor personality systems are here conceived as concrete entities.

8

The distinctions among the four subsystems of action are functional. We draw them in terms of the four primary functions which we impute to all systems of action, namely pattern-maintenance, integration, goal-attainment, and adaptation.

An action system's primary integrative problem is the co-ordination of its constituent units, in the first instance human individuals, though for certain purposes collectivities may be treated as actors. Hence, we attribute primacy of integrative function to the social system.

We attribute primacy of pattern-maintenance – and of creative pattern change – to the cultural system. Whereas social systems are organized with primary reference to the articulation of social relationships, cultural systems are organized around the characteristics of complexes of symbolic meaning – the codes in terms of which they are structured, the particular clusters of symbols they employ, and the conditions of their utilization, maintenance, and change as parts of action systems.

We attribute primacy of goal-attainment to the personality of the individual. The personality system is the primary *agency* of action processes, hence of the implementation of cultural principles and requirements. On the level of reward in the motivational sense, the optimization of gratification or satisfaction to personalities is the primary goal of action.

The behavioral organism is conceived as the adaptive subsystem, the locus of the primary human facilities which underlie the other systems. It embodies sets of conditions to which action must adapt and comprises the

185

primary mechanism of interrelation with the physical environment, especially through the input and processing of information in the central
nervous system and through motor activity in coping with exigencies of the
physical environment.

The System of Modern Societies, Englewood Cliffs, New Jersey, Prentice-Hall, 1971,
pp. 4–6.

9 Contrary to many current views, I do not treat sociology as the discipline
dealing with the total social system, even in this analytically abstracted sense.
This would either deny to economics and political science the title of being
social science disciplines in the strictest sense or would make them subsidiary
branches of sociology. Neither alternative would be acceptable. I therefore
conceive sociology as concerned with one primary functional aspect of social
systems, namely the understanding of the structures and processes especially
concerned with the *integration* of social systems, which of course includes
the failures of integration and understanding of the forces impeding as well
as favoring integration. By integration in this context I mean the structures
and processes by which the relations among the parts of the social system
– persons in roles, collectivities, and normative pattern components –
either become so ordered as to promote harmonious functioning in their
respective involvements with each other in the system, or in specific and
understandable ways fail to do so. Integration has both a negative and a
positive aspect. The negative concerns the prevention or minimization of
action which would disrupt the integration of the system, by mutual destruc-
tiveness or blockage. It is important to realize that consequences of actions
in the integration are to an important degree independent of the intentions
of the participant units. The traffic jam is a classic example. It is safe to say
that very seldom does any group of drivers intend to create a jam, but the
consequence of too many of them trying to use the same road system at
the same time, in the absence of adequate traffic control, is to create such a
jam. Positive integration, on the other hand, is the phenomenon of mutual
support and facilitation among the units of a social system, seen in the
perspective of the functioning of the system as a whole. The typical
phenomenon of co-operation in the accomplishment of a group task is a case
in point . . .

The main substantive focus of sociological analysis, seen in the above
context, may be said to lie in the *institutional* aspect of social action. In the
most general terms, this is the area in which the *normative expectations*
operating in the social systems, which are grounded in the culture and which
define what people in various statuses and roles in *one* or more of various
senses, *ought* to do under various circumstances, are articulated. These
expectations are integrated with the *motives* of actors, i.e., the kinds of
things the actors are, in the relevant positions and circumstances, 'driven' to
do, or 'want' to do. Since, however, the system reference of sociology is to

social systems rather than to the personality of the individual, it is *collectivities* composed of individuals rather than individuals even in roles as such in which the most important sociological interest lies. Where motivation is concerned, therefore, it is the types and rates of motives and the resultant behavior, rather than the individual case, which are the primary focus.
'An Overview', in T. Parsons (ed.), *American Sociology*, New York, Basic Books, 1968, pp. 322–4.

Professions and social structure

The importance of the professions to social structure may be summed up as **10** follows: The professional type is the institutional framework in which many of our most important social functions are carried on, notably the pursuit of science and liberal learning and its practical application in medicine, technology, law and teaching. This depends on an institutional structure, the maintenance of which is not an automatic consequence of belief in the importance of the functions as such, but involves a complex balance of diverse social forces. Certain features of this pattern are peculiar to professional activities, but others, and not the least important ones, are shared by this field with the other most important branches of our occupational structure, notably business and bureaucratic administration. Certain features of our received traditions of thought, notably concentration of attention on the problem of self-interest with its related false dichotomy of concrete egoistic and altruistic motives, has served seriously to obscure the importance of these other elements, notably rationality, specificity of function and universalism.
'The Professions and Social Structure', in T. Parsons, *Essays in Sociological Theory* [1954], New York, Free Press, 1964 (pbk edn), p. 48.

Illness and the role of the physician

The sick person is, by definition, in some respect disabled from fulfilling **11** normal social obligations, and the motivation of the sick person as being or staying sick has some reference to this fact. Conversely, since being a normally satisfactory member of social groups is always one aspect of health, mental or physical, the therapeutic process must always have as one dimension the restoration of capacity to play social roles in a normal way.
'Illness and the Role of the Physician: A Sociological Perspective', *American Journal of Orthopsychiatry*, vol. 2, 1951, pp. 452–60.

[I]llness is not merely a 'condition' but also a social role. The essential cri- **12** teria of a social role concern the attitudes both of the incumbent and of others with whom he interacts, in relation to a set of social norms defining expectations of appropriate or proper behavior for persons in that role. In

187

this respect we may distinguish four main features of the 'sick role' in our society. The first of these is the exemption of the sick person from the performance of certain of his normal social obligations ...

Secondly, the sick person is, in a very specific sense, also exempted from a certain type of responsibility for his own state ... This exemption from obligations and from a certain kind of responsibility, however, is given at a price.

The third aspect of the sick role is the partial character of its legitimation, hence the deprivation of a claim to full legitimacy. To be sick, that is, is to be in a state which is socially defined as undesirable, to be gotten out of as expeditiously as possible ...

Finally, fourth, being sick is also defined, except for the mildest of cases, as being 'in need of help'. Moreover, the type of help which is needed is presumptively defined; it is that of persons specially qualified to care for illness, above all, of physicians. Thus from being defined as the incumbent of a role relative to people who are not sick, the sick person makes the transition to the additional role of patient. He thereby, as in all social roles, incurs certain obligations, especially that of 'co-operating' with his physician – or other therapist – in the process of trying to get well.
Ibid.

13 [T]he physician is, by the definition of his role, positively enjoined not to enter into certain reciprocities with his patients, or he is protected against the pressures which they exert upon him. Thus, giving of confidential information is, in ordinary relationships, a symbol of reciprocal intimacy, but the physician does not tell about his own private affairs. Many features of the physician–patient relationship, such as the physician's access to the body, might arouse erotic reactions, but the role is defined so as to inhibit such developments even if they are initiated by the patient. In general the definition of the physician's role as specifically limited to concern with matters of health, and the injunction to observe an 'impersonal', matter-of-fact attitude without personal emotional involvement, serve to justify and legitimize his refusal to reciprocate his patient's deviant expectations. Finally, the prestige of the physician's scientific training, his reputation for technical competence, give authority to his approval, a basis for the acceptance of his interpretations.
Ibid.

SCHUTZ, ALFRED (1899–1959)

The world, as has been shown by Husserl, is from the outset experienced in the pre-scientific thinking of everyday life in the mode of typicality. The unique objects and events given to us in a unique aspect are unique within a horizon of typical familiarity and pre-acquaintanceship. There are

mountains, trees, animals, dogs – in particular Irish setters and among
them my Irish setter, Rover. Now I may look at Rover either as this unique
individual, my irreplaceable friend and comrade or just as a typical example
of 'Irish setter', 'dog', 'mammal', 'animal', 'organism' or 'object of the outer
world'. Starting from here, it can be shown that whether I do one or the
other, and also which traits or qualities of a given object or event I consider
as individually unique and which as typical, depend upon my actual interest
and the system of relevances involved – briefly, upon my practical or theoretical 'problem at hand'. This 'problem at hand', in turn, originates in the
circumstances within which I find myself at any moment of my daily life
and which I propose to call my biographically determined situation.
Thus, typification depends upon my problem at hand for the definition and
solution of which the type has been formed. It can be further shown that at
least one aspect of the biographically and situationally determined systems
of interests and relevances is subjectively experienced in the thinking
of everyday life as systems of motives for action, of choices to be made, of
projects to be carried out, of goals to be reached. It is this insight of the actor
into the dependencies of the motives and goals of his actions upon his
biographically determined situation which social scientists have in view
when speaking of the subjective meaning which the actor 'bestows upon' or
'connects with' his action. This implies that, strictly speaking, the actor and
he alone knows what he does, why he does it, and when and where his action
starts and ends.

But the world of everyday life is from the outset also a social cultural
world in which I am interrelated in manifold ways of interaction with
fellow-men known to me in varying degrees of intimacy and anonymity
... Yet only in particular situations, and then only fragmentarily, can I
experience the Others' motives, goals, etc. – briefly, the subjective meanings
they bestow upon their actions, in their uniqueness. I can, however, experience them in their typicality. In order to do so I construct typical patterns
of the actors' motives and ends, even of their attitudes and personalities, of
which their actual conduct is just an instance or example. These typified
patterns of the Others' behavior become in turn motives of my own actions,
and this leads to the phenomenon of self-typification well known to social
scientists under various names.

Here, I submit, in the common-sense thinking of everyday life, is the
origin of the so-called constructive or ideal types ...

The world of nature, as explored by the natural sciences, does not
'mean' anything to molecules, atoms and electrons. But the observational
field of the social scientist – social reality – has a specific meaning and
relevance structure for the human beings living, acting and thinking within
it. By a series of common-sense constructs they have pre-selected and pre-
interpreted this world which they experience as the reality of their daily
lives. It is these thought objects of theirs which determine their behaviour,

by motivating it. The thought objects constructed by the social scientists, in order to grasp this social reality, have to be founded upon the thought objects constructed by the common-sense thinking of men, living their daily life within this social world. Thus, the constructs of the social sciences are, so to speak, constructs of the second degree, that is, constructs of the constructs made by the actors on the social scene, whose behaviour the social scientist has to observe and to explain in accordance with the procedural rules of his science. Thus, the exploration of the general principles according to which man in daily life organizes his experiences, and especially those of the social world, is the first task of the methodology of the social sciences.

'Concept and Theory Formation in the Social Sciences', *Journal of Philosophy*, vol. 51, 1954, pp. 257–73.

SIMMEL, GEORG (1858–1918)

Society and sociology

1   Society is merely the name for a number of individuals, connected by interaction.

Fundamental Problems of Sociology: Individual and Society (first published in German, 1917); ed. and trans. Kurt H.Wolff, *The Sociology of Georg Simmel*, New York, Free Press, 1950, p. 10.

2   Sociology asks what happens to men and by what rules they behave, not insofar as they unfold their understandable individual existences in their totalities, but insofar as they form groups and are determined by their group existence because of interaction.

Ibid., p. 11.

3   If society is conceived as interaction among individuals, the description of the forms of this interaction is the task of the science of society in its strictest and most essential sense.

Ibid., pp. 21–2.

4   Sociology as the history of society and all its contents, i.e. in the sense of an explanation of all events by means of social forces and configurations, is no more a specific science than, for instance, induction. Like the latter – though not in the same formal sense – it is a method of acquiring knowledge, a heuristic principle . . .

   Just as the differentiation of the specifically psychological from objective matter produces psychology as a science, so a genuine sociology can only deal with what is specifically societal, the form and forms of sociation as such, as distinct from the particular interests and contents in and through which sociation is realised.

'The Problem of Sociology', *Annals of the American Academy of Political and Social Science*, vol. 16, 1895, pp. 412–23. Essay first published in German in 1894.

The metropolis and mental life

The feeling of isolation is rarely as decisive and intense when one actually **5** finds oneself physically alone, as when one is a stranger, without relations, among many physically close persons, at a party, on a train, or in the traffic of a large city.
'The Isolated Individual', in Wolff (ed.), op. cit., p. 119.

The psychological basis of the metropolitan type of individuality consists **6** in the intensification of nervous stimulation which results from the swift and uninterrupted change of outer and inner stimuli.
'The Metropolis and Mental Life', in Wolff (ed.), op. cit., pp. 409–10.

The metropolis has always been the seat of the money economy. Here the **7** multiplicity and concentration of economic exchange gives an importance to the means of exchange which the scantiness of rural commerce would not have allowed. Money economy and the dominance of the intellect are intrinsically connected. They share a matter-of-fact attitude in dealing with men and with things; and, in this attitude, a formal justice is often coupled with an inconsiderate hardness.
Ibid., p. 411.

The philosophy of money

We experience in the nature of money itself something of the essence of **8** prostitution. The indifference as to its use, the lack of attachment to any individual because it is unrelated to any of them, the objectivity inherent in money as a means which excludes any emotional relationship – all this produces an ominous analogy between money and prostitution.
The Philosophy of Money, trans. T. Bottomore and D. Frisby, London and Boston, Routledge, 1978, p. 377. First published in German in 1900.

Money, more than any other form of value, makes possible the secrecy, **9** invisibility and silence of exchange ... money's formlessness and abstractness makes it possible to invest it in the most varied and most remote values and thereby to remove it completely from the gaze of neighbours. Its anonymity and colourlessness does not reveal the source from which it came.
Ibid., p. 385.

[S]ince money measures all objects with merciless objectivity, and since its **10** standards of value so measured determines their relationship, a web of objective and personal aspects of life emerges which is similar to the natural cosmos with its continuous cohesion and strict causality. This web is held together by the all-pervasive money value, just as nature is held together by the energy that gives life to everything.
Ibid., p. 431.

The stranger

11 If wandering, considered as a state of detachment from every given point
in space, is the conceptual opposite of attachment to any point, then the
sociological form of 'the stranger' presents the synthesis, as it were, of both
of these properties. (This is another indication that spatial relations not
only are determining conditions of relationships among men, but are also
symbolic of those relationships.) The stranger will thus not be considered
here in the usual sense of the term, as the wanderer who comes today
and goes tomorrow, but rather as the man who comes today and stays
tomorrow – the potential wanderer, so to speak, who, although he has gone
no further, has not quite got over the freedom of coming and going. He is
fixed within a certain spatial circle – or within a group whose boundaries
are analogous to spatial boundaries – but his position within it is fundamentally affected by the fact that he does not belong in it initially and
that he brings qualities into it that are not, and cannot be, indigenous to it.

The following statements about the stranger are intended to suggest
how factors of repulsion and distance work to create a form of being
together, a form of union based on interaction.

In the whole history of economic activity the stranger makes his appearance everywhere as a trader, and the trader makes his as a stranger. As long
as production for one's own needs is the general rule, or products are
exchanged within a relatively small circle, there is no need for a middleman
within the group. A trader is required only for goods produced outside the
group. Unless there are people who wander out into foreign lands to buy
these necessities, in which case they are themselves 'strange' merchants in
this other region, the trader *must* be a stranger, there is no opportunity for
anyone else to make a living at it . . .

Although in the sphere of intimate personal relations the stranger may
be attractive and meaningful in many ways, so long as he is regarded as a
stranger he is no 'landowner' in the eyes of the other. Restriction to intermediary trade and often (as though sublimated from it) to pure finance
gives the stranger the specific character of *mobility*. The appearance of this
mobility within a bounded group occasions that synthesis of nearness
and remoteness which constitutes the formal position of the stranger. The
purely mobile person comes incidentally into contact with *every* single
element but is not bound up organically, through established ties of kinship,
locality, or occupation, with any single one.

Another expression of this constellation is to be found in the objectivity
of the stranger. Because he is not bound by roots to the particular constituents and particular dispositions of the group, he confronts all of these
with a distinctly 'objective' attitude, an attitude that does not signify mere
detachment and nonparticipation, but is a distinct structure composed of
remoteness and nearness, indifference and involvement . . .

Connected with the characteristic of objectivity is a phenomenon that is found chiefly, though not exclusively, in the stranger who moves on. This is that he often receives the most surprising revelations and confidences, at times reminiscent of a confessional, about matters which are kept carefully hidden from everybody with whom one is close . . .

The Stranger (first published in German in 1908). Extract in *On Individuality and Social Forms: Selected Writings*, ed. D. K. Levine, Chicago, University of Chicago Press, 1971, pp. 143–9.

The triad vs. the dyad

This peculiar closeness between two is most clearly revealed if the dyad is contrasted with the triad. For among three elements, each one operates as an intermediary between the other two, exhibiting the twofold function of such an organ, which is to unite and to separate.   **12**

'Quantitative Aspects of the Group', in Wolff (ed.), op. cit., p. 135.

SPENCER, HERBERT (1820–1903)

Spencer and Comte

What is Comte's professed aim? To give a coherent account of the progress of human conceptions. What is my aim? To give a coherent account of the progress of the external world. Comte proposes to describe the necessary, and the actual, filiation of ideas. I propose to describe the necessary, and the actual, filiation of things. Comte professes to interpret the genesis of our knowledge of nature. My aim is to interpret . . . the genesis of the phenomena which constitute nature. The one is subjective. The other is objective.   **1**

An Autobiography (2 vols), New York, Appleton, 1904, vol. 2, p. 570.

The study of sociology

The average opinion in every age and country is a function of the social structure in that age and country.   **2**

The Study of Sociology, New York, Appleton, 1891, p. 390.

The study of Sociology is the study of evolution in its most complex form.   **3**

Ibid., p. 385.

There can be no complete acceptance of sociology as a science, so long as the belief in a social order not conforming to natural law, survives.   **4**

Ibid., p. 394.

Social evolution and progress

5   The many facts contemplated unite in proving that social evolution forms a part of evolution at large. Like evolving aggregates in general, societies show integration, both by simple increase of mass and by coalescence and re-coalescence of masses. The change from homogeneity to heterogeneity is multitudinously exemplified; up from the simple tribe, alike in all its parts, to the civilized nation, full of structural and functional unlikenesses. With progressing integration and heterogeneity goes increasing coherence.
    The Principles of Sociology, vol. 1, 1876.

6   Like other kinds of progress, social progress is not linear but divergent and re-divergent.
    Ibid., vol. 3, 1897.

7   The society exists for the benefit of its members; not its members for the benefit of society.
    Ibid., vol. 1, 1876.

WEBER, MAX (1864–1920)

Sociology, methods and concepts

1   Sociology (in the sense in which this highly ambiguous word is used here) is a science concerning itself with the interpretive understanding [*Verstehen*] of social action and thereby with a causal explanation of its course and consequences. We shall speak of 'action' insofar as the acting individual attaches a subjective meaning to his behaviour – be it overt or covert, omission or acquiescence. Action is 'social' insofar as its subjective meaning takes account of the behaviour of others and is thereby oriented in its course.
    Economy and Society (3 vols), ed. Guenther Roth and Claus Wittich, New York, Bedminster Press, 1968, vol. 1, p. 4. First published in German in 1925.

2   For the purposes of a typological scientific analysis it is convenient to treat all irrational, affectually determined elements of behaviour as factors of deviation from a conceptually pure type of rational action . . . It is naturally not legitimate to interpret this procedure as involving a rationalistic bias in sociology, but only as a methodological device.
    Ibid., p. 6.

3   A correct causal interpretation of a concrete course of action is arrived at when the overt action and the motives have been correctly apprehended and at the same time their relation has become meaningfully comprehensible. A correct causal interpretation of typical action means that the process which is claimed to be typical is shown to be both adequately grasped at the level of meaning and at the same time the interpretation is to some degree causally adequate.
    Ibid., p. 12.

In the case of social collectivities, precisely as distinguished from organ- **4**
isms, we are in a position to go beyond merely demonstrating functional
relationships and uniformities. We can accomplish something which is
never attainable in the natural sciences, namely, the subjective understanding of the action of the component individuals.
Ibid., p. 15.

Not every type of contact of human beings has a social character; this is **5**
rather confined to cases where the actor's behaviour is meaningfully oriented to that of others. For example, a mere collision of two cyclists may
be compared to a natural event. On the other hand, their attempt to avoid
hitting each other, or whatever insults, blows, or friendly discussion might
follow the collision, would constitute 'social action'.
Ibid., p. 23.

Social action, like all action, may be oriented in four ways. It may be: **6**

1 *instrumentally rational* [*zweckrational*], that is, determined by expectations as to the behaviour of objects in the environment and of other
   human beings; these expectations are used as 'conditions' or 'means' for
   the attainment of the actor's own rationally pursued and calculated
   ends;
2 *value-rational* [*wertrational*], that is, determined by a conscious belief in
   the value for its own sake of some ethical, aesthetic, religious, or other
   form of behaviour, independently of its prospects of success;
3 *affectual* (especially emotional), that is, determined by the actor's
   specific affects and feeling states;
4 *traditional*, that is, determined by ingrained habit.

Ibid., p. 25.

Power, authority and organization

There are three pure types of legitimate authority. The validity of their **7**
claims to legitimacy may be based on:

1 Rational grounds – resting on a belief in the 'legality' of patterns of normative rules and the right of those elevated to authority under such rules
   to issue commands (legal authority).
2 Traditional grounds – resting on an established belief in the sanctity of
   immemorial traditions and the legitimacy of the status of those exercising authority under them (traditional authority).
3 Charismatic grounds – resting on devotion to the specific and exceptional
   sanctity, heroism or exemplary character of an individual person, and of
   the normative patterns of order revealed or ordained by him (charismatic
   authority).

Ibid., pp. 24–5.

8 Power [*Macht*] is the probability that one actor within a social relationship will be in a position to carry out his own will despite resistance, regardless of the basis on which this probability rests. Domination [*Herrschaft*] is the probability that a command with a given specific content will be obeyed by a given group of persons.
Ibid., p. 53.

9 Bureaucratic administration means fundamentally the exercise of control on the basis of knowledge. This is the feature of it which makes it specifically rational.
   This consists on the one hand in technical knowledge which, by itself, is sufficient to ensure it a position of extraordinary power. But in addition to this, bureaucratic organizations, or the holders of power who make use of them, have the tendency to increase their power still further by the knowledge growing out of experience in the service.
Economy and Society [1925], in Max Weber, *The Theory of Social and Economic Organization*, ed. T. Parsons, New York, Oxford University Press, 1947, p. 339.

10 Experience tends universally to show that the purely bureaucratic type of administrative organization – that is, the monocratic variety of bureaucracy – is, from a purely technical point of view, capable of attaining the highest degree of efficiency and is in this sense formally the most rational known means of carrying out imperative control over human beings.
Ibid., p. 357.

11 The development of the modern form of organization of corporate groups in all fields is nothing less than identical with the development and continual spread of bureaucratic administration. This is true of church and state, of armies, political parties, economic enterprises, organizations to promote all kinds of causes, private associations, clubs, and many others.
Ibid.

12 Though by no means alone, the capitalistic system has undeniably played a major role in the development of bureaucracy. Indeed, without it capitalistic production could not continue and any rational type of socialism would have simply to take it over and increase its importance. Its development, largely under capitalistic auspices, has created an urgent need for stable, strict, intensive, and calculable administration. It is this need which gives bureaucracy a crucial role in our society as the central element in any kind of large-scale administration. Only by reversion in every field – political, religious, economic, etc. – to small-scale organization would it be possible to any considerable extent to escape its influence.
Ibid., p. 338.

13 The term 'charisma' will be applied to a certain quality of an individual personality by virtue of which he is set apart from ordinary men and

treated as endowed with supernatural, superhuman, or at least specifically exceptional powers or qualities.
Ibid., p. 358.

Social stratification

'Classes', 'status groups' and 'parties' are phenomena of the distribution of **14** power within a community.
Economy and Society [1925]; ed. and trans. Hans Gerth and C. Wright Mills, *From Max Weber: Essays in Sociology*, London, Routledge and Kegan Paul, 1948, p. 181.

In our terminology, 'classes' are not communities; they merely represent **15** possible and frequent bases for communal action. We may speak of a 'class' when (a) a number of people have in common a specific causal component of their life chances, in so far as (b) this component is represented exclusively by economic interests in the possession of goods and opportunities for income, and (c) is represented under the conditions of the commodity or labour markets.
Ibid., p. 181.

In contrast to classes, *status groups* are normally communities. They are, **16** however, often of an amorphous kind. In contrast to the purely economically determined 'class situation' we wish to designate as 'status situations' every typical component of the life fate of men that is determined by a specific, positive or negative, social estimation of *honour* ... In content, status honour is normally expressed by the fact that above all else a specific *style of life* can be expected from all those who wish to belong to the circle.
Ibid., pp. 186–7.

The development of status is essentially a question of stratification resting **17** upon usurpation.
Ibid., p. 188.

Where the consequences have been realized to their full extent, the status **18** group evolves into a closed 'caste'. Status distinctions are then guaranteed not merely by conventions and laws, but also by *rituals* ... A 'status' segregation grown into a 'caste' differs in its structure from a mere 'ethnic' segregation: the caste structure transforms the horizontal and unconnected coexistence of ethnically segregated groups into a vertical social system of super- and subordination.
Ibid., pp. 188–9.

With some over-simplification, one might thus say that 'classes' are stratified **19** according to their relations to the production and acquisition of goods; whereas 'status groups' that are stratified according to the principles of their *consumption* of goods are represented by special 'styles of life'.
Ibid., p. 193.

20 Whereas the genuine place of 'classes' is within the economic order, the place of 'status groups' is within the social order, that is, within the sphere of the distribution of 'honour' . . . But 'parties' live in a house of 'power'. Their action is oriented toward the acquisition of social 'power', that is to say, toward a communal action no matter what its content may be.
Ibid., p. 194.

Religion and economy

21 The impulse to acquisition, pursuit of gain, of money, of the greatest possible amount of money, has in itself nothing to do with capitalism. This impulse exists and has existed among waiters, physicians, coachmen, artists, prostitutes, dishonest officials, soldiers, nobles, crusaders, gamblers, and beggars. One may say that it has been common to all sorts and conditions of men at all times and in all countries of the earth, wherever the objective possibility of it is or has been given. It should be taught in the kindergarten of cultural history that this naive idea of capitalism must be given up once and for all. Unlimited greed for gain is not in the least identical with capitalism, and is still less its spirit. Capitalism *may* even be identical with the restraint, or at least a rational tempering, of this irrational impulse. But capitalism is identical with the pursuit of profit, and forever *renewed* profit, by means of continuous, rational, capitalistic enterprise.
The Protestant Ethic and the Spirit of Capitalism, trans. T. Parsons, London, Allen & Unwin, 1930, p. 17. First published in German in 1904.

22 In this case we are dealing with the connection of the spirit of modern economic life with the rational ethics of ascetic Protestantism. Thus we treat here only one side of the causal chain.
Ibid., p. 27.

23 The capitalistic economy of the present day is an immense cosmos into which the individual is born, and which presents itself to him, at least as an individual, as an unalterable order of things in which he must live. It forces the individual, in so far as he is involved in the system of market relationships, to conform to capitalistic rules of action. The manufacturer who, in the long run, acts contrary to these norms, will just as inevitably be eliminated from the economic scene as the worker who cannot or will not adapt himself to them will be thrown into the streets without a job.
Ibid., pp. 54–5.

24 The religious valuation of restless, continuous, systematic work in a worldly calling, as the highest means to asceticism, and at the same time the surest and most evident proof of rebirth and genuine faith, must have been the most powerful conceivable lever for the expansion of that attitude toward life which we have here called the spirit of capitalism.
Ibid., p. 172.

The Puritan wanted to work in a calling; we are forced to do so. For when **25**
asceticism was carried out of monastic cells into everyday life, and began
to dominate worldly morality, it did its part in building the tremendous
cosmos of the modern economic order. This order is now bound to the
technical and economic conditions of machine production which today
determine the lives of all individuals who are born into this mechanism, not
only those directly concerned with economic acquisition, with irresistible
force. Perhaps it will so determine them until the last ton of fossilized coal
is burnt. In Baxter's view the care for external goods should only lie on the
shoulders of the 'saint like a light cloak, which can be thrown aside at any
moment'. But fate decreed that the cloak should become an iron cage.
Ibid., p. 181.

But it is, of course, not my aim to substitute for a one-sided materialistic **26**
an equally one-sided spiritualistic causal interpretation of culture and of
history. Each is equally possible.
Ibid., p. 183.

It is not our thesis that the specific nature of a religion is a simple 'func- **27**
tion' of the social situation of the stratum which appears as its characteris-
tic bearer, or that it represents the stratum's 'ideology', or that it is a
'reflection' of a stratum's material or ideal interest-situation.
The Economic Ethic of the World Religions, published in German in 1915.
Translation under the title 'The Social Psychology of the World Religions' in H.
Gerth and C. Wright Mills (eds), *From Max Weber: Essays in Sociology*, London,
Routledge & Kegan Paul, 1948, pp. 269–70.

Not ideas, but material and ideal interests, directly govern men's conduct. **28**
Yet very frequently the 'world images' that have been created by 'ideas'
have, like switchmen, determined the tracks along which action has been
pushed by the dynamic of interest. 'From what' and 'for what' one wished
to be redeemed and, let us not forget, 'could be' redeemed, depended upon
one's image of the world.
Ibid., p. 280.

The fortunate is seldom satisfied with the fact of being fortunate. Beyond **29**
this he needs to know that he has a right to his good fortune . . . In short,
religion provides the theodicy of good fortune for those who are fortunate.
Ibid., p. 271.

To define 'religion', to say what it is, is not possible at the start of a **30**
presentation such as this. Definition can be attempted, if at all, only at the
conclusion of the study. The essence of religion is not even our concern, as
we make it our task to study the conditions and effects of a particular type
of social behaviour. The external courses of religious behaviour are so
diverse that an understanding of this behaviour can only be achieved
from the viewpoint of the subjective experiences, ideas, and purposes of

the individuals concerned – in short, from the viewpoint of the religious behaviour's 'meaning' [*Sinn*] . . . .The most elementary forms of behavior motivated by religious or magical factors are oriented to *this* world.
The Sociology of Religion, ed. Talcott Parsons, trans. E. Fischoff, London, Methuen, 1965, p. 1. First published in German in 1922, as part of *Economy and Society*.

31 Since every need for salvation is an expression of some distress, social or economic oppression is an effective source of salvation beliefs, though by no means the exclusive source. Other things being equal, classes with high social and economic privilege will scarcely be prone to evolve the idea of salvation. Rather, they assign to religion the primary function of legitimizing their own life pattern and situation in the world.
Ibid., p. 107.

32 From the time of its inception, ancient Christianity was characteristically a religion of artisans. Its saviour was a semi-rural artisan, and his missionaries were wandering apprentices, the greatest of them a wandering tent maker, so alien to the land that in his epistles he actually employs in a reverse sense a metaphor relating to the process of grafting.
Ibid., p. 95.

NAME INDEX

SUBJECT INDEX

205